THE I.B.TAURIS HISTORY OF THE CHRISTIAN CHURCH

The Church in the Early Middle Ages

THE I.B.TAURIS HISTORY OF THE CHRISTIAN CHURCH
GENERAL EDITOR: G.R. EVANS

The Early Church
Morwenna Ludlow, University of Exeter

The Church in the Early Middle Ages
G.R. Evans, University of Cambridge

The Church in the Later Middle Ages
Norman Tanner, Gregorian University, Rome

Early Modern Christianity
Patrick Provost-Smith, Harvard University

The Church in the Long Eighteenth Century
David Hempton, Harvard University

The Church in the Nineteenth Century
Frances Knight, University of Wales, Lampeter

The Church in the Modern Age
Jeremy Morris, University of Cambridge

THE I.B.TAURIS HISTORY OF THE CHRISTIAN CHURCH

The Church in the Early Middle Ages

G.R. Evans

I.B.TAURIS
LONDON · NEW YORK

Published in 2007 by I.B.Tauris & Co. Ltd
6 Salem Road, London W2 4BU
175 Fifth Avenue, New York, NY 10010
www.ibtauris.com

Copyright © 2007 G.R. Evans

Vol 1: *The Early Church*   978 1 84511 366 7
Vol 2: *The Church in the Early Middle Ages*   978 1 84511 150 2
Vol 3: *The Church in the Later Middle Ages*   978 1 84511 438 1
Vol 4: *Early Modern Christianity*   978 1 84511 439 8
Vol 5: *The Church in the Long Eighteenth Century*   978 1 84511 440 4
Vol 6: *The Church in the Nineteenth Century*   978 1 85043 899 1
Vol 7: *The Church in the Modern Age*   978 1 84511 317 9

A full CIP record for this book is available from the British Library

Typeset in Adobe Caslon Pro by A. & D. Worthington, Newmarket, Suffolk
Printed and bound in Great Britain by CPI Bath

THE I.B.TAURIS HISTORY OF THE CHRISTIAN CHURCH

Since the first disciples were sent out by Jesus, Christianity has been of its essence a missionary religion. That religion has proved to be an ideology and a subversive one. Profoundly though it became 'inculturated' in the societies it converted, it was never syncretistic. It had, by the twentieth century, brought its own view of things to the ends of the earth. The Christian Church, first defined as a religion of love, has interacted with Judaism, Islam and other world religions in ways in which there has been as much warfare as charity. Some of the results are seen in the tensions of the modern world, tensions which are proving very hard to resolve – not least because of a lack of awareness of the history behind the thinking which has brought the Church to where it is now.

In the light of that lack, a new history of the Christian Church is badly needed. There is much to be said for restoring to the general reader a familiarity with the network of ideas about what the Church 'is' and what it should be 'doing' as a vessel of Christian life and thought. This series aims to be both fresh and traditional. It will be organized so that the boundary-dates between volumes fall in some unexpected places. It will attempt to look at its conventional subject matter from the critical perspective of the early twenty-first century, where the Church has a confusing myriad of faces. Behind all these manifestations is a rich history of thinking, effort and struggle. And within it, at the heart of matters, is the Church. *The I.B.Tauris History of the Christian Church* seeks to discover that innermost self through the layers of its multiple manifestations over twenty centuries.

SERIES EDITOR'S PREFACE

Against the background of global conflict involving interfaith resentments and misunderstandings, threatening 'religious wars' on a scale possibly unprecedented in history, Christians and the Christian Church are locked in internal disputes. On 2 November 2003, a practising homosexual was made a bishop in the Episcopal Church in the United States, America's 'province' of the Anglican Communion. This was done in defiance of the strong opinion in other parts of the 'Communion' that if it happened Anglicanism would fall apart into schism. A few years earlier there had been similar rumblings over the ordination of women to ministry in the same Church. A century before that period, the Roman Catholic Church had pronounced all Anglican ordination to the priestly or episcopal ministry to be utterly null and void because of an alleged breach of communion and continuity in the sixteenth century. And the Orthodox Churches watched all this in the secure conviction that Roman Catholic, Anglican and all other Christian communities were not communions at all because they had departed from the truth as it had been defined in the ecumenical Councils of the first few centuries. Orthodoxy alone was orthodox. Even the baptism of other Christians was of dubious validity.

Those heated by the consecration of a 'gay' bishop spoke on the one side of faithfulness to the teaching of the Bible and on the other of the leading of the Holy Spirit into a new world which knew no discrimination. Yet both the notion of faithfulness to Scripture and the idea that Jesus particularly wanted to draw the outcasts and disadvantaged to himself have a long and complex history which makes it impossible to make either statement in simple black-and-white terms.

One of the most significant factors in the frightening failures of communication and goodwill which make daily headlines is a loss of contact with the past on the part of those taking a stand on one side or another of such disagreements. The study of 'history' is fashionable as this series is launched, but the colourful narrative of past lives and episodes does not necessarily make familiar the patterns of thought and assumption in the minds of those involved. A modern history of the Church must embody that awareness in every sinew. Those embattled in disputes within the Church and disputes involving Christian and other-faith communities have tended to take their stand on principles they claim to be of eternal validity, and to represent the will of God. But as they appear in front of television cameras or speak to journalists the accounts they give – on either side – frequently reflect a lack of knowledge of the tradition they seek to protect or to challenge.

The creation of a new history of the Church at the beginning of the third millennium is an ambitious project, but it is needed. The cultural, social and political dominance of Christendom in what we now call 'the West' during the first two millennia made the Christian Church a shaper of the modern world in respects which go far beyond its strictly religious influence. Since the first disciples were sent out to preach the Gospel by Jesus, Christianity has been of its essence a missionary religion. It took the faith across the world in a style which has rightly been criticized as 'imperialist'. Christianity has proved to be an ideology and a subversive one. Profoundly though it became 'inculturated' in the societies converted, it was never syncretistic. It had, by the twentieth century, brought its own view of things to the ends of the earth. The Christian Church, first defined as a religion of love, has interacted with Judaism, Islam and the other world religions in ways in which there has been as much warfare as charity. We see some of the results in tensions in the modern world which are now proving very hard to resolve, not least because of the sheer failure of awareness of the history of the thinking which has brought the Church to where it is now.

Such a history has of course purposes more fundamental, more positive, more universal, but no less timely. There may not be a danger of the loss of the full picture while the libraries of the world and its historic buildings and pictures and music preserve the evidence. But the connecting thread in living minds is easily broken. There is much to be said for restoring as familiar to the general reader, whether Christian or not, a command of the sequence and network of ideas about what the Church *is* and what it should be *doing* as a vessel of Christian thought and life.

This new series aims, then, to be both new and traditional. It is organized so that the boundary-dates between volumes come in some unexpected places. It attempts to look at the conventional subject matter of histories of the Church from the vantage-point of the early twenty-first century, where the Church has confusingly many faces: from Vatican strictures on the use of birth-control and the indissolubility of marriage, and the condemnation of outspoken German academic theologians who challenge the Churches' authority to tell them what to think and write, to the enthusiasm of Black Baptist congregations in the USA joyously affirming a faith with few defining parameters. Behind all these variations is a history of thought and effort and struggle. And within, at the heart of matters, is the Church. It is to be discovered in its innermost self through the layers of its multiple manifestations over twenty centuries. That is the subject of this series.

Contents

Preface

A modern history of the Church must embody the patterns of thought and assumption in the minds of those involved in the life of the Church at the time in question. There are perennial and repeating questions which challenge the Church generation by generation, but there have also been questions peculiar to each age. Matters which demand discussion in one period leave little mark on the fabric of another. It is, to later eyes, remarkable that the early creeds contain no statement on the relationship of Bible and Church, and puzzling to find God's creation of 'things visible' being stressed.

The launch of a new history of the Church at the beginning of the third millennium is a bold enterprise, and perhaps nowhere is it needed more than in the description of the development of the Church and its life and thought in the period after the end of the 'early Church' in the ancient world. The cultural, social and political dominance of Christendom in what we now call 'the West' during the period from about 600 to 1300 made the Christian Church a shaper of the modern world in respects which go far beyond its strictly religious influence. There may not be a danger of the loss of the full picture while the libraries of the world and its historic buildings and pictures and music preserve the evidence. But the connecting thread in living minds is easily broken. There is much to recommend making it possible for general readers, whether or not they are Christian, to get a sense of the various conceptions about the Church (and the events and occurrences leading up to those ideas) which unfolded during this defining period, and place them within a framework of understanding.

The era from the end of late antiquity to the high Middle Ages was the formative period for the doctrine of the Church. It was also a determinative period in the practical resolution of the endless difficulties of running the Church locally, in a society which had its own developing ideas about the holding of property and obedience to secular law. There is a wealth of discussion and commentary and also of episodes and human histories, pictures and buildings, which illustrate the new difficulties and the way they were identified and approached.

With the overall purpose of pointing up the aspects which have become constitutive for the modern framing of the issues, within the context of the events of these medieval centuries, this new history of the Church in the period 600–1300 seeks to trace in a series of topically focused chapters the story of devotional and theological thought and of ecclesiastical and pastoral life.

Abbreviations

AHDLMA	Archives d'histoire doctrinale et littéraire du môyen age
CCCM	Corpus Christianorum Continuatio Medievalis
CCSL	Corpus Christianorum Series Latina
CSEL	Corpus Scriptorum Ecclesiasticorum Latinorum
LTR	Bernard of Clairvaux, *Opera omnia*, ed. J. Leclerq, C.H. Talbot and L.M. Rochais (Rome, 1967–77), 8 volumes
MGH	Monumenta Germaniae Historica
PG	Patrologia Graeca
PL	Patrologia Latina
RS	Rolls Series
SC	Sources chrétiennes
SSLov	Spicilegium Sacrum Lovaniense
ST	Thomas Aquinas, *Summa theologiae*
Tanner	*Conciliorum oecumenicorum decreta*, ed Norman Tanner (Georgetown, 1990), 2 volumes

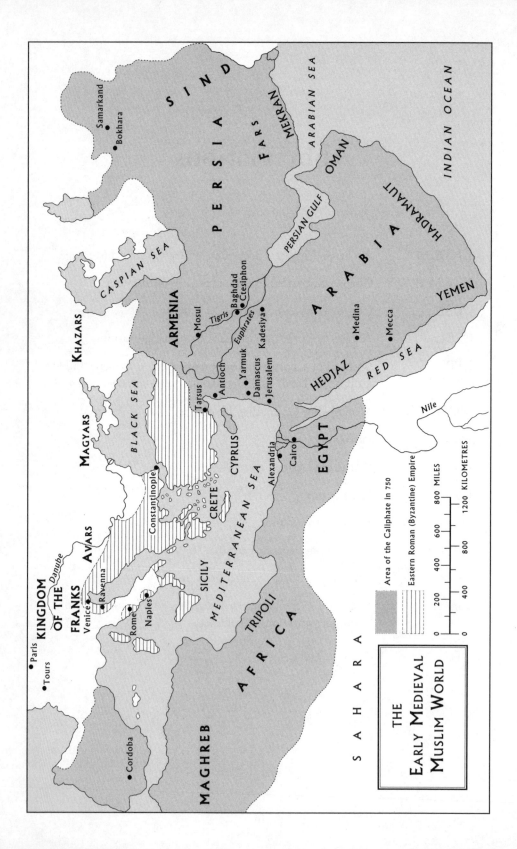

THE
EARLY MEDIEVAL
MUSLIM WORLD

Area of the Caliphate in 750

Eastern Roman (Byzantine) Empire

MILES
0   200   400   600   800

KILOMETRES
0   400   800   1200

SIND

PERSIA

FARS

MEKRAN

ARABIAN SEA

OMAN

HADRAMAUT

INDIAN OCEAN

Samarkand
Bokhara

CASPIAN SEA

KHAZARS

ARMENIA

Mosul
Tigris
Baghdad
Ctesiphon
Euphrates

PERSIAN GULF

ARABIA

YEMEN

Medina
Mecca

HEDJAZ

RED SEA

MAGYARS

FRANKS

AVARS

BLACK SEA

Antioch
Tarsus
Yarmuk
Damascus
Kadesiya
Jerusalem

CYPRUS

CRETE

MEDITERRANEAN SEA

Constantinople

Nile

Alexandria
Cairo

EGYPT

KINGDOM
OF THE

Danube

Paris
Tours

Venice
Ravenna
Rome
Naples

SICILY

TRIPOLI

AFRICA

MAGHREB

Cordoba

SAHARA

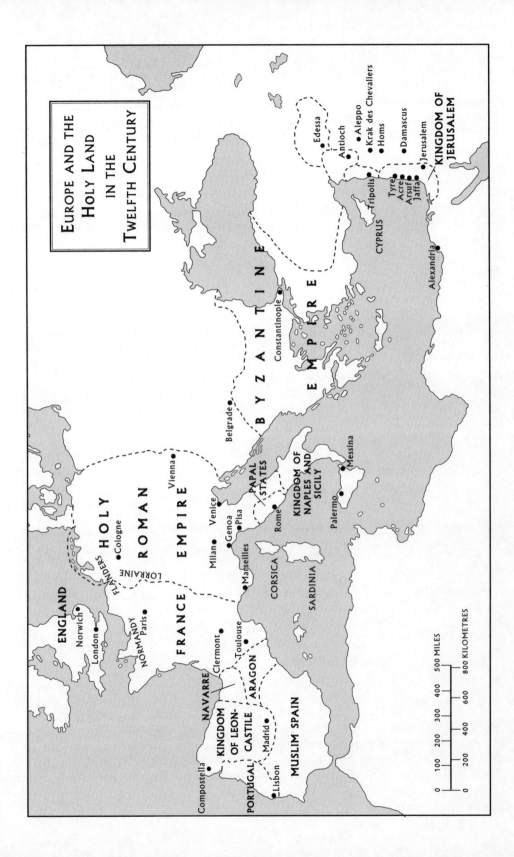

EUROPE AND THE
HOLY LAND
IN THE
TWELFTH CENTURY

ENGLAND
Norwich
London
NORMANDY
Paris
FRANCE
Clermont
Toulouse
NAVARRE
Compostella
KINGDOM
OF LEON-
CASTILE
ARAGON
PORTUGAL
Madrid
Lisbon
MUSLIM SPAIN

FLANDERS
Cologne
LORRAINE
HOLY
ROMAN
EMPIRE
Vienna
Milan
Venice
Genoa
Pisa
Marseilles
CORSICA
SARDINIA
PAPAL
STATES
Rome
KINGDOM OF
NAPLES AND
SICILY
Palermo
Messina

Belgrade
BYZANTINE
EMPIRE
Constantinople

CYPRUS
Alexandria

Edessa
Antioch
Aleppo
Krak des Chevaliers
Homs
Damascus
Jerusalem
KINGDOM OF
JERUSALEM
Tyre
Acre
Arsuf
Jaffa
Tripolis

0   100   200   300   400   500 MILES
0   200   400   600   800 KILOMETRES

INTRODUCTION

Out of the Ancient World

Changing ideas of multiculturalism

Europe was formed by two great empires, that of ancient Rome and the perhaps even more complex and sophisticated ecclesiastical 'empire' of the medieval Christian Church – which might, if it was honest, have had to confess to increasingly imperialist ambitions of its own by the end of the period covered by this book. Even at the beginning of our period the Church was perforce left to do a good deal of the practical administration which the secular government was increasingly unable to carry out. A thousand years on, it was confidently challenging the secular authorities for 'world supremacy'. The balance to be struck was a fine one, and not easily maintained. Bernard of Clairvaux (1090–1153) reminds Pope Eugenius III that he should above all see the Church of which God had made him supreme as the 'mother' (*mater*) not the 'mistress' (*domina*) of all other churches and himself not as the lord of other bishops but as one of them, a brother-bishop.[1] Nevertheless he is the one responsible for the well being of the Church in all the aspects of its life.[2] As the vicar of Christ on earth, he has to put into operation in the world the principle of Psalm 49.1: 'The world is the Lord's and its fullness', and that of Numbers 24.18: 'All the world shall be his possession'.

The Christian Church became in intention a 'world religion' from the earliest days when, as the Acts of the Apostles records (Acts 15), the young Church took the decision that it was going to see itself as something distinct from Judaism. That line of thought had clearly not grown less ambitious by the twelfth century. Equally clearly it had been affected by the changed priorities of a later age. But there are many kinds of world-picture, and part of the interest and importance of the period covered by this book lies in the shifting of assumptions and expectations, the jostling for space and position and the rationalizations which followed. These were the centuries during which the doctrines of the Church and of the sacraments were fully worked out in the West, with new institutional structures unknown to the age of Constantine, when papal primacy was asserted and anti-clericalism and anti-establishment dissidence emerged.

Within this institutional 'power structure' modest pious lives could be led, and with its established position in society the Church served as a protective shell for ordinary Christians. But it also actively controlled their lives. Moreover the Church in the West defined itself in many respects by its power-relationship with the secular world. Church–state relations lay at the heart of Bernard's advice to Pope Eugenius. This was most notably a phenomenon of the Western end of the old Roman Empire. There were plenty of moments when the Patriarch of Constantinople quarrelled dramatically with the Emperor. Nevertheless in the Greek-speaking East the medieval politics turned out to be different in flavour, and so was the ecclesiastical 'lifestyle'.

For some centuries it was the Greek which predominated. The major 'ecumenical' councils of Nicaea (325), Constantinople (381), Ephesus (431) and Chalcedon (451) may have been described as 'universal', but they all took place at the eastern end of the Mediterranean and were attended mainly by the Greek bishops. Christian writers arose at both ends of the Roman world in the first Christian centuries, some thinking and preaching and writing in Greek, some in Latin. While the Empire lasted the Church was busy giving its own account of both the Greek and the Latin ways of thinking through a series of ecumenical Councils and writings by individuals. But as we shall see, Greek and Latin traditions took off down different tracks when the Roman Empire collapsed and a gulf opened between Latin and Greek speakers so that the two halves of the old Empire effectively ceased to talk to one another except when they had a disagreement to resolve. The Church in the Eastern half of the former Roman Empire tended to protect its old ways and thus a corresponding gulf opened up in theological thinking between East and West.

The young Church grew to its medieval maturity in what we should now call a multicultural society, but one which did not necessarily share modern assumptions about the way distinct cultures should work out their differences. The constructions the Romans placed on the endeavours of the conquered Greeks had had the effect of transforming them into something which was useful to their own 'Latin' world. Rome had thus successfully absorbed and communicated the culture of ancient Greece, subtly changing it in the process. The relationship between the two halves of the culture of the classical world went on colouring the history of the Church throughout the Middle Ages, and the layering of these influences continued for many centuries. 'We cannot now read Pope's *Iliad* without feeling the English eighteenth century descend like a thick curtain between us and Homer's

Greece', regretted Dorothy Sayers as she struggled to translate the thirteenth-century Dante for the twentieth century.[3]

Once an educated population ceased to be to some degree bilingual at the end of the Roman Empire, as happened during the fifth and sixth centuries, communication of the subtleties of Christian belief met practical impediments. It had never been easy to translate Greek ideas directly or literally into Latin. The languages were different in style and character as well as in vocabulary and grammar. Bilingual education was a great help here, a monoglot population distinctly disadvantaged, whichever language they were born to.

At its best, the Roman Empire had the virtues of its own most highly regarded citizens. These were the 'Ciceronian' virtues of justice, prudence, temperance and fortitude which made its military might potent but kept it under control.[4] It remained for some centuries a protective oppressor, generally maintaining good order for its conquered peoples. Yet it was no more altruistic and enlightened than any more recent imperialist power. In rather the way the modern West has exploited Third World economies in our own day, Rome carried some of the conquered off into slavery and treated the products of their economies as a source of cheap food and luxury goods for themselves as conquerors. This book begins with the way this world changed when the Roman Empire, with its dominant virtues and vices, collapsed and the Christian Church – despite its internal divisions – became the presiding and unifying force in Europe. But we shall also see the Church in Europe learning how to engage with the new 'world religion' of Islam in North Africa, the Middle East and modern Spain.

Those who ran first the Roman Republic and later the Empire had been astute in the way they treated the religious sensitivities of the peoples they conquered as 'Rome' expanded. Rome's custom had always been to allow people to continue with their existing religious beliefs. They imposed a governmental structure but they allowed the local pagan religions to continue, merely suggesting firmly that in a polytheistic system there need be no rivalry among the gods. The members of the Greek pantheon, with its king god Zeus and its queen goddess Hera, could be equated readily enough with the members of the Roman pantheon, with its king god Jupiter and its queen goddess Juno. Pallas Athene could be Minerva, and so on. No interfaith dialogue was necessary. The local people were allowed to keep their friendly familiar local deities and continue to worship them. The old polytheism could easily accommodate any additional gods without difficulty, although it strained at some of the Middle Eastern cults of the 'dying and rising' god.[5]

Within paganism there was a wide range of options, from the sophisticated speculative thought and ethical systems of the philosophers to the comfortable placating and bribing of household and local gods. Augustine of Hippo (354–430) described the scene in Book VIII of *De civitate Dei* ('The City of God'), classifying religions into the philosophical, the popular and the 'civic'. He meant by this: beliefs of an intellectually sophisticated kind which embodied a moral system, the simple folk-worship of pagan gods, and the showing of respect for the Emperor, which blurred the line between civic obedience and worship.

Christians, like Jews, understood that for them there could be no hedging of bets, no holding of the Christian faith while continuing in the beliefs of paganism. The exceptions were the Jews and the Christians, who would not go along with syncretism[6] and who were, from time to time, persecuted because they would not show the respect for the Emperor amounting to worship which 'civic' religion required. That persecution had come to an end before this book begins, with the conversion of Constantine, the first Christian Emperor, and the setting up of the Christian Empire. The third exception was to be Islam, which stood just as firm on the question of monotheism.

As the pressures of *romanitas* eased and Europe transformed itself into a new kind of multicultural unity, the Church in both East and West came face to face with a changing Asia and a renewed North Africa. The Roman Empire had extended into the modern Middle East, and the lands which have become modern Israel and Palestine were under Roman domination when Christianity began. So the interface with Asia was nothing geographically new. North Africa, too, had had an important place in the history of the Church from the earliest stages. Cyprian, Bishop of Carthage, wrote and preached there and so did Augustine, Bishop of Hippo. But the emergence of Islam presented a wholly new experience for the Church, in both Eastern and Western Europe. Attitudes and expectations had to change.

It was by no means easy for one faith community to understand another. Throughout the period covered by this book there was mutual incomprehension and a sometimes constructive misunderstanding; pictures of things were based on positions taken up, sometimes unconsciously, sometimes deliberately, but almost never with a neutral wish to see things objectively and in a way other communities could readily share. It would be anachronistic to expect anything else. Modern talk of world peace and mutual tolerance arises from quite different expectations. 'Unanimity' was insisted on by the ecumenical Councils of the early Church, but that did not and could not include 'agreeing to disagree', or allowing other religions an equal respect. Society was almost perpetually at war for many centuries and only the Roman Empire for a time – and that time was now past – had had the power to 'keep the peace' physically speaking, and it had been ineffective at keeping the peace when it came to differences of religious opinion within Christianity itself.

The idea of a 'religion' in the Middle Ages

When the World Council of Churches was formed in 1948 as a 'fellowship of Churches', two movements of the earlier twentieth century were merged, 'Faith and Order' and 'Life and Work'. The area of concern represented by the first was by far the most prominent in the Middle Ages. The medieval period had a 'social conscience' only insofar as it recognized the importance of almsgiving and general personal support of the kind Jesus had called for, for widows and orphans and the poor and afflicted. Medieval movements for social change tended to work from the bottom up, when anti-establishment dissidents preached 'popular' religion. Agreeing what was to be believed by Christians (the content of the faith), forming a 'body' of believers into an institution and creating rules under which they would live and worship together (Church order and its institutional features), became the defining tasks of the medieval Church. And it had new kinds of encounter to engage with, of sorts unknown in the ancient world.

In its first centuries Christianity had not only to define its beliefs; it also had to determine what kind of thing the Christian 'religion' was to be,[7] what Christians meant by 'religion'. In the Middle Ages it had to think that through in the face of the need to define itself in relation to Islam too. Neither of the chief conceptions of pagan antiquity about the nature of 'religion' quite fitted the Christian self-image. The Roman *pietas*, which is not quite rendered by the modern English 'piety', meant an attitude of dutiful respect. Jesus encouraged his disciples to think of God as their Father and themselves as his children, but the resulting relationship was to go far beyond Roman *pietas*. It was to involve something of the depth of intellectual companionship which ancient societies brought to the idea of friendship. This notion was moderated in medieval religious life. Fulbert of Chartres wrote to Abbo, the Abbot of Fleury, in the early summer of 1004: 'How can I suitably return your greeting, O holy abbot and great philosopher, what can I give you in return for the gift of holy friendship?'[8] A more developed theory of Christian friendship appeared in the first half of the twelfth century in the book 'On Spiritual Friendship' written by Ailred of Rievaulx. Ailred's idea was that Christian friends were always in the presence of Christ, who made a third whenever they met as friends.[9] *Religio*, on the other hand, connoted divine sanction, a feeling of supernatural constraint in the Roman world. It had to do with fear and awe. Here, too,

Christianity was subtly different. Jesus's emphasis was on the freedom of the children of God (John 8.32; Galatians 5.1).

As the confidence of the ancient world was lost and with it the scaffolding of society, there were many things to consider. *Ecclesia* originally meant an assembly of the people in a Greek city. In Christianity the term was to evolve to connote a mystical unity as well as a physical gathering, and a unity in which Christ himself was head to the 'body' of the assembled faithful.[10] For example, was the Christian community, which was calling itself the Church from New Testament times (Acts 8.3), a branch of Judaism or something quite distinct? The events recorded in Acts 15 led to a decision that the Church was not to require its members to keep the Judaic law. Was Christianity to define membership of the Church and set an entrance test so that those who wished to call themselves Christians must demonstrate their commitment? Was it to discipline those who apostatized? Decisions had been taken on all these points as the ancient world moved into the medieval period,[11] but they arose again in the melting together of tribes and belief-systems when the invading 'barbarians' took over the Empire. Where formerly Roman *imperium* had made top–down decisions about the way 'other faiths' were to be regarded and had deemed syncretism politically and pragmatically best, now no one was 'in charge' in the same way, and various views of the religious life had to jockey for position.

Was it going to be possible to be a Christian and at the same time continue to worship the pagan gods? The early Christians had got into a good deal of trouble over their refusal to throw their own beliefs into the syncretistic mix of the Roman Empire, worshipping the Emperor when called upon to do so. Nevertheless, it proved hard for ordinary people to break decisively with the comforts of the old local gods, and there were worrying indications that they were simply transferring their loyalty from the local gods to the local saints, with little real difference in the religious emotion involved and considerable unclarity about the theology. Augustine had commented with a mixture of exasperation and affection on his own mother's habit of pouring libations and tippling some of the wine herself. On the face of it, superstition, the nervous attempt to propitiate potentially hostile supernatural powers, was incompatible with faith in Christ, although ordinary people in late antiquity and even in the Middle Ages commonly hedged their bets on that point. Caesarius of Heisterbach, writing in the first half of the thirteenth century, describes a woman who took home in her mouth the consecrated host she was given at the Eucharist and put it into her beehive for safe keeping, having in mind some magic spells she hoped to perform with its powers. The bees, more respectful than she, built it a little shrine of wax.

But for the educated classes, the problem had another face. The late antique philosopher thought he stood eye to eye with the gods in a conversation of intellectual equals. 'Superstition was a social *gaffe* committed in the presence of the gods. It betrayed a lack of the ease and candour that were supposed to characterise a free man's relations with any persons, human or divine.'[12] Despite the emergence of a stronger sense of the humanity of the incarnate Christ – a conception which was uncomfortable for the philosophically educated of the ancient world – that sense of personal dignity and equality with God did not come so naturally in the Middle Ages. The medieval Christian theologian read Augustine on the subject of an intellectual exchange with God, capable of engaging soul and mind, *anima* and *animus*, but his own culture encouraged him to quake, to abase himself. The medieval mind found it more natural to talk of the dung-heap of human desires (*stercora*) to emphasize a person's unworthiness rather than his status as a free intellectual being walking the courts of heaven in energetic conversation with his friend and God.

Pagan and Jew and Christian and Muslim and 'dualist' and 'dissident' not only had different systems of belief in the Middle Ages; they had contrasting ideas of the very nature and purpose of religion both for the individual and for the society in which he or she lived. Already a generation or two before Augustine's time that scene had changed irrevocably. The Emperor Constantine the Great, in a tight corner politically, had chosen to become Christian, which meant that the Empire itself was now officially 'Christian' and the Church had a 'position' within the imperial constitutional framework. That story is told in a previous volume of this series, but its consequences were to run on into the present one. The relationship between Church and state was not to be off the agenda for a thousand years.

For this period of the first Christian Empire coincided with the first serious challenge to the imperial hegemony, the successive incursions of 'barbarians', the settlement of some of these new conquerors within the borders of the Empire with a licence to stay and with a good many pragmatic arrangements made to allow them to do so.[13] The people who lived in the variously conquered territories of the former Roman Empire had to make what adaptation they could or migrate away. By the sixth century the fragile persistence of the fiction that the Greek-speaking East and the Latin-speaking West were a single world was gradually breaking down. The Church was left at the 'end of Empire' as the only continuing institution with an administrative framework capable of holding together the delivery of supplies and some semblance of order, while the barbarian invaders made themselves comfortable in the conquered territories of proud old Rome.

The Empire in its last period had become bipolar, with a Latin capital city in Rome and a Greek capital in Constantine's new city of Constantinople. The contact between the two halves of the old Empire was now to be much slighter and more episodic for many centuries, often with mutual misunderstanding arising from the widening language barrier and the divergence of political needs. The East was forced to look further east as well as towards the West, for its other frontier in the Middle Ages was with Islam. This division proved important for the centuries with which we are concerned. The history of the Church in the Middle Ages becomes largely two parallel histories.

This story proved to be important for the Church in the modern world, for it was now that the interpenetration of communities created the conditions in the Balkans which made it so explosive an area. The break up of Yugoslavia was disastrous in the 1990s because the juxtapositions of the communities of Greek and Latin Christians and Muslims there had never been satisfactorily made to work. Other developments of the medieval period have cast equally long shadows.

CHAPTER I

The Medieval History of the Church in Time and Space

The Church: time and eternity, space and infinity

Why write a history? The medieval historian did not see this question in the same way as a modern historian would do. He was always aware of time as a slot in eternity, a kind of quantitative anomaly in something which had no quantities or durations, and that made him sensitive to the cosmic implications of whatever story he had to tell about events in time. It encouraged him to be conscious of the story's power to edify the reader. This question of its 'place in eternity' provided the supreme reference point of historical 'truth'.

Keeping a written record was recognized to be important. The author of the *Life* of the late twelfth-century Hugh of Lincoln says in his Prologue that he is writing in order that the record may be preserved 'in letters which will endure' (*tenacibus scribendo litteris*).[1] The chronicler was also, pragmatically, often concerned with proving a legal title to property, pinning down the right to land or some other form of grant. One should keep a written record of a transaction 'because the life of man is brief and it makes it easier to prove the gift was made', said Bracton (d.1268), the English legal authority.[2] Charters granting land to monasteries, for example, were frequently renewed, with the insistence that this was a mere continuation of an existing state of affairs, nothing new but simply a reminder to contemporaries. So another reference point of 'truth' might be the preservation of a state of affairs, even when it related to something as mundane as the right to hold a small piece of land. In the absence of a documentary record it was not uncommon to forge what was missing. The record had simply not been made at the time, so the gap was filled; this was not taken to amount to falsification, for there was no fraud, just the filling of a gap in the written record.

This approach to 'accurate' record keeping, which placed more reliance on recording what ought have been said than the authenticity of the copy which said so, could affect the keeping of records at a much higher level. The canon law of the Church embodied a vast collection of 'Ps-Decretals' of invented popes, put together by a figure to whom the name of the sixth-century encyclopaedist Isidore became attached, lending this Ps-Isidore further credibility by association.[3] It was not unknown for an author who wished to claim reliance on an older document to confess that, although he insisted that he or someone else had certainly once seen it, he could no longer produce it. Matthew Paris described how the original document on which he was relying in telling one story had been found in a hole in the wall, but had sadly crumbled to dust as soon as a fair copy (translation?) had been made in Latin.[4] Giraldus Cambrensis (Gerald of Wales) defends his own account of the ancient privileges of the see of St David against any attempt to suggest that he had made them up with *quod non res ficta vel frivola, non Arturi fibula.*[5]

So 'what is the truth' is a question with certain nuances when it comes to reconstructing the history of the medieval Church. Contemporary writers might well take the view that it was more important to preserve the story than to be honest about admitting to gaps in the record. *Historia* was first and foremost 'story', in the double sense of being a narrative and an explanation. The aim was to give an account which would make the reader see things in a certain light, the light of a spiritual and edifying 'truth' which need not necessarily coincide with what we should now regard as 'the facts'.

In any case, historical 'fact' was not limited to events of the sort to which history now restricts itself. There was no objection to including miracle and legend. When Geoffrey of Monmouth set out to write the *History of the Kings of Britain* in the 1130s, it was with the objective of linking the Anglo-Norman dynasty of English kings, who were really invaders from France and originally from the even more un-British Viking territories, with the legendary King Arthur, saviour of Britain. Improving and exemplary story could merge into 'real' history. The Norman poet Wace put Geoffrey of Monmouth's story into Old French for presentation to the erstwhile French queen, Eleanor of Aquitaine, when she divorced the French king and married Henry II of England.[6] Wace added the Round Table to the tale. It was further developed by Chrétien de Troyes who inserted the story of the quest for the Holy Grail (both the vessel used at the Last Supper and the cup in which Jesus's blood was said to have been caught when his side was pierced as he hung on the Cross), with its insistence on the importance of purity to the successful finding of the Grail. Galahad, the knight whose special quest this was, was said to have been the son of Lancelot and the daughter of King Pelles, the Grail King. She could trace her ancestry back to Joseph of Arimathea and King David. Wolfram von Eschenbach's *Parzival* describes the Grail differently, as a stone or perhaps 'bread', recalling the consecrated bread of the Mass, which prevents anyone who beholds it from dying for at least a week.[7] 'Real' history could travel into story too. The life of Charlemagne becomes an Old Norse *Karlamagnus Saga* in the late thirteenth century.[8]

Medieval ecclesiastical (and secular) historians saw no objection to including miracles in their histories because that was in comfortable accordance with the assumption that the story to be told was 'really' set in the supernatural world and in the context of eternity. Bede did not for a moment imagine that a historian who wished to do his job properly was required to leave out the supernatural or the miraculous.[9] Miracles, or at least marvels, had a place even in the historiography that is apparently addressed to a non-clerical readership, and in presentations of mere amusing anecdote. Gervase of Tilbury's *Otia imperialia* ('The Emperor at Leisure')[10] is the work of a twelfth-century English scholar-nobleman, a lawyer trained at Bologna, for a time a royal civil servant, who spent time at the court of Henry II of England, and wrote a book of amusements for the young prince Henry (which does not survive).[11] This larger work, *Otia imperialia*, intended for the amusement of the Emperor Otto IV, became a huge encyclopaedia of geography and marvels. He describes the 'marvels' in much the same spirit of straightforward acceptance as the authors of saints' lives describe miracles. They serve a similar purpose of heightening excitement and awakening awe.

The inclusion of miracles also has implications for the conception of *evidence* with which these authors were working. The very drama and impact of the miraculous could make a story seem more reliable. It altered or added to the acceptable range of chains of cause and effect that the marvellous could be that which is predictable within the laws of nature. But most important is the understanding that the divine plan can be seen to unfold in events. There is always a story behind the story, going beyond the recalling of the good examples set in previous generations, and that is the great narrative of salvation history which binds all together. Accordingly authors of medieval ecclesiastical histories commonly tell their tale as though it continued the historical narrative of Scripture. Orderic Vitalis (1075–1142) begins his *Ecclesiastical History* there and continues to the coming of the Holy Spirit, adding material in his first two books from apocryphal acts of the apostles. It is not until Book III of his *History* that he begins to set out the detailed information he has about the monasteries of Normandy.

John of Salisbury reviews the earlier historians of the Church to whom he proposes to add himself as the chronicler of its most recent days. Luke wrote the Acts of the Apostles. Eusebius told the story of the young Church (*adolescentis ecclesie*). Then came Cassiodorus and Orosius and Isidore and Bede and others 'it would be too tedious to list'. In John's own times there have been several, whose names he gives with a detailed explanation of the part of the story each has covered. John's proposal is to confine himself to *pontificalis historia*, papal history, and recent papal history since the Council of Rheims in 1148 at that, omitting everything else, for as a papal civil servant he is peculiarly well informed on that subject.[12] This sort of historiography is a close cousin to an exegesis of Scripture which also sees a march of ages against an eternal backdrop. Rupert of Deutz composed enormous commentaries in which he endeavoured to bring out such a pattern.[13]

Medieval historians often begin with a review of events since the creation of the world, not only so as to include the Scriptural narrative in their chronology, but also so as to go forward into eternity. As they look forward beyond the present day, the history turns to prophecy. Although they fully recognized the divine inspiration of the biblical narrative, they see no reason to draw a hard line between the historical events narrated in Scripture and those of more recent times or even the future. Some things belong to this world. Some are eternal. The medieval Christian world took the Church to belong to the cosmic dimension; they did not consider it merely an institution of this world.

Another twelfth-century author, Hugh of St Victor, proposes in his *De sacramentis ecclesiae* to distinguish two 'works' of God, the 'work of creation' (*opus creationis*) and the 'work of restauration' (*opus restaurationis*). The story of the first, he says, is told in the Bible's account, and the story of the second also unfolds there.[14] But the second cannot be arrived at by reasoning alone. It is historical. And it continues. The story the Bible has to tell goes on into the present and future.[15] Another notable example of the same approach is the work of the 'prophet Abbot' Joachim of Fiore (*c*.1135–1202). He organized all history into three periods (*status*). The first, described in the Old Testament, was the Age of the Father and ran from the creation of the world. The second, outlined in the New Testament and continuing for 42 generations, was the Age of the Son. The last, the Age of the Spirit, stretched into the future and was to be introduced by the rise of a new spiritual order. He prophesied the end of the world as we know it, which he believed would happen in the time of the 'Last World Emperor' of his own day.[16] Joachim eventually toppled over the edge of Christian intellectual respectability, to be condemned by the Fourth Lateran Council (1215), but it was not his approach to history that got him into trouble.

Against these ambitious habits of thought, and this reaching for ideal examples and something beyond current events, we must set a very different reality when it comes to the question of what medieval authors writing about the Church knew of the geography and physical extent of the world they lived in. The understanding of the workings of the 'real world' which was possible for an individual medieval author was very limited. Some writers frankly admit to a rather local view of the Church and its doings. Ralph Glaber (c.980–c.1046) lived his life in the monasteries of Burgundy, and his view of the world gives special prominence to the rise and establishment of the Capetian dynasty of French kings.[17] He contends that since Bede (c.672–735) in England and Paul the Deacon (c.730–c.799) in Italy there has been no one anxious to leave a history for posterity and each of these wrote only about his own geographical area. He knows that many things have happened in far-flung places and especially about the time of the millennium of the birth of Christ.[18] The occurrence of the millennium stimulates him to remark on various most unusual events, and to stretch beyond the local history he really knows about.[19]

Orderic Vitalis (1075?–1142) says he has a knowledge narrowed by the fact that 'monastic observance' keeps him at home, but within those limitations he has done his best to describe ecclesiastical affairs (res ecclesiasticae). In particular he recognizes that matters Egyptian, Greek and Roman (res alexandrinas seu grecas vel romanas) are out of his reach. But his story of local events has its larger implications nevertheless. He learned while writing a commissioned history of Saint-Evroul that he needed to comment on the 'good and evil' in the behaviour of the great of the land.[20]

The approach of such historians shows how keenly they strove to give their local story a wider scene, and at the same time it is an indication of the unavoidable lack of evenness of texture in the resources they had available to them.

We shall see in later chapters the growth of the realization that the world looked different from the vantage point of the Islamic rulers of parts of North Africa and southern Europe, and also from Greek-speaking Eastern Europe. The big picture, the prophetic picture, was very big indeed and there writers felt able to move more freely in their imaginations. They did not have the same confidence when it came to the power blocks of the contemporary world. Nevertheless looking at history like this encouraged a view of the Church in which the particular and familiar is always seen against the immensities of eternity and infinity.

Historiography

The purpose of the medieval historian of the Church 'in society' was the edification of his readers. When John of Salisbury cited Cato, 'The lives of others are our teachers',[21] he wanted to draw his reader's attention to the lessons to be learned from the examples set by leading figures of the past. The idea was that the holding up of earlier spiritual heroes would encourage people to become spiritual heroes themselves. Thomas of Marlborough's *History of the Abbey of Evesham*[22] begins with the explanation of the purpose of historical writing. It is to ensure that the outstanding deeds of good men and the evil deeds of bad men alike should not die with them but should be recorded for the edification of future generations. Had this not been done, he points out, we should not know how to imitate the Fathers of the early Church, for we should know nothing of the example they set.

In a study such as this, concerned with interfaith as well as Christian issues in the history of Christianity and the Church, it is important not to lose sight of the historiographical questions which were occurring to those of other faiths. The preoccupation with the basis of the knowledge of historians became pervasive in Islam. Al-Biruni, who described Judaic, Christian, Manichee and Indian religions, wrote a *Chronology* in which he began from the principle that 'the simplest method ... is to acquire a knowledge of the history of ancient nations ... most of which consists of historical reports about them and vestiges of their culture and customs'. But to get the necessary information one can 'only adopt what authors of books and men of religion ... have themselves used in this regard'.[23]

The comparative method relied on reasoning and the assessment of probabilities. For example, in the thirteenth century, Yaqut was considering the likelihood that Alexander the Great could have acquired the necessary leadership skills, marched throughout the earth and established 'all these cities' by the age of 20 (sic). 'And yet, in our own days ... and in the years 616 and 618 [i.e. the thirteenth century] ... there occurred such events, associated with the Mongols who came from China, as, had they continued to unfold, would have led to their occupation of the earth in a few years. ... In less than two years, they came to rule and ruin vast tracts of Moslem territory.' So perhaps it is true about Alexander.[24] The viewpoint of Muslims, their understanding of the events which had brought them where they were, geographically and in their beliefs, might, then, be very different from the way it was all seen by their Christian contemporaries, while they shared similar preoccupations about the nature and reliability of the evidence available to them.

So to set out to write a history of the medieval Church is to imitate many contemporary authors, who moved with varying degrees of sure footedness as they tried to understand the nature of their task, but who shared a different sense of the overriding purpose from the Church historians of both the ancient and the modern world. Medieval Church historians wrote a great deal – chronicle, memoir, biography and experimental work – which is a hybrid of history, exegesis and theology. Orderic Vitalis explains that he has called his work an 'ecclesiastical history' because it is his purpose 'to speak truthfully about ecclesiastical affairs as a simple son of the Church; eagerly striving to follow the early Fathers according to the small measure of my ability'.[25] In the mid-twelfth-century John of Salisbury's 'memoirs' of his time at the papal court, the *Historia pontificalis*, there are numerous digressions from this theme. He includes sharp personal comments so that what he writes seems now and then more like a memoir; he is visibly in pursuit of his own fame and glory. But these things were secondary to his notion of the reason for writing at all, which is that the history of the world is really the history of the Church, in which divine providence unfolds its purposes.

Some of the thinking of medieval historians of the Church concerned questions of methodology, of a kind with which modern historians still have to engage. Even if they would not have taken the same view of what a fact was, they examined (though not all of them) their duty to get the facts right. Bede, for example, tried to be careful to identify his sources; he emphasizes how much of what he relates derives from eyewitnesses or has been checked with written records.[26] They recognized another duty which they share with the modern scholar, which was to ensure that the coverage of events was completed, gaps filled, new happenings recorded, the work of previous scholars recognized, attributed, evaluated, corrected. John of Salisbury, twelfth-century raconteur of Church affairs, provides a critical analysis which aims to explain the chain of cause and effect and to evoke as fully as can be contrived the flavour and context and assumptions which make sense of what is narrated.[27]

CHAPTER 2

Spreading the Gospel:
The Missionary Centuries

What is mission?

Jesus sent his disciples out to spread the Gospel. He told them exactly what
to do. They were to take nothing for the journey, no luggage, not even a
walking stick, no food, no money. They were to preach to whoever would
receive them, eat the food they were given and move on, shaking the dust of
each place from their feet. This was the apostolic life in its first and purest
form, involving an absolute poverty and simplicity and dedication (Luke
9.3–5; cf. Matthew 10.14; Mark 6.11).

But as the first centuries passed, and Christianity became more deeply
interfused in society, society's tensions and the realities of politics made this
instruction seem not at all straightforward. The first Apostles would have
been objects of social disapproval to later generations, with their simple
garb and lack of formal education. Wild-haired 'charismatic' figures began
to look dangerous, a threat to the institutional stability of the Church. It
began to be asked what 'mission' meant beyond this first simple 'sending',
who was to be allowed to do it and on what authority, and what assurance there was that self-appointed missionaries would not teach misleading
things and lead the faithful astray at the very beginning of their conversion.

It also had to be asked how Christianity was to conduct its mission
within a changed and changing world. It is hard to set limits to expansion, especially when it is tinged with imperial ambitions. It was as difficult
for Rome in the ancient world as for Britain in South Africa, or Russia in
Afghanistan in the nineteenth century, or the USA in its 'war on terror' at
the beginning of the new millennium, to stop once they had begun, because
each piece of territory attained in the name of 'liberation' created a fresh
raw interface with angry and restless potential opposition from the as yet
unconquered.[1] It was an irony which will not be lost on the modern reader

that the justification for the additional expansion had often been that it was the only way to ensure the 'security' of an empire. The transitions between the defensive and the offensive could be as subtle as they were crucial. This all grew much more challenging with the collapse of the Roman Empire and the transition to a 'multicultural' world in which the relationship of Christians with the state could be of many kinds.

The main area of the old Roman Empire had, in the end, been officially Christian, in the sense that there had been a series of Christian emperors, with some interruptions, since the time of Constantine (d.337). During the period of the first Christian Empire, from the reign of Constantine, Christianity nominally extended to the boundaries of empire, though the Christianization seems to have been patchy or superficial in many places. Objects surviving from the Roman occupation of Britain show that there were Christians there, but the indigenous people were not apparently comprehensively converted, for Augustine of Canterbury came in 597 to people he understood to be pagans.

The infection of missions with contemporary political assumptions was inescapable in the flux of the period when the ancient world was mutating into the medieval world. In the fifth century, before the founding of Islam, protection money already had to be paid to Arabian chieftains to prevent raids on Byzantine territory. It was a matter of geographical advantage, not of religion.[2] Powers came and went, invasions too. It is easy enough to see now with hindsight that this was a period of decline of empire, and the pervasive sense that the world was in its old age (*senectus mundi*) was to be overtaken by a sense of new dawnings. At the time appearances were very differently interpreted.

It is impossible to separate the story of Christian missions from the movements of peoples and their beliefs across the face of Europe, as the early medieval centuries progressed. Charlemagne (714–814) was to rule an empire whose boundaries were defined as much by the recent endeavours of Christian missionaries as by politics and warfare. For when the invading tribes came down on the Empire, some pagan, some Christian from the communities holding an 'Arian'[3] version of the faith which was declared heretical by the Council of Nicaea in 325, they had proved quite capable of shaking up the hold of Christianity as the official imperial religion.

When the Roman Empire collapsed the institutions, the legal framework and structures of governance fell away with it in many parts of Europe. It was the Church, with its institutional framework, its network of diocesan bishops, its relatively good communications, which helped to keep food supplies moving. Pope Gregory the Great (*c.*540–604) had had responsibility for that kind of thing before and during his papacy, as his letters show.

The urge to expand was not confined to Christians in the late antique world and the early Middle Ages, and it could come in the form of a diffuse 'inculturation' of conquered lands as well as through conscious imposition of a new religion upon new territory, just as easily when other religions were 'spreading' as in the case of Christianity. The Germanic invaders who had been pressing down upon the Empire had the Western half largely under their control by 476. In the middle decades of the seventh century Islamic armies captured Egypt, Palestine, Lebanon and Syria from the Byzantine half of the old Roman Empire, which had survived the collapse of the Empire in the West. To the north the Slavs and the Turks hemmed the Byzantines in. So the pattern of migration, which was observable for several centuries after Charlemagne's day, brought new rulers and new systems of government and administration, some of which adopted Roman ways, at least in part, or adapted their own tribal structures to their new possessions. It would be unwise ever to forget the interconnectedness of politics and religion in this era of early medieval Christian expansion. On the northern front the pagan Saxons were pushing at the Rhine border in 778; in the east, the River Elbe, natural boundary though it was, signally failed to keep the Slavs from being a problem for many centuries. In the late 770s the Arabs in Spain were a threat as far north as Aquitaine. Charlemagne unwisely took sides in some internal Muslim disputes while hemmed in on all these sides, with the horsemen of the Steppes (known as Huns to the Carolingians) raiding and robbing from the north.

The Viking invaders from the Nordic pagan cultures presented challenges of 'inculturation' in England during the ninth and tenth centuries, and also in Normandy (so-called after the 'northmen'). These were even sometimes seen as the terrorists of their time. The Annals of Fulda record how in 845 the Nordmanni came as far as Paris, laying waste (*vastantes*), and left peacefully only after receiving a substantial monetary bribe. In the eleventh and twelfth centuries they conquered England and Sicily. We shall meet them as a worry sufficiently urgent to get the estranged leaders of the East and West corresponding about what to do. Ironically, once Christianized, the Normans became some of the most notable crusading leaders. Northern and eastern frontiers of Europe were brought into Christendom in the eleventh century (Norway, Sweden, Denmark, Poland, Bohemia, Hungary). (The boundaries with the Eastern Empire and its own struggles to establish an interface boundary with Islam in the East and with the non-Chalcedonian Churches, the contentions about control of Sicily, and of the areas of Eastern Europe which gave rise to Yugoslavia and Macedonia in more modern times, and the relations of Christians with Muslims in Spain as control of the land moved up and down, must wait for later chapters.)

Pushing against this inward and westward movement of non-Christian and anti-Christian interests went Christian missions, often led by individuals rather than carried along as part of the political package that came with an invasion. Patrick probably converted Ireland in this do-it-yourself way. He has been described as an ill-educated wandering bishop with a paid retinue of young nobles, giving gifts to petty kings.[4] He has also been seen as the spearhead of an ecclesiologically sophisticated system of institutionalization of Christianity in Ireland. It is difficult to resolve this dilemma, for it is impossible to determine whether he tried to establish an episcopal structure of dioceses in Ireland or preferred to encourage a monasticism which could remain independent of any such ecclesiological structure.[5] In his purported 'Confession' Patrick calls himself *peccator rusticissimus* (the most uneducated of sinners), while evincing some theological understanding. His attempt to define the deity shows no influence of the Nicene Creed, and leaves him struggling. 'For God never was nor ever will be anything but the Unbegotten Father without beginning, from which all things take their origin.'[6]

Other missionaries were definitely 'sent', with the full backing of the Roman support system, but still as individuals or small groups unconnected with invasions or tribal movements. Bede describes in his *Ecclesiastical History* how Pope Gregory the Great, happening to see some beautiful fair-haired slaves for sale in Rome and being told that they were 'Angles', sent the Augustine who became known as Augustine of Canterbury as a missionary to England. Thanks to Bede, we have a picture of what happened on Augustine's mission, which indicates that there was careful planning and use of resources and backup from adjacent Continental Christian organizations. There was a language problem of course, but up to a point Latin was a common language, and the missionaries had equipped themselves with Frankish interpreters and with arguments which would appeal to the self-interest of their potential converts. The message was conveyed to the King of Kent that the missionaries had come with good news, the promise of joys in heaven and a kingdom without end for those who would receive the Gospel. The King had a Christian wife, the daughter of a Frankish king, so this was not entirely new to him. She had been given to him as his wife only on condition that he allowed her to practise her religion, so he must have had some notion of what it involved.

The King struck a bargain with the missionaries. They were to be given accommodation and allowed to go about preaching and try what success they could have with the people. The missionary party settled down to a life which set an example, in imitation of the Apostles, and this simple and innocent way of life – a true approximation of the original purity of mission

Christianity fostered – proved so attractive that it won converts. The King himself was won over by what he saw and by the sweetness of what they promised and also by the evidence of the miracles they worked. The people flocked to hear and see in ever increasing numbers, abandoning, says Bede, the pagan ways of life in which they had lived before.[7] We do not know of course how clear an idea they had of their faith or how deep or exclusive Christianity became in this early period.

Once the 'conversion' appeared to be secure, Augustine travelled to Arles to be consecrated as a bishop for the English people.[8] There was a manifest will to act within the Church's proper 'order' in the planting of new churches. The complications of doing so are spelt out in the list of questions Augustine sent to Pope Gregory[9] and the answers he received. Augustine first asked how a bishop ought to behave. Gregory referred him to Scripture (I Timothy 3.15), but he added instructions which presume that the bishop will be living with his priest-helpers in a monastic community in which all things could be held in common and where any surplus gifts could be applied conscientiously to the needs of the poor.

The sixth question is whether the normal rule that three bishops must participate in the ordination of a new bishop may be waived if geography makes it difficult to get the requisite number together. Augustine, the new bishop, realized that he was going to be in difficulties about creating any extra bishops for England. The Pope recognizes that to begin with, his missionary will be in an emergency situation, 'for how often do bishops come from Gaul who can assist?' But he should make sure that at least priests are present, and as soon as possible he should ensure that a suffi-cient number of bishops is ordained to allow future episcopal ordinations to follow the normal rules.

Then comes the question of jurisdiction (question seven), which under-lines the territoriality of the local church. Augustine can have no jurisdic-tion over the bishops of Gaul, any more than he could legitimately harvest someone else's standing corn (Deuteronomy 23.25). But the Pope entrusts to him the existing British bishops (from the Irish mission) and encour-ages him to attend to their discipline and instruction. There is a group of pastoral questions framed in ways which suggest that Augustine was find-ing himself in real difficulties on such points. The third question Augustine asked the Pope concerns the discipline of the faithful, with reference to the particular problem of the way someone is to be treated if he robs a church. The Pope said that love must dictate the measure of correction. The thieves must restore what they have stolen of course, but the objective is to save their souls. The fourth and fifth questions, apparently also dealing with a practical pastoral matter but one which allows the Pope room to answer it by reference to broader principles, concern the prohibited degrees of marriage (for example, whether two brothers may marry two sisters if their families are not related). Gregory says he can find no reason in canon law why that should not be done, but he sets out rules for other circumstances in which marriage should not be allowed. Questions eight and nine are pastoral too, and concerned with a series of cleanliness questions relating to sexual intercourse and the sacraments, but also with matters of theological importance. (Beginning with 'Should a pregnant woman be baptized?', a knotty question if it could not be settled whether her unborn infant would automatically be baptized at the same time.)[10]

Problems arising from an attempt to superimpose one Christian mission upon another without taking thought beforehand about the need to accommodate the views and practices of any Christians who were there already, quickly became apparent. The earlier conversion of parts of what are now the British Isles by independent missionaries from Ireland may or may not have been known about in Rome when Gregory dispatched this mission, but the fact was that Augustine was being sent to lands where the Christian faith was already quite well established. Ireland was Christian. Irish missionaries had reached the northern parts of mainland Britain. Augustine landed in the south of the island, while these existing Christian missions were at work mainly in the north. There was no lack of communication between the two once Augustine's conversion had settled down. At least one well-known dynastic marriage among the 'royal' families of the English tribal 'kingdoms' involved partners from the different traditions. Bede gives a lengthy account in his *Ecclesiastical History* of the holding of a Synod at Whitby, when the strains on the royal marriage became too great and it became desirable to establish who was 'right'. One section of the population, those converted by Irish missionaries, was celebrating Easter according to one calendar, while those converted according to the rites of the mission of Augustine of Canterbury sent from Rome were celebrating on a different day, which could be many weeks apart. Queen Eanfled, who came from Kent, took the Roman date but her husband, the King of Northumbria, kept to the Celtic one. This made the differences pressing in a practical way. It created discomfort at court.

The Synod of Whitby demonstrates a tendency common in the centuries of the Reformation and after. A continuing loyalty to the leader or founder or missionary who first won the believer to the faith or to a particular version of the faith could be so strong that adherents almost lost sight of the common faith. Called to give account of themselves, spokesmen for the two sides at Whitby explained that they did as they had been taught by those who had converted them, though it was commented that it was fitting that those who serve one God should keep one rule of life (*unam vivendi regulam tenere*).[11] Some of the southern Irish Churches had celebrated the Roman Easter from the mid-sixth century. The Synod persuaded the Northumbrian Church to adopt the Roman calendar. Iona and its dependants remained of the Celtic persuasion until 716.[12] The Easter controversy had a further dimension too, one far more international than Bede perhaps realized. It divided Europe, for it was indeed felt that the common celebration of so important a feast must be essential to the unity of the Church.

Augustine asked Gregory whether variation was allowed in the forms of the liturgy. Traditionally variation of rites had been acceptable provided it did not imply differences of faith. Gregory advised him to select from the best of the Gallic and any other rite, modifying the Roman rite with which he is familiar in the way he thinks will best meet the needs of his new English Christians. Yet it could be hard to say what constituted a difference of detail in worship, or conduct of life, and what was a substantive and potentially divisive difference. Some differences were very obvious. Bede quotes correspondence on the differences of hairstyle between monks of the Irish mission and those of the Roman conversion. It is known that the Apostles did not all use the same style of tonsure. This might seem trivial, and surely not a Church-dividing matter. The imperative that there should be one faith, one hope, one love for God, does not extend to a requirement that there should be 'one mode of dressing the hair', it is suggested.[13] Yet such things could divide in exactly that way, as the controversy over the date of Easter and the controversy over the use of leavened or unleavened bread in Holy Communion show. Both had the same characteristic of being noticeable to people in their daily lives, and having symbolic importance far deeper than might seem.

Missions tend to breed missions, for the convert, excited about his new view of things, tends to be full of zeal. Less than a century after Augustine of Canterbury's successful conversion of the southern English kingdoms, from 677 to 678, Wilfrid, Bishop of York, was in Frisia in a failed attempt to win the people there over to Christianity. Willibrord (658–739) was one of his disciples, a Northumbrian and a monk who had 12 years' experience in an Irish monastery. Boniface (*c*.675–754) was one of Willibrord's followers. Only after a first abortive attempt to convert Frisia in 716 did his mission work 'officially', with papal blessing. His idea was to cultivate with the plough of his preaching the uncultivated hearts of the people of Germany.[14]

Such preaching could still, in the nature of things, be directed in the first instance only to princely ears and the ears of those who held power. When the prince is Christian the community is Christian, in the sense that that is how it identifies itself, though not of course in any sense which allows us to get the feel of the understanding the ordinary faithful were likely to have of their new faith. When Boniface addressed Thuringia, with his papal mandate, it was the leaders of the people he was consciously speaking to.[15] The sixteenth-century principle that the ruler determines the official religion (*cuius regio eius religio*) was a pragmatic truth long before it became a political one in the sixteenth century.

The strongest argument, and perhaps the one most likely to convince a ruler, was that the Christian God was more powerful and more effective than the one he had been worshipping. A God who could deliver victories, children, wealth, was the God to choose, Bishop Daniel of Winchester, who had come of Germanic blood himself, told Boniface in a letter to stress this point.[16] Here is a notion complementary to the assumption that if a ruler becomes a Christian his realm is 'converted' too, in an early form of *cuius regio eius religio*. Yet it was obvious in the flow of changing hegemonies in the late antique and early medieval worlds that those dwelling in a given 'place', realm, region, kingdom, empire, will not necessarily be solidly of the same religion as their prince or government.

Such missionary work could be dangerous. Boniface was killed in Frisia in 754. But to die spreading the Word was martyrdom.

The old 'Roman' boundaries of Christendom expanded during the Middle Ages as 'missionaries' arrived in more and more of the lands which had lain on the fringes of the old Roman Empire. Here, too, politics and commerce had vested interests in converting unbelievers to the faith. The Church prudently formed the habit of putting down local churches and instituting bishoprics wherever they made conversions, as though they were footprints on the land, bringing the new communities of the faithful within the existing institutional framework.

It is not at all easy to be sure what understanding of membership and belonging went with these successful missions at first. *Metanoia*, a true change of mind, is rarely to be achieved at the point of the sword, or as a politically advantageous move. It takes dialogue and the winning of hearts and minds. Something of the sort was going on in the missionary preaching just described, but these tales of changed religious stance are unsatisfactory. They do not help us to distinguish between a relatively simple change of commitment and a thought-through new theological position; they tell us little about what happened in the mind and soul of someone when he understood that polytheism would not longer do, and how many continued to hedge their bets in adherence to the old ways as well as the new.

Pilgrimage: a gentler journeying and the broadening of horizons

A pilgrimage is a journey to a holy place, undertaken as a meritorious act or as a direct means of getting into contact with the numinous with the objective of benefiting from supernatural help. It is not a missionary activity but it was still understood in the Middle Ages as a Christian journeying, an adventure of faith. Pilgrimage was not a wholly new idea. The paganism of the ancient world had featured many shrines to the gods, where the pious would come in search of help. But Christianity introduced new elements as well as new shrines and holy places.

One of the most notable early Christian pilgrims had been Helena, the mother of the Emperor Constantine. Her fame reached the late eleventh-century writer Guibert of Nogent, who refers to her in his book *Gesta Dei per Francos* ('Deeds of God through the Franks').[17] Pilgrimages became newly fashionable in the early eleventh century. Richard II, Duke of Normandy, provided the funding for one in 1026, which was to be led by Richard Abbot of St Vanne at Verdun.[18] Once news got about, numbers grew as other groups joined them, and they had encounters which suggest that there were avenues of communication by which the notion of such pious travelling could spread. On their journey the pilgrims met the Venetian Gerard, who was living as a hermit in Hungary. Simeon from Syracuse, now a monk on Mount Sinai, was waiting for them at Antioch to collect alms which they were bringing from Normandy to support his monastery. This indicates a considerable degree of organization, even if Simeon had had a number of vicissitudes on his journey. Certain shrines and places became especially attractive to pilgrims, and Jerusalem, Compostela and later Canterbury became significant marks on the map of the Church's life.

Although most people probably never strayed far from their birthplaces, there was travelling for various purposes, commercial, diplomatic and administrative. It was practical for a king or great baron to travel through his lands with his household consuming the more perishable of the produce he was owed in return for the use of his properties by his tenants. So feudal lordship could be peripatetic. Abbots of great abbeys made journeys to keep an eye on the monastery's lands, which might become far-flung, as noble benefactors made gifts from their own extensive estates over the generations. It was this kind of journeying which had brought Anselm, the Abbot of Bec, to England in a year when the archbishopric of Canterbury became vacant with the death of Lanfranc.

These incidental broadenings of perspective cannot be said to have provided a systematic geography any more than they did a complete chronology, still less a real insight into the way things looked to others elsewhere. The problem of mutual incomprehension will be a repeating theme of this book. Liutprand (*c*.922–72)[19] had no understanding of the way Constanti-nople fitted into the power blocs of his time, and the Western funders and leaders of the Fourth Crusade (1204) had no real conception of what would be involved in capturing Byzantium and dividing the spoils of empire. It may, for the modern reader, be reminiscent of the attitudes struck in the 'war on terror' of the early twenty-first century. The Iraq war of 2003 and its aftermath demonstrated the difficulty of seeing ahead or of understand-ing the realities of a course of action in another place or civilization even when information is comparatively plentiful. A medieval observer could travel widely in his mind, but however well read he was, and however well travelled in the physical world, it was impossible for an individual writer to approach the sophistication of up-to-the-minute understanding which could be aspired to by any casual modern newspaper reader.

CHAPTER 3

The Church Defines
the Outsider

'He who is not with me is against me,' said Jesus, and 'he who
does not gather with me scatters' (Matthew 12.30).

The notion that there is 'no salvation outside the Church' appears as early as
Cyprian[1] and grew stronger with his North African successor Augustine.[2]
Ecclesia, the word that both Greek and Latin Christians adopted as the word
for 'Church', began as a Greek word for 'assembly' or 'gathering'. The early
Christians developed a theory of community (*koinonia*) in which Christ was
the Head and his faithful people were the Body (Ephesians 1.22–3, 4.15–16;
Colossians 1.18–24), in a relationship organic in its structure and unified in
the profound level which that image implies. Its lived reality might be – for
most – within a local church, the kind of 'gathered community' so important in sixteenth-century reforming thinking. But the mystical whole, the
'Idea of Church', formed the macrocosm for these microcosms. It was in
this total context that it was so strongly felt that those who were not insid-
ers were outsiders.

Yet on the face of it, the medieval Church displayed inconsistent attitudes to being an outsider. *Proscriptus* in classical Latin conveys enforced
exile or being outlawed. It applied to someone whose life and property were
forfeit.[3] Jesus is called *proscriptus* in the Vulgate translation of Galatians 3.1.
Being *peregrinus et hospes*, a wanderer from home, and thus making yourself
an outsider for Jesus's sake (Matthew 19.29; Mark 10.29; Luke 18.29), was
praiseworthy and the stimulus for many 'extreme lives' in the Middle Ages,
but only because the exile was longing to return to the *patria*, the homeland, where his father would welcome him back.

There were various ways in which a Christian could come to look like an
outsider in the sense of being not an unwilling exile but wilful and obstinate
in his refusal to remain within the Church. One was a complete lapse of

faith, the apostasy which was identified in the early Church as one of the three serious sins (along with murder and adultery). Another was apathy or evil living, which could be put right by amendment of life. Another was adherence to Judaism or Islam. Another was schism, encouraging division in the one Church, which was a breach of order. Another was disagreement with the Church's teaching on one or more particular points of doctrine which, if persisted in, became heresy.

Up to a point, it could be acceptable to consider all these sorts of non-Christian, if not in the same breath, at least as falling in the same general area of concern from the Church's point of view. Alan of Lille recognized this when he wrote *Contra haereticos* ('Against the Heretics') at the end of the twelfth century, with chapters on dualists, popular dissidents, Jews and Muslims.[4] Alan sets out the opinions of heretics and the way to refute them in four books, with a preface alleging that not only are old heresies reappearing as new heresies but the true faith is also being contaminated by philosophical speculations.[5] His first class of heretics is the dualists; here his principal anxiety is to establish that God is the creator of the material as well as the immaterial world. Book II is concerned with the Waldensians, and in it he is chiefly concerned to show the necessity of obedience to the ordained ministry and proper observance of the sacraments.

Thomas Aquinas did something similar, though in a more sophisticated way, when he wrote his *Summa contra gentiles* a century later. All known ways of misbelieving were arranged so as to enable an apologist for the official Church position to identify and classify what he was being told and select the correct rejoinder. Just as heretics tended to be 'tarred with the same brush', so too did communities which were perceived, for one reason or another, as being 'outside' the Church. It was as though the most important thing about them was their being outsiders. A passage in the Song of Songs (2.15) about foxes became a standard textual authority for the idea that although heretics may seem to be saying different things, they are really all the same. They are like foxes with their tails all tied together. Bernard of Clairvaux devoted several sermons in his long cycle of the Song of Songs to this idea[6] and it found its way into the decrees of the Fourth Lateran Council.

As Christendom expanded and consolidated itself it became increasingly important to clarify what ought to be done about outsiders in this collective sense of being somehow, in various ways, beyond the bounds of the Christian community.[7] Was it right to look inward and concentrate on the Christian community? Bernard of Clairvaux argued, during the period in which he remained reluctant to encourage people to join the Second Crusade, that bringing back its own straying sheep and keeping them in the fold was the proper work of the Church and its ministers, not mounting military expeditions against those who were not of Christ's flock. Peter the Venerable, Abbot of Cluny, eventually persuaded Bernard that he was wrong, and it was appropriate to stir up Christendom to military effort, so as to drive Muslims out of the holy places of Christendom. Once convinced, Bernard became indefatigable in preaching the Second Crusade, until its failure had him apologizing and returning to his earlier contention that the first priority was to make people better Christians, in the belief that God would then reward his Christian soldiers with success.

A variety of outsiders: the rationalists

What, then, was the range of 'outsiders' with which the medieval Church had to deal and about whom it had to make this important decision whether to turn its back on them or engage with them? There is not much evidence for medieval atheism. Most people probably believed in God after a fashion, or said they did. Society expected it. There were probably few so far 'outside' that they had no time for religion at all.

The role played by atheists and agnostics in modern theological debates fell to certain intellectuals, who could be loosely identified for the purposes of discussion with the 'philosophers' of the ancient world. There were plenty of thinkers and writers 'doing philosophy' as an intellectual exercise, as part of a foundation course of study of the liberal arts, and for its helpfulness to their task as Christian theologians. Nevertheless the ancient philosopher, for whom a rational metaphysics supporting moral principles took the place that the Christian religion occupied for Christian believers, had no real medieval counterpart, though he was to be met with in considerable numbers as late as Augustine's day in the fourth and fifth centuries.

Gilbert Crispin, in his *Disputation with a Gentile*, describes a philosophical society which he says used to meet in London at the turn of the eleventh century. Gilbert evidently expected his readers to be able to enter into the spirit of the idea of a 'talking club' or 'debating society'. One day as he entered, he says, he found the members discussing whether to rely on reason and authority, and which 'authority', Old Testament or New.[8] It is just possible that this was a real debating society, but even if it was, the members arguing the philosophers' position would be doing so merely as role-play in the debate. Such intellectual guides, who invited others to scepticism, were not the real threat to the faith they became from the eighteenth century onwards. Their role in Christian theology was to provide a background of rational argument into which material derived from classical philosophy could be slotted for educational purposes.

Judaism

Real living and arguing 'outsiders' were plentiful enough. Literally closest to home for medieval Christians were the Jews. Jews and Christians lived in the same cities throughout Europe, and had done so since Roman times, though not without episodes of conflict. Severus of Minorca's early fifth-century *Letter on the Conversion of the Jews* underlines the potential explosiveness of even the most seemingly settled scenes of harmonious 'living together' by adherents of different faiths. Mutual tolerance could readily turn into a crusading zeal for enforced conversion if something happened to disturb the balance. The Jews and the Christians in Minorca had become practised at mutual tolerance within a socially integrated way of life. Then the alleged 'relics' of Stephen, the first Christian martyr (Acts 7.58–9), arrived, having recently been 'identified' in their resting place in the Holy Land and brought by a passing priest who was on a journey from Jerusalem to Spain. The effect was dramatic. The local Christians awoke to a new pride in their faith and were filled with a burning zeal (*tepor noster incaluit*). Friendly greeting of Jews in the street abruptly ceased, and love turned to hatred driven by the new 'greater love of salvation', says Severus. There were street battles, he adds,[9] and eventually the local synagogue was destroyed and the Jewish community was converted *en masse* to the Christian faith.[10]

In the early summer of 576, Avitus, Bishop of Clermont, allegedly induced several hundred Jews to become Christians. The historian Gregory of Tours had been born in the city and knew Avitus. Gregory's own account survives in his *Histories*. He describes the entry of King Guntram into Orléans, and how his arrival was greeted in customary fashion by enthusiastic crowds waving banners in the streets and shouting the praises of their king. The Jews were visible among them, waving like the rest. The King is reported to have been unimpressed by this display. He later remarked at dinner that he thought the Jews had been there merely because they hoped he would pay for the rebuilding of their synagogue; their enthusiasm had been nothing but a false display.

What such claims of mass 'conversion' really meant is another matter. Of all those 'outcast' because they were not orthodox Christians, the Jewish community were in the most 'impossible' position when it came to integration into the community. There were innumerable questions of Jewish identity and practice standing in the way, not least the fact that Judaism is a system of custom and ritual as much as a belief-system. From the 'theological' point of view there remained the insuperable barrier that Jews felt that they could not accept Christ as the Son of God as the Christians did and still remain Jews. This became the central issue between Jews and Christians, reappearing again and again. Guibert of Nogent (*c*.1053/65–*c*.1125) wrote a *Treatise on the Incarnation* because he saw the Incarnation as central. Alan of Lille identifies the same key issue of dispute in his book against the heretics.[11]

Real conversions from Judaism did of course occur. That can be seen to take place in several personal accounts, though such tales are written with an emphasis designed to be pleasing to the Christian reader. They seem to be for self-congratulatory Christian consumption rather than a serious effort to draw more Jews to Christianity. They are sanitized and focused. Such autobiographical accounts of the pros and cons may even have helped to spur the anti-Semitism that is arguably present in the twelfth century, by adding to the armoury of the Christian apologists. Peter Abelard advances an argument from 'rewarded suffering' in his fictional debate, the *Collationes*, where a Christian and a Philosopher both argue with a Jew. The Jews are persecuted, and it seems to the Jewish speaker into whose mouth Abelard puts this idea unjust that they should receive no reward for their sufferings. They make their way in pilgrimage (*peregrinatio*) among people who hate them. The laws they have to obey lay a heavy yoke on them.[12] The Philosopher's response is to point to natural law. Before the Judaic law was laid down, he says, people knew that they should love God and their neighbours and live lives acceptable to God. Abel knew that, and Noah, and his children.[13]

The role of Jews as financiers may have added to their unpopularity in anti-Semitic quarters, but the core of the matter seems to have been the claim that the Jews had murdered Jesus, that the *synagoga* was opposed to the *ecclesia* in every way and that the Jews were the enemy. This prejudice against the Jews is noticeable in the 'Confession of Faith' of Bruno the Carthusian, where he adds to the usual elements of the creed: 'I believe that that same Son of God was captured by the "perfidious" Jews, injured, unjustly bound, spat on, beaten, died and was buried.'[14]

Arguably what we have here is *apologia* treated as polemic, in rather the spirit of the hostilities arising out of mutual incomprehension between Greeks and Latins. One of these dialogues was written by Hermannus Judaeus in the twelfth century. He builds up to the high drama of his eventual capitulation by describing how long and hard he resisted. That enables him to heighten the contrast between the sweet kernel which the Christian finds by penetrating to the heart of Scripture's 'spiritual' or 'figurative' senses, and the husk of the literal sense with which the Jews content themselves. He explains how long it took him to realize this and how hard he resisted while the truth pressed itself upon him. He also contrasts the ritual observances of the Jews with the 'apostolic life' the Christian lives.[15] Peter Alfonsi was another Jew who became a Christian in 1106. His *Disciplina clericalis* was probably written in his native Spain.[16] He, like Hermannus, writes with all the zeal of a new convert about his reasons for embracing Christianity and rejecting Judaism.

Yet there is evidence of real interfaith conversation, on various levels, where we may glimpse something closer to the actual debate needed to clarify the differences between 'Judaic' and 'Christian' options. In the Middle Ages, Jews lived among Christians, in the same towns and cities, and had commercial and conversational dealings with them. Gilbert Crispin, as Abbot of Westminster, was also the author of *Disputation with a Jew*. This may possibly have its origins in contacts with the Jews who would have been approached as money lenders for building work at the abbey. In Gilbert Crispin's *Disputation with a Jew* the theological complexity of the debate is greater than that to be found in his briefer *Disputation with a Gentile* (or pretend-philosopher).[17] Peter Abelard's *Collationes* is a dialogue involving all three, a Christian, a Philosopher and a Jew, in which the level of debate is more profound.[18] The Philosopher raises an important and realistic question at the outset. He asks the Jew and the Christian whether they have reasons for what they believe or whether they had adopted their positions just because they are beliefs current among their own people. Is this merely what a parent brought them up to believe? Unthinking acceptance of a 'cradle faith' is not only a social or sociological reality but, he suggests, a cause of lack of progress in human knowledge. He observes that human understanding grows (*crescat*) age by age, yet he notices that among the adherents of a given religion orthodox 'faith' is that which does not go beyond what everyone believes, the ordinary people, the leaders of society and the ignorant and the educated alike. Investigation and analysis of the faith is discouraged, even punished, because it raises doubts about the common opinion.[19]

The Jew in the dialogue responds with an illustrative 'story' underlining the importance of Scriptural 'authority' in all such transactions. Supposing he is the servant of a lord of whom he stands greatly in fear. His fellow servants tell him that this lord has given certain commandments at a time when he himself was not present. Will he not be wise to obey those commandments just as they do, even though he did not personally hear them delivered? Whether or not the lord gave such a command is a matter of historical fact and cannot be proved by reasoning. But neither can it be disproved, and the Jew considers it prudent and rational to accept the veracity of what he is told, just in case.[20]

The interlocutors discuss what each is prepared to accept by way of proof in the debate they are going to have. What would convince each that one of the others is right? The Jew can accept only the Old Testament, the Christian both Old and New and the Philosopher only what reason tells him.[21]

A modern controversialist in this situation might be expected to enquire about the Hebrew text in the original language. Peter Abelard may have asked the advice of Jewish Hebrew speakers on puzzling Hebrew terminology in the Old Testament.[22] It was a feature of the elementary failure to take the obvious steps towards achieving mutual understanding that he did not set about learning Hebrew but apparently merely asked advice on difficult words. Andrew of St Victor perhaps did the same in compiling his Old Testament commentaries for Christian use, which concentrated in the Jewish fashion on the literal interpretation.

There certainly were exchanges and conversations, if only for business purposes. As the Middle Ages progressed and a middle-class bourgeoisie grew up and prosperity increased, there was a growing practical need for banking facilities. Yet Christians were in a difficult position. They read Leviticus 25.36–7 ('Do not make a profit out of helping your kinsfolk'), Deuteronomy 23.19–20 ('You may not charge interest except on loans to a foreigner') and Luke 6.35 ('Lend and expect nothing in return'). The Third Lateran Council of 1179 and the Second Council of Lyons in the West forbade Christians to practise usury. Thomas Aquinas was against charging interest, but Hostiensis thought it might be justifiable if the lender was going to be inconvenienced by doing without his money for a time. Moreover fees could be charged for carrying out transactions without its counting as usury.[23] The Fourth Lateran Council of 1215 permitted usury to Jews, with the proviso that if they exacted unreasonable rates of interest they would be subject to a Christian boycott (Canon 67). The Jewish communities living in towns served a useful purpose as money lenders willing to accommodate scruples and facilitate Christian trade.

In the mid-1230s Pope Gregory IX was sent a treatise containing 35 alleged dangerous falsehoods in the Talmud, compiled by Nicholas Donin, a convert from Judaism. A mythology evolved, taking forward ideas which had been current in previous centuries, but focusing on the notion that present-day Judaism was a perversion and that the Jews had been misled by demonic persuasion. The growing renewed interest in this derived partly from the fact that the Christians were beginning to study Hebrew seriously and to read the Talmud for themselves, especially in Spain. Secular authorities such as Louis IX of France took an interest and were keen to see action against the Talmud. The papacy looked on all this with an uncertain eye. It responded at first by an Inquisitorial approach, seizing books, condemning them and having them burned. But in 1247 a delegation of Jews went to see Innocent IV and persuaded him that he was in danger of countenancing an injustice if this continued, and he ruled that Jewish scholars must be allowed to consult books such as the Talmud, which they needed for the interpretation of their laws and the text of the Old Testament. Thomas Aquinas, writing about the Jews,[24] stressed the importance of recognizing the indispensable place of the Jews in the economy of salvation.

Islam

What did medieval Christians understand about Muslims? Like the Jews, Muslims became embedded in a mythology which treated them unfavourably and encouraged hostilities. It was customary to identify them with the Ishmaelites of Genesis 16. Ishmael is described by Genesis as the 'wild' son of Abraham. Isidore of Seville, of the same generation as Mohammed himself, suggested that they were also known as 'Saracens' because they 'falsely pretended' to be descended from Sarah, Abraham's wife, although they were really the descendants of his slave and concubine, Hagar, who was Ishmael's mother.[25] The usual vocabulary used in the Middle Ages to describe Muslims was 'Saracen', 'Arab', 'Turk', 'Moor' or simply 'pagan'.[26]

Christians in the Eastern half of the old Roman Empire had been familiar with Arab civilization before the founding of Islam. There the Arabs were, on the border, a powerful military threat and a successful invading and occupying force in some areas. It was only later that it became apparent that they might also present a challenge to Christian faith. Christians living in the conquered territories found it expedient to convert to Islam if they wished to progress in their careers in the service of the government. It was only with the realization in the seventh and eighth centuries that this was a threat to Christianity that polemicists got to work, as far apart as Syria and Spain, explaining and justifying. The most important of their themes mirrored the argument Augustine had put forward in *The City of God*, when educated pagans fleeing for safety to North Africa asked how he could claim that the Christian God was all-powerful when he was allowing a Christian empire to fall under the control of the 'barbarians'. Augustine had explained what was happening in terms of a divine providential plan, in which the education and stirring up of apathetic Christians was a significant need. Now, in a new context and with a new religion presenting a challenge, it once more seemed the strongest argument to say that God's purpose was educational and edificatory, and that he was revealing the imminence of the end of the world by allowing the long-prophesied mass conversion to error to take place.[27]

The religion of Islam – which means 'submission' – was 'founded' by Mohammed (*c*.570–632), after the end of the ancient world. It may be that Mohammed saw himself as no more than a messenger sent by God to recall his people to the truth and warn them of God's judgement soon to come. His message in the first instance was to the Arabian peninsula where idolatry and polytheism were rife.[28] Islam regarded itself from the first as the primal religion, from which Judaism and Christianity had strayed. At first it was a religion of simple core beliefs and straightforward required practice. Its central idea was the oneness of God and the importance of accepting the Prophet Mohammed as the last and greatest prophet. Islam has no priests and no institutional or organized Church. It regards secular and sacred authority as one, a single continuum. Prayer five times a day was expected of all the faithful, together with almsgiving, fasting during the holy month of Ramadan and pilgrimage to Mecca at least once in a lifetime, but that was all. The fundamental notions were therefore different from Christianity not only in the details of requirements of observance but also in the general idea of what a 'religion' was, and most particularly in the assumptions about the way adherents should be organized. There is no real counterpart to the Christian Church.

Mohammed taught the warring tribes of Arabs that they must stop fighting one another. His followers must live in peace. On the other hand, they had a duty to strive to persuade unbelievers to adhere to Islam. This striving (*jihad*) could be interpreted so as to allow scope for the use of violence. Both these objectives accorded with the notion that all the Arabs should aim to come together into a single great *umma*, with its capital in the holy city of Jerusalem.

The Islamic lands of the mid-eighth century were vastly more extensive than those of the Eastern, Byzantine half of the old Roman Empire. The latter extended round Greece, parts of north and south Italy, Sicily and into Asia Minor, but south of Antioch, along the coast of North Africa, into Egypt and across the Middle East as far as the borders of modern India and north to the Caspian Sea, was Muslim territory. The old Persian Empire, always fearsome to Rome, had been absorbed into this new empire.[29]

Intellectually speaking, the unity of the movement was short lived. Its holy Book was the Koran. The Koran drew on the Old and New Testaments, but selectively. The relative simplicity of the early inspiration and of the writing of the Koran itself proved, much as in Christianity, an irresistible challenge to intellectuals. Once scholars got to work and debates began, 'schools of thought' emerged. A division arose. Shi'ites were the 'party' of Ali, Mohammed's son-in-law. They would not accept the authority of the first three caliphs who came after the Prophet. The Sunnis, now by far the most numerous group in world Islam, respect these early caliphs and do not accept that Ali and his descendants deserve special reverence. But for the Sunnis, interpretation of the Koran and the *Sunna*, the original body of tradition and practice according to the consensus of the faithful, had ended with the ninth century.

The contrast was not wholly dissimilar to that between Greek and Latin Christians, with the Greeks much more reluctant than the Latins to entertain any idea of 'development' of doctrine beyond the very early period. For some Muslims any record which seemed to 'add' to the Koran presented a difficulty. The *Hadith*,[30] which included more than one kind of account of the progress of Islam, began to evolve in the Umayyad period[31] into something more closely resembling Christian historiography in its inclusion of threads of sacred, local and universal history. The Christian acceptance of 'ecclesiastical authors' as authoritative, though to a lesser degree than the Bible, was more easily negotiated because of the slow progress of the canon of the Bible to its position of acceptance roughly by the end of the fourth century. By then a considerable body of Christian writing was already in active use and being relied upon.

These divisions of a theological kind led to divisions of communities and to political and geographical consequences. In the tenth century there was a deepening of the internal schism in Islam between the Sunni and the Shi'ite Muslims, with the Shi'ites taking over Egypt and setting up a new dynasty there in 972.[32]

Christian knowledge of the world of Islam was derived in the first instance by direct encounter, in unpromising circumstances. For the progressive invasion of 'Christian' territory in the post-Empire world was alarming. Muslim forces, at first merely small tribal groups seeking booty, began to expand after the death of Mohammed. As early as 634 Byzantium was sufficiently uneasy about this to engage them in battle in southern Palestine. The Greek forces came off worst. Emboldened, Arab Muslim armies moved into Syria, then a Byzantine province, and captured Damascus in 636 and Jerusalem in 638. To the north, Byzantium held on to Anatolia and the Balkans, though they had to fight off major assaults in 660, 668 and 717 when the Arabs made a bid for Constantinople. The next region to be conquered was Egypt, which fell much more easily to the Arabs in the early 640s. Muslims had taken North Africa by 711, and then moved up into Spain, generally tolerating the continuing presence of Christians, who seem to have accepted the occupation, for the great military powers of Roman Christendom were now a spent force and the Ostrogothic and Visgothic kingdoms which had succeeded them (in the fifth to the seventh centuries) were also passing.

An uneasy accommodation was arrived at, in rather the way we have just seen happening between Christians and Jews. Muslim Arabs seem to have adopted some of the Greco-Roman patterns of government and habits of city life.[33] Two broad notions of the role of a 'caliph' emerged, one inspired by Islam and essentially religious, the other a more secular notion. Christians living under Muslim rule were not as a rule forced to convert (for Mohammed had not made that a requirement), but if they did not their status in the new society was low and that perhaps encouraged a tendency to do so. There was some 'moving on' and 'moving elsewhere' too. A proportion of those who preferred to go into exile rather than change their faith arrived in Italy, including monks, nuns and clergy as well as laity, and some of them proved to be notable in the Christian Church.

Living in the same places did not necessarily lead to mutual understanding, still less to mutual respect. While the Jews were a known quantity, their Scriptures familiar to Christians in their own Old Testament, the Muslims were not. Their Koran remained for some time a new and unknown text in the world of Christian scholarship.

Yet Islam must have seemed more coherent as a threat than any 'paganism' of Augustine's time, for early polemicists embarked on a campaign of vilification of the Prophet for which there seems no exact counterpart in the way the earlier varieties of barbarian invader had been characterized. There are parallels in the attempts to demonize Arius.[34] For some centuries Muslims converting to Christianity in the Greek Church had been required to assent to a formula of abjuration, which included a forswearing of 'the God of Mohammed'. Manuel Comnenus (1142–80) gave instructions that this anathema was to be deleted and provoked strong opposition from the Patriarch and the bishops.[35]

About 830, Al Kindy, possibly a Nestorian[36] Christian with scholarly interests lying within the Syriac tradition, who knew Greek and translated Aristotle, wrote a defence of Christianity against Islam, which relied heavily on the Old Testament. The reason he gives for composing this account was that a Muslim friend had asked for it, a cousin of the caliph.[37] It is similar to the account of Jewish conversions to Christianity in that it represents Christianity as higher and better and not merely more 'true' or 'accurate'.

In his account, he describes the life of Mohammed. True prophecy is a divine commission, he argues, but Mohammed deliberately refrained from making miraculous claims. Mohammed said that God had told him he was not going to send miracles to prove that what he was doing and saying had divine authority. Accordingly the Koran dismisses that kind of evidence. Jesus, on the other hand, did perform miracles and had implied that authentic prophecy would continue until his coming and then cease (John 10; Acts 20.29). It must follow that no one coming after Jesus and claiming to be a prophet could be a true prophet.[38] This contention, if true, would have undermined one of the central tenets of Islam, that Mohammed was *the* Prophet. There is also critical comment on Muslim teaching. Al Kindy touches disapprovingly on the worldly and materialist inducements in the Koran[39] and its alleged contradictions.[40]

Al Kindy has an alternative explanation for the way Mohammed became a teacher, though not, as he alleges, a prophet. His story is that Sergius, an excommunicated Nestorian monk, went to Mecca in Arabia and there met Mohammed, to whom he taught Nestorianism. He made Mohammed his disciple. Then Sergius died and Mohammed was taken in hand by two learned Jews. Thus he was able to acquire sufficient learning to account for the quality of the Koran, without resort to the explanation that it is divinely inspired. And thus too is explained how he came to occupy a position somewhere between Judaism and Christianity, because he was in fact drawing on both.[41]

Whatever the influence of this account in its day, it is of importance as an illustration of the perhaps greater understanding of Judaism and Christianity by Islamic scholars than Jewish and Christian scholars could claim in the reverse direction. The verse *Life of Mahomet* by Embricon de Mayence[42] is a highly coloured and critical account. It begins with a challenge to that 'pernicious people' who sneer at Christ, 'irrationally' obeying Mohammed and fighting to defend their 'folly'.[43] Along comes Simon Magus, bent on doing harm like a wicked bear (*ut impius ursus*), and he comes to Libya, where at that time, as throughout Africa, devotion to Christ flourished. He meets Mohammed.[44]

There was also comparative work on the Christian, Judaic and Muslim versions of events. In the eleventh century Abd al-Qahir al-Baghdadi (d.1037) queried the Christian and other 'infidel' accounts both of their own claims and of Islamic beliefs, on the grounds of the inadequate basis of their knowledge. The most reliable knowledge (*tawatur*) is transmitted at the time when the events happened by those who observed them directly or had completely reliable knowledge of what they were describing.[45] There was a risk that historians would place reliance on reports which were wrong.[46]

Christian–Muslim relations remained uneasy. The Islamic potentates could seem arrogant. In the tenth century Liutprand[47] sets his description of the way Christians were received by Muslims in a context. His reflections are coloured by unpleasant memories of the slave trade with Spain, which seems chiefly to have involved people captured in Eastern Europe by Verdun merchants.

A 'mission' could be diplomatic as well as religious. Even more important persons were treated with disdain, it appears. On an embassy to the Caliph of Cordoba in 953, John of Gorze found that he had to approach the Caliph through a slave. He had been sent with letters of introduction containing remarks on Islam which were, though the authors presumably did not realize it since they wished it to ease his way, dangerously likely to cause offence. John had to wait until fresh and safer introductions could be procured.[48] Even when he acquired new ones it still took him three years to reach the Caliph in person.

Understanding of Islam and its beliefs remained patchy in the West until the twelfth century. Only on the judgement of isolated authors about sources which were themselves remote from Muslim tradition was an understanding of Islam transmitted.[49] That encouraged the tendency to demonize Muslims which was already dangerously tempting, and echoed anti-Semitic tendencies in attitudes to the Jews.

William of Malmesbury (c.1090–c.1143) was a keen compiler of materials, and a collection he made (towards a 'continuous history ' of the Roman Emperors) survives.[50] He used a copy of Hugh of Fleury's *Ecclesiastical History*, in the version which Hugh had completed in 1110. Hugh had described how Mohammed, who was once a merchant, often travelled with his camels into Egypt and Palestine and talked with Jews and Christians, from whom he learned both the Old and the New Testaments. He relates a number of popular tales and some of the principal facts, relying, he explains, on the *Historia tripartita* of Anastasius, though in fact he allows himself considerable freedom to depart from it. William of Malmesbury edited and selected from Hugh's account in writing his own.

He was unusual in possessing some apparently quite sophisticated knowledge. He understood how central Christology was to maintaining the distinction between the great monotheistic faiths. In his *Commentary on Lamentations* (before the end of the 1130s) he comments that 'although Christians and Jews and Saracens have conflicting views of the Son, they all believe in their hearts and confess with their lips that God the Father is the creator'.[51] William was, in his way, not unsympathetic to Islam. He considered it rather in the light of a 'world religion' with real miracles to show for itself, if not quite a fully respectable alternative to Christianity.[52]

The only too evident reality of the Muslim conquest of territory in the early centuries of Islam had led to the emergence of a mythology that Islam was greedy for conquest. For why should it stop at present boundaries? Among the convictions which struck terror into Christians was the idea that Islam wanted to take over the world. This was an important difference between the Muslims and the Jews in common perception. According to Liutprand in the *Antapodosis*, a mysterious judgement of God had sent 20 Saracens in a small boat from Spain who landed in Christian territory and murdered the local Christians, turning the place, Fraxinetum, into a Moorish settlement. They grew a cactus hedge as a defence. Then they made raids into the surrounding country, sending for another 100 men from Spain to assist them. William of Malmesbury knew from a letter of Alcuin (c.740–

804) that there had been concern even in the reign of Charlemagne about
the Islamic conquest of the Middle East and Africa. William had an idea
that the number of Muslims was considerable, and this worried him. He
describes how Urban II had expressed a similar anxiety about the fewness
of Christians and the huge numbers of Muslims in the world:

> They dwell in Asia as their ancestral home, the third part of the earth, which
> our forefathers not without reason regarded, for its wide open spaces and the
> greatness of its provinces, as the equal of the other two combined. ... There,
> the Christians of today, those who remain, eke out a starveling livelihood by
> pitiful tillage of the soil. ... They [the Muslims] hold Africa, the second part
> of the world, having won it two hundred and more years ago by force of arms.
> ... There remains Europe, the third division of the world; and how small a
> part of that do we Christians live in. ... This small part, then, or our world,
> is threatened by Turks and Saracens with war. For three hundred years ago
> they overran Spain and the Balearic Islands; now they fully expect to devour
> what remains.[53]

'If you let the Turks and Arabs alone, they will invade the territories of
the faithful further still,' Urban was reported to have warned in his Clermont sermon. He portrays them as 'The Lord's enemies'.[54] The underlying
anxiety here seems to have been similar to that which Augustine's contemporaries faced with the fall of a Christian Empire to 'infidel' invaders. How
could this be? Why did God allow it? Was the survival of Christianity
really at risk?

In the twelfth century there were moves by Westerners to go out among
the Muslims and make a serious effort to learn more about their scholarship
and beliefs. In 1141 Peter the Venerable, Abbot of Cluny, went on a tour of
the Benedictine monasteries of Spain. This kind of journey was quite usual
for the abbot of a wealthy house. It made possible an inspection of the abba-
tial lands which might be attached to a house a long way off, and Peter had
a particular reason for wishing to create good relations in this part of the
world. The Muslim domination of southern Spain was coming to an end
with its 'reconquest' by Christian rulers. Alfonso VII had been proclaimed
ruler of Spain in 1135 and Peter was anxious to win his favour towards Cluny
and its connections.[55]

Spain was an area of peculiar interest to scholars because at the interface
between Muslim and Christian territories it was possible to meet those who
were familiar with Arabic scholarship on the ancient Greek philosophers
and to get copies of Arabic writings. It was also possible to arrange for translation, even if that sometimes involved bringing together a mixed committee of merchants who spoke Spanish and commercial Arabic and clerics
who spoke Spanish and Latin.[56] Merchants made journeys for commercial

reasons which brought into contact speakers of different languages and adherents of different religions. Though there is little reason to suppose that that often led to talk about matters of faith, it did create a pool of basic linguistic competence in more than one tongue.

Peter the Venerable had his own concerns, which were mainly about the consequences of the continuing widespread ignorance of the beliefs of Islam in the Christian West. He put together a party to translate the Koran: Peter of Poitiers, now his own secretary and a former academic; Peter of Toledo, a competent Arabist (for many in the area were bilingual) but who was probably a less secure Latinist; Robert of Ketton and Herbert the Dalmatian, whom he met on their travels in search of the philosophical writings of the ancient world. He added a Saracen called Mohammed to ensure the fidelity of the translations from the Arabic.[57] Robert may in fact have done much of the work alone and it was completed in a mere two years.[58]

In one of his letters, Peter provides for the edification of Bernard of Clairvaux to whom he is writing, a summary account of the origins of Islam and a biography of Mohammed.[59] This occurs in similar form in Peter's 'Digest of the Whole Heresy of the Saracens' (*Summa totius haeresis Saracenorum*). He says, 'I have sent our new translation, which it was my care to get translated from the Arabic language on my recent sojourn in Spain.' He describes his translation team and the methodology adopted, which was to create a summary of points arising which will need to be countered in future debates with Muslims about their beliefs. The idea has been to provide apologists with a pack of information and relevant authorities with which they may demonstrate the truth on every point.[60] He gives his own view of the Koran. It is a collection of precepts which 'that wicked man' pretended had been revealed to him from heaven bit by bit.

Mutual misunderstandings persisted, however, and so did the demonizing of Muslims. In the twelfth century, Giraldus Cambrensis gives an account of the history of Islam as it was 'known' in northern Europe in his day. He associates Islam with 'great evil' (*nimis mala*) and, in the same 'demonizing' spirit, he reports that the Prophet Mohammed perished in a drunken stupor, being eaten by pigs. But he knows better, he assures his readers. He knows that Muslims do not drink wine 'because of the heat of the regions in which they live', and that the abstinence from pork is not occasioned by horror at the story of the Prophet's end but is the result of Jewish influence. He is conscious that Muslims draw 'some of their beliefs from the Jews and some from the Christians'.[61]

Book IV, the slightest of the four books of Alan of Lille's late twelfth-century 'Against the Heretics' – an indication perhaps that this is where his own knowledge was most limited – is concerned with the Muslim faith, to which he is extremely hostile. 'A monstrous life; a still more monstrous sect; a most monstrous purpose.' 'Mahommed, inspired by the evil spirit, began an abominable sect, given to carnal pleasures.'[62] He calls them *Saracanos vel paganos*. He says that they select from the Scriptures at their whim, that although they accept that Christ was born of the Virgin by the Spirit of God they do not accept that the Holy Spirit is a person or that Christ himself is a person or that there is a Trinity.[63]

A quite differently flavoured slant on the understanding Western authors achieved is to be found in the letters of Jacques de Vitry (*c*.1165–1240), given a bishopric at Acre in the period of the Fifth Crusade. Letter II, written to various Paris masters in 1216–17, describes his voyage to the Middle East, how he sailed past Crete and Cyprus, mentally noting a classical reference, that he was leaving Scilla on the left and Charybdis on the right, and a Scriptural one, that in Malta Paul suffered his shipwreck and stayed for the winter. He also describes with apparent pleasure the dolphins who leapt in front of the ship at Cyprus. He is delighted to say that merchants and important persons received the cross from his hand as he travelled.[64]

At Acre he preached to the Jacobites, Syrians of a sect founded in the sixth century by a Monophysite monk from Constantinople. He used as interpreter someone who could 'speak the Saracen language'. He showed them that they were wrong to circumcise their children and persuaded some to agree to confess to a priest instead of directly to God, as had been their practice.[65] 'I also met Nestorians, Georgians and Armenians,' he relates. These could not be brought together in a meeting or assembly because they had no bishop or other leader. He says he met some Armenians who used leavened bread in the Eucharist but did not mix water with the wine, so he evidently explored differences of rite as well as differences of belief with those he encountered. Others in the population he had come to serve were unsatisfactory sheep for his flock for quite different reasons. There were communities of Pisans, Genoese and Venetians who did not acknowledge the jurisdiction of Rome and placed themselves under chaplains of their own appointing. They would not come to Jacques' sermons but that did not stop him going and standing outside their homes to preach to them whether they wished it or not.[66] He found lay people and even religious communities letting lodgings to prostitutes.[67]

The interface with Islam further compounded itself during the thirteenth century in different ways in different parts of Europe, the Middle East and North Africa. At the beginning of 1200, the annual flooding of the Nile failed and there was a crisis and a famine in Egypt. Since his death in 1193, internal disputes had divided the realm of Saladin, who had been the chief enemy of the Third Crusade, and the Mamluks were coming to prominence. They had been a mere army of slave soldiers, but under the leadership of Saladin's brother they became a power in the land, Kurdish by origin but increasingly controlling the Arab rulers who formed the Ayyubid dynasty.

Meanwhile in the West of Europe the Maghrib (the Muslim West) was still powerful and successful at the beginning of the thirteenth century, though this was to be the century in which Islam was obliged to withdraw from Spain. From the late 1220s the soldiers of the Abbasid caliphs and other groups were embattled, and this made them vulnerable to the determined onslaught of the Christian forces which began to win ground in the 1230s and eventually captured Córdoba in 1236. The kingdom of Granada survived as an enclave of Muslim domination into the next century.

Western ideas of Islam were largely formed in these conflicts of ideology and weaponry during the twelfth and thirteenth centuries, and became something of an orthodoxy in their own right.[68] There was a pragmatic alliance of the West with Islam against the Mongol hordes in the thirteenth century, but when it came to conversions the Buddhists who made a change mostly turned to Islam not Christianity. The conversion of Muslims to Christianity turned out to be a vexed question. While they were not Christians it was relatively easy to know how to treat them, said some of the locals, for they were manifestly outsiders. But what was to happen if they were Christian? Jacques is glad to report that some of them did come to be baptized, claiming to have had dreams in which Jesus or Mary or a saint had appeared to them, and the Virgin had warned them that they should die in battle if they did not agree to be Christians. Such attitudes Jacques finds intelligible, for the Saracens were fearful of the arrival of pilgrims, let alone crusaders. He himself seems to have been quite fearful too, for he reports that he has been afraid to visit the holy places himself so far because of the Saracens.[69]

The three faiths which would now be described as 'world religions' thus reached an accommodation, in which questions of geography and politics and social life jostled matters of theology and practice. There were 'interfaith dialogues' but of a kind which could be deemed successful only when one of the participants converted to the views of another. It was a reluctant *modus vivendi*, in which there was no place for modern notions of mutual respect and letting be.

Dualisms

There could be no question to Christians but that adherents of Islam and Judaism were 'outsiders', and that these were 'other faiths'. Less easy to classify – though they are sometimes described loosely as 'heretics' – were the various sorts of 'dualists'. This has been one of the most persistent unorthodoxies throughout Christian history. Dualists, so-called because they believed that there are two 'first principles' or supreme powers in the universe, formed a series of groups or sects over the centuries but never achieved a continuing identity as an organization. Dualist Gnostics were already to be found before the Christian era. Dualism had a new wave of popularity with the rise of Manicheeism. The decade Augustine of Hippo spent as a Manichee and his continuing struggles with dualist ideas throughout his life, ensured that such themes lingered in the consciousness of the medieval West.

The Paulicians, a Byzantine sect which appeared in Armenia in the seventh century, were persecuted on imperial orders and their founder was stoned about 684. They were still present in the ninth century and seem to have made common cause with the Bogomils in Bulgaria from the tenth century. Other groups within Christianity also continued to be influenced by the ancient dualism and the more recent Manicheeism, which regarded matter, and therefore material images, as evil. The Monophysite heresy may also have had its effect. Leo III was influenced by the Paulicians and began to believe that the use of icons by Christian worshippers was standing in the way of the conversion of Muslims and also Jews. The political consequences were lively.

The next important phase occurred in the late twelfth and early thirteenth centuries. The underlying dualist theology may have persisted in the interim or reappeared spontaneously,[70] but now, in the south of France, northern Spain and parts of north Italy, dualist adherents began to appear again in some numbers. The term 'Cathar' seems to have been first used in about 1150 by a German author.[71] The Albigensians clustered in the south of France and northern Spain and the Bogomils appeared further east. The Albigensians were dualists, in the long tradition of the 'medieval Manichee' which began with the Gnostics who predate the Christian era, continued with the Manichees of the time of Augustine of Hippo and reappeared with the medieval Bogomils, Cathars and Albigensians.

The details of dualist teaching varied, but among the core ideas were that there are two first principles, two supreme and opposed powers in the universe: spirit, which is good, and matter, which is evil. The distinctive feature of this heresy was its denial of the omnipotence of God. It postulates that there are two powers in the universe, a spiritual 'good' power, the God of the New Testament, and a material 'bad' power, whom they identified with the God of the Old Testament. These powers the dualists believed to be eternally at war, in a great battle of good and evil, whose outcome was not certain, for evil might win.[72] The dualists rejected orthodox Christology.

It seemed to them inconceivable that a good God could have sent his Son to die. Jesus was only a messenger, they claimed; the Redeemer was the Holy Spirit, for it is he who reminds people of their spiritual origins. A concomitant puritanism accompanies these ideas, for the followers of the good are expected to detach themselves from fleshly pleasures and material wealth.

Adherents were divided into two categories, the 'hearers' or postulants and the *perfecti*. The belief was that those who were perfect could make their own contribution to the winning of the war of good and evil by transmuting the material food they ate into 'spirit'; and the hearers could do their part by making donations of material things for the *perfecti* to transmute.

The single sacrament of the dualists, performing some of the functions of baptism in their theology, was the *consolamentum*. A 'hearer' who was to receive it had to be able to answer the 'catechetical' questions which showed that he understood and held the faith. The ceremony involved the placing of a copy of St John's Gospel on the postulant's head and the imposition of the hands of the minister upon the Gospel. The idea was that this marked the bestowing of the Holy Spirit on the postulant and was a baptism of the Spirit, requiring no (material) water as baptism did.[73] The dualists did not recognize the other sacraments of the Catholics, for each involved an outward and visible (material) sign of the inward and spiritual grace (spiritual).

Unusually among medieval heretics (as far as can be known, for often it is only the accusations of the Church's apologists which survive, caricaturing the beliefs which they condemn), some of the Albigensians left their own accounts of themselves. The Cistercians had attempted to preach them into submission during the later twelfth century without success. The Dominicans were founded for the purpose.

Caesarius of Heisterbach gives a summary of the origins of the Albigensian heresy, with particular feeling because, as he relates, the Cistercians had mounted preaching expeditions against it with little success:

> Their leaders had collected some points from the Manichaean dogma, and some of the errors which Origen is said to have written against Periarchon, and very many which they had fashioned out of their own heads. They follow Manicheus in believing that there are two sources of life, a good God and a wicked God, i.e. the devil; and they say that the wicked God created all bodies and the good God all souls. ... They say that they look forward to the glory of the spirit.[74]

In the *Compendium ad instructionem rudium*, a Latin summary of the essentials for beginners, it is explained that since God is good and cannot do evil there must be another God, an evil power, which balances the good power in the universe. The evil power is the source of all bad behaviour

and it is his fault that so many men, women and children die.[75] The dualist dissidents, who tended to be ordinary people and not highly educated,
needed theological explanations and texts of the New Testament in their
own language. Cathar New Testaments in Provençale survive from the
thirteenth century.[76]

The *Livre des deux principes* sets out in detail, underpinning the argument comprehensively with biblical quotations, the case for saying that
there are two gods, a good and an evil one. This is persuasive argument
and the uneducated might easily be swayed by a set of beliefs which seemed
to set love of Christ higher even than did the orthodox preachers. They
were taught to expect persecution and to embrace it gladly. Martyrdom is
frequently attractive to dissidents.

The Church adopted an attitude of official disapproval, sending preachers, culminating in the Dominicans, an order founded especially to convert
such heretics.[77] Ultimately it treated them as proper objects of an Albigensian 'crusade', beginning in 1209 and ending in 1229 with the Peace of
Paris.

Divisions within Christendom

It was often remarked that it was characteristic of dissidence and heresy
and 'unbelief' of all kinds that it tended to create further divisions, subdi-
viding the faithful as it misled them, and fragmenting that unity which
was of the essence of the Church. This may seem a paradoxical idea when
it is set beside the equally firmly held view that those who were not of one
mind with the Church were all to be regarded, collectively and generically,
as 'outsiders'. Nevertheless it is important to the Church's sense of itself as
repository, maintainer and protector of the true faith, 'one, holy, catholic
and apostolic'.

Gervase of Tilbury is reported as having played a part in a scene which
shows how difficult it could be to be sure whether one was dealing with
a muddled ignorance or hardened heresy. William of the White Hands,
the Archbishop of Rheims (1176–1202), in whose service Gervase then was,
was strolling in the countryside with some of his household when Gervase
noticed a solitary girl in a vineyard. He tried to flirt with her. She defended
herself by saying that she feared that loss of her virginity would lead to
her damnation. Gervase, alert to theological unsoundness even in such
circumstances, thought he spied a member of the sect of the Publicani, who
preached that sexual intercourse was evil because it led to procreation. He
was deep in theological argument with her on this point when the Archbishop came up. The girl was eventually burned at the stake for heresy.[78]

Heresy, strictly defined, is not muddle-headedness or the raising of challenging questions, but obstinate perseverance in an officially recognized

error of faith. Schism divides the Church. The difference may be less clear than it looks, however. Augustine, for whom unity was of supreme importance, argued that division was itself a heresy, indeed the greatest heresy of all. And when schism occurred, as it did in 1054 between Greek and Latin Christians, each side claimed to be the true Church and regarded the others as heretical. In that instance each half of Christendom maintained its ancient formal structures, its bishops and primates and its local liturgies, in which was embedded the theology a liturgy always carries within it.

But there were other divisions arising from expressions of dissidence within the community in the West, which threatened the structural integrity of the institutional Church. The Waldensians or 'Poor Men of Lyons' challenged the institutional order, saying in effect that sacraments and ministry as insisted upon in the West in their day were not necessary to salvation. Walter Map reports that he has seen with his own eyes the inferior education and intellectual quality of these dissidents at the Third Lateran Council. There were Waldensians, *homines idiotas, illiteratos*, called 'Waldensians' after Waldes their 'Primate', he mockingly comments.[79] Their lack of education causes him to raise the question whether allowing such people to read the Bible is not casting pearl before swine. No one exercises any control over them, yet they themselves have a dangerous appetite to be rulers of others.[80]

Waldes or Valdes and his followers had mounted a challenge to the established order of the Church. They too had rediscovered the idea of the apostolic life, with its emphasis on poverty and simplicity. They were lay people, but bourgeois. They were perhaps the first generation of articulate townspeople to question the claim that the ordained had a claim to special access to the Bible and to the mysteries of Christian doctrine, that the Church should conduct its life in Latin, even its worship, when ordinary lay people could not understand the words, that the Church controlled the way to salvation and there was 'no salvation outside the Church' (*nulla salus extra ecclesiam*), that the priesthood gave powers to the ordained that the laity were denied. Moreover they objected to the corruption and conspicuous wealth of the some of the clergy.

Caesarius of Heisterbach outlines the origins of the Waldensian heresy, pitching it at a level where the ordinary monastic novice could understand it and presenting it as the work of the devil in the section of his *Dialogue on Miracles* which is devoted to demons. The ringleaders were identified as demons, who answered back when challenged by the bishop and 'gathered a crowd round them and preached their errors to them'. Some of the clergy who saw this asked them by what authority they preached, citing Romans 10.15. They replied that they were sent by the Holy Spirit. But really, says

Caesarius, they had been sent by 'the Spirit of error' and it was only because of certain vested and influential interests locally that the bishop was unable to suppress them and the Waldensian heresy was planted in the city of Metz, where it still persists.[81]

The Humiliati were one of the more long-lasting of several groups with similar ideals which emerged in the second half of the twelfth century. They believed in simplicity of life and refused to swear oaths because they believed they should take literally Jesus's instruction that the conversation of his disciples should include no assertion stronger than a simple yes or no (Matthew 5.37). They were condemned along with the Waldensians and Cathars in 1184 but there seems to have been a change of heart in official circles in the Church, and in 1201 Innocent II approved a threefold arrangement under which Humiliati might live apart in houses of canons, or live apart in lay communities or even 'practise' at home while living ordinary family lives with husbands or wives. They were in some respects forerunners of the Franciscans. Their history demonstrates that a hardline view that a group's members were outsiders might not be irreversible, at least where there were not clearly defined points of contention. The Humiliati were perceived as threatening chiefly because they insisted that lay people could preach.

Giraldus Cambrensis's account of the history of Islam as it was 'known' in northern Europe in his day is positioned after his description of the defeat of the Arian heresy and it contains a digression about some 'old-style heretics of our own time' (*antiqui haeretici nostri temporis*), the Patari. Hugh Eteriano's *Contra Patarenos* was written in Constantinople between 1165 and 1180, and was probably directed against dissidents who were to be found in the 'Latin rite' population, rather than among Greek Christians as such. These Patarenes could have been Cathars. The Cathars, being dualists, were also a 'purity' movement. Some of these Patarenes were apparently saying that sacraments could not be valid if celebrated by an unworthy priest. A further clue pointing in the same direction was that Patarenes would not venerate images.[82] Walter Map also mentions them in his *De nugis curialium* ('On Courtiers' Trifles'),[83] along with a sect of violent marauders who say that there is no God.[84] The Patarenes, he explains, are also known as the Publicani, and they are descended from those who reject Christ's initiation of the Eucharist, and have lain low ever since, as 'sleepers' in their villages, but have now awakened into active heresy. He reports that those who have been converted from this sect and returned to the orthodox Christian fold describe how at their meetings at night, with all the doors and windows locked, the members of the sect wait, and there descends down a rope in their midst a monstrous black cat.[85]

Tolerance and the multicultural society?

Gratian's *Decretum* of 1140 and the *Decretales* (1234) discuss the status of Jews and Muslims living alongside Christians in the same places. The objective at this period was, it seems, to keep the communities separate. Innocent III instructed Jews and Muslims living in Christian lands to dress distinctively.[86] Mixed marriages are discouraged. Forced baptism is frowned on but non-Christian subjects can be required to attend sermons. The Muezzin could be forbidden to call Muslims to prayer. In reality there was a good deal of variation of practice in different places.[87] But none of these accommodations and practical arrangements can really be said to amount to an enthusiasm for anything approaching a modern multiculturalism. It is a nervous compromise to keep the peace.

CHAPTER 4

Imposing Order

The need for order

When he spoke of a new light yoke (Matthew 11.29–30), Jesus promised that the faith he was preaching would not be burdensome. One of the most noticeable developments of the Middle Ages in the West was a growth in the number of what began to be described as 'impositions' on the faithful, and of 'human laws' the Church told them they must obey if they were to be saved.

There were several drivers of this change. Shifts in the balance of power between Church and state, and within the Church, especially from the late eleventh century, brought questions of pastoral authority to the forefront of debate. Some of the practices later condemned as impositions had begun in response to pastoral need particularly vigorously in the eleventh and twelfth centuries. The expansion and much greater complexity of the penitential system is a case in point. There was a rise in dissident protest from the twelfth century, which was treated by the ecclesiastical authorities as a danger to the souls of the faithful. In a medieval version of the 'war on terrorism', the community of the Church was encouraged to look over its collective shoulder for threats from the 'outsiders', from dissidence within and from the world of the demons. The authorities reacted repressively.

There were both historical and theological reasons for these shifts. The movement of peoples westward which had brought about the fall of the Roman Empire went on for some centuries after its collapse. The structural and governmental integrity of Europe became patchy once the dominating but reassuring presence of the ancient Roman Empire was gone. An interim stage saw Christians working in a civil service capacity for the new rulers of the old Empire. Theodoric (475–527) employed both Boethius and Cassiodorus in his Ostrogothic kingdom. Further into the sixth century, the bishops were obliged to maintain civic order. Gregory, Bishop of Tours (540–94) and Gregory the Great (540–604), Pope and Bishop of Rome, ran the legal and financial affairs of their dioceses as well as the spiritual. In these unsettled times, when the Holy Roman Empire was emerging out of the 'real' Roman Empire – Charlemagne was crowned Emperor by Pope Leo I in Rome at Christmas 800 – the regime of the Church extended more uniformly than most, and over a far greater area than any single secular authority.

A variety of systems of government now came into existence as the dust settled on the dismembered Empire. In Italy city states persisted. In northern Europe feudalism emerged. In parts of Europe from time to time there were strong competent rulers, but the threat of new invasions or disruption by envious and ambitious barons or factions perpetuated an uneasy sense that nothing could be relied upon for long.[1] There were real problems in maintaining order in the Church in a violent society. Thierry of Orleans complained to Fulbert of Chartres that he had not been consecrated on the date planned. Why not? Because, explains Fulbert, the required number of bishops of the province were not there, and, anyway, a letter had been received at the last minute from the Pope in which he said he had heard that Thierry had been charged with homicide. There was also the matter of the use of intimidation to secure the election. Fulbert sets out the conciliar canons which provide the ground-rules in such cases.[2]

The institutional structure of the Church evolved during this period both as a practical reality and as an 'ecclesiology', or theology of order in the Church. Either the Church claims to reflect the principles and practices of an 'eternal' Church, or it seeks to adapt itself to the needs of the times, and opens itself to accusations that it is abandoning truth for expediency, or allowing vested interests to control its behaviour. In the later part of the period we are concerned with, when things were settling down, there remained a contrast between the structures intended to embody good practice and the actual behaviour of the individuals who held office. In the ninth century at Winchester there seems to have been a rota of the wealthier clergy, some of whom were married.

Historians of the Middle Ages who saw the Church in its 'place' in the economy of salvation envisaged it as both an 'institution' and a 'mystery', something both visible and invisible. They used the word equivocally. The church is a building in the village, town or city. At the same time, the Church is a wider institution, that is to say, a structure with a recognized mode of governance, conditions of membership and an increasingly well-defined power-structure which could exercise sanctions against those who broke its rules. An institutional 'order' embodying certain structural principles began to be formed from the earliest times, and in most respects it was common to East and West, though there were points of heated dispute. It included a recognized sacramental ministry, exercised within a territorially based organization which placed local groups of Christians under a local pastor. It developed a method for making collective decisions and enforcing disciplinary rules. Because the practice was to determine who was 'in' and who was 'out' by reference to the institutional framework, some of the most troublesome challenges faced by the medieval Church were those which raised questions about that framework, as the Waldensians, or Poor Men of Lyons, did in the twelfth century.

But 'mystically', too, the Church is a community (the New Testament word is *koinonia*). The Church is a vessel of grace. The Bride of the Song of Songs became identified with the Church and the Bridegroom with Christ in early Christian exegesis of the Old Testament. The New Testament adds that the Church is the body of Christ, and Christ is its head (Ephesians 5.23). Both the institutional and visible order and the invisible spiritual order were aspects of a conception of 'order' which was immensely strong to medieval minds and reflected the deep reality of the universe. 'The very word "church" – and it is the only place where the true sacrifice can be offered – signifies more than one; and the priest's greeting where he says, "The Lord be with you" is addressed not to just one, but to several persons. … I think it is safer for you to stop celebrating mass rather than to celebrate it without at least two or three of the faithful present.'[3]

Paul's first letter to the Corinthians explores in some detail the image of the body which makes it both an organism and a 'body politic'. The body has many parts. The hand does not disclaim its connection with the body because it is not a foot. It would not be for the general good for the parts of the body to be the same or to do the same thing; there has to be some differentiation of function. This differentiation enables the body as a whole to function well. Each part cares for the others and for the whole, and that ought to rule out dissension, for it is for the benefit of no part to pull against the rest. There is, however, room for some parts of the body to have more 'honour' than others. (I Corinthians 12.12–31). The 'body' image lent itself very readily to a doctrine of social differentiation of role and even to the need for a hierarchy.

This sort of extended analogy was very congenial to the Middle Ages, which saw it as reflecting the deep structure of things. Order seemed to commentators of the medieval West to reflect the relations of things as they most profoundly are 'in themselves'. They expected 'order' to be hierarchical, because it was under divine governance (*gubernatio*); they thought of it as harmonious; a *rectus ordo* or 'right order' held together a relationship of differentiated parts, such as head and body; they expected some of the structures to be common to both secular and spiritual communities. Although he was writing in a feudal England which did not have the sort of citizens he describes, John of Salisbury's *Policraticus* includes a discussion of the various tasks of the citizenry. He says he got the idea from a work by a classical author, Trajan, in which he remarks, 'So the citizens have various occupations and as long as each discharges his duties for the general good the city will run sweetly as honey.'[4] Dante argues in a similar way in his *Monarchia* that the parts of a whole have different purposes. Thus the hand does not have the same purpose as the foot. In order to find out what something has as its purpose one must ask what sort of *operatio* is special to it. One individual human being may have a different *operatio* from another and each a different *operatio* from the human race as a whole. For example, each individual person cannot do all the things necessary to maintain himself; he cannot grow all the food and make all the goods he needs. Nor can one village be self-sufficient in that way.[5]

The three planes of the Church's life

The structural model which had evolved by the early Middle Ages envisaged the intersection of three 'planes' of the Church's life, in the person of the 'local bishop'. As Christian missionaries took the faith out into the wider world, they established local churches. The ecumenical Councils of the first centuries were concerned to ensure that these local churches did not behave as though they were completely independent entities and could do as they liked. So the first 'plane' was that of the local pastoral community in a given territorial area which was, throughout the Middle Ages in both East and West, the diocese, headed by a bishop who was its local pastor. His locality of jurisdiction was of significant importance to the preservation of the presumption that the Church had territorial units or parts. The early Councils were insistent that priests should not travel to minister in other dioceses without carrying a letter of recommendation from their own bishop. In this way one bishop handed on a satisfactory priest to another, who would then grant him a licence or permission to minister within his own 'cure'. If a bishop excommunicates someone that same bishop must restore him. No one else must give him communion until that has been done.[6] Some scholars have asserted that St Patrick (in the mid- or late fifth century) had introduced dioceses in Ireland on this model, though this is disputed;[7] but bishoprics were certainly set up all over Europe as lands were converted to Christianity.

In feudal society bishops (like abbots) were expected to provide so many days of military or 'knight' service a year for the king as 'rent' for their lands just like a secular baron, for all land ultimately belonged to the king. So the politics of Europe had bishops heavily involved in a purely secular capacity and discovering conflicts of interest between their secular and spiritual functions. This localized arrangement of the Church into territorial 'parts' was sometimes interfered with by a certain amount of 'private enterprise' from the secular side, too. Private churches were built by landlords for the use of their own peasants, and by monasteries for the people working on the lands which belonged to them.

Various arrangements were possible for the care of a growing Christian community in a new diocese, for it could soon outgrow the capacity of a single minister to exercise proper pastoral care. One, the institution of *chorepiscopoi*, 'country bishops', or assistant bishops, was favoured in the Eastern half of the former Roman Empire. It is not easy to say for sure whether these were priests or bishops. Another, the provision of suffragan bishops, was more usual in the West. As the Middle Ages wore on, the parish emerged, with its priest, who was the 'vicar' of the bishop, exercising his pastoral care on his behalf, but by no definition himself a bishop. These developments sharpened the question what the difference was between a priest and a bishop, which we shall come to in a moment.

The second and third planes of the Church's life linked the churches of a given time and ensured the continuity of the Church over time. This way of looking at things tended to strengthen the presumptions about the importance of bishops in the institutional scheme, for three planes intersect at a point, and the 'point' was the person of the bishop. The Eastern Church tended to see the local church as a microcosm of the whole, so that it *was* 'the Church in each place'. In the West it was more natural to think of local churches as 'parts of a whole'. But in both the principle was accepted that local churches were not independent entities which could do as they liked, and it was quickly found to be important that their relationship to one another should be clear. Ecclesiological theory began to insist that they could best ensure that by meeting in the persons of their bishops, who acted as their representatives. The early Church established that the convening and dismissal of a council might be done by a lay person, and that a lay person could even preside. But no lay person could join in the deliberations or vote. Local churches were thus related to one another in the second plane, that of the whole Church of a given time, in the sense that all the bishops could meet in synods or councils (which are Greek and Latin terms respectively for essentially the same thing) and agree on behalf of their local communities the 'decrees' their council would put out.

Bishops were expected to meet regularly in this capacity of representatives of their dioceses. The Second Council of Nicaea of 787 confirms that a provincial synod should be held once a year to discuss canonical and evangelical matters as well as the disciplinary details and the maintenance of good order which make up the ordinary business of councils, and no excuses about the inconvenience or expense of attending should be accepted.[8] Such meetings might be fairly local, and their decisions were considered to be binding only on those whose episcopal representatives had been present. A council of bishops from Gaul could not bind the English, for example. An ecumenical or universal council was a rarity. The decrees of each council were deemed to be binding only on churches which were present in the persons of their episcopal representatives. This strengthened rather than weakened the conception of a linking of churches at local level which formed part of a great network or mesh of linked churches of the day. Councils of bishops thus became a living demonstration that the churches must work together and agree on matters of faith. It was accepted from the early centuries that although it was essential for the Church to be of one mind about the faith, it did not matter whether there was some variation of practice. Lanfranc, preparing constitutions or house-rules for his monks while he was Archbishop of Canterbury, emphasized the need to adjust requirements to the circumstances in which a particular community was living.[9]

In the era of the first ecumenical Councils the presumption persisted that when bishops met together they arrived (or they always said they did) at 'unanimous' agreements. The idea was that at a properly convened and conducted council the Holy Spirit would be present, and that of course would make the decisions absolutely binding. It was just a question of being sure that he had been heard correctly. It was also assumed that the Holy Spirit would guide the deliberations. In reality, especially in the Middle Ages, there do not seem to have been many deliberations. The Fourth Lateran Council of 1215, for example, probably met with its conclusions already conveniently before it.[10]

The Middle Ages saw a testing of these old presumptions about the bishops and their functions. Whether conciliar decrees were binding at all became a complex question, as a parallel and complementary doctrine of the *consensus fidelium* emerged.[11] For it might turn out that the council's views would need to be adjusted when the faithful as a whole received or did not receive them. More urgent for the earlier and high Middle Ages were questions of the respective powers of Church and state and of the position of primates and whether there was a supreme primate over the whole Church.

Primacy

There was a growing awareness in the early centuries that it was going to be necessary to find some means of ensuring that each local Church or diocese would stay in line with the wider Church in matters of faith. Provision had

been made for that from an early date through the emergence of metropoli-
tan bishoprics, known as patriarchates or provinces. In the early Church
five patriarchates emerged, four of them in the Eastern Greek-speaking
half of the Empire: Jerusalem, Antioch, Alexandria and Constantinople,
the latter founded by the Emperor Constantine the Great and taking its
place among them from the early fourth century. The fifth patriarchate was
the see of St Peter. It was the only one in the Latin-speaking West and it
could claim supremacy because its first bishop was the 'rock' on which Jesus
himself had said he would found his Church (Matthew 16.18).

What did primacy really mean? Under each of these primates or principal bishops a pyramid structure began to form. Below them were the
local bishops, each with his diocese, and below the local bishops their own
priests. But at the same time, the continuation of councils meant that all
the bishops in a province were collegial equals, and when they met they
made up their minds together in a cooperative way rather than in obedience
to the directive of their senior bishop. And there was a rivalry among the
patriarchs as to which was greatest.

Gregory the Great recognized that he was the subject of the Emperor of
the East and that he must accept his rulings on many matters of ecclesiastical policy. However, he objected to the Patriarch of Constantinople using
the title 'ecumenical patriarch', for he did not consider that that implied
that he was a subject of the Patriarch of Constantinople. The Council of
Chalcedon (451) had granted Constantinople the same status as a patriarchate that Rome enjoyed (Canon 28) on the principle that both were imperial cities. Gregory tried to insist that the Bishop of Rome, the Pope, had a
unique position. He was successful in protecting the appellate jurisdiction
of Rome, but the larger question was the subject of continuing correspondence throughout his reign. In a letter of June 595 to the Emperor Maurice he
insisted that it was inappropriate for John, the Patriarch of Constantinople,
to be calling himself 'universalis'. He argued fiercely that no one can rule
the earth rightly unless he knows how to deal with *divina*; that the peace of
the state depends on the peace of the universal Church; that Christ gave the
care of the whole Church to Peter; and that a consequence of the making
of rival claims by other authorities is confusion and disorder everywhere in
Europe.[12] In 603 he was still pressing the point, when he wrote to congratu-
late Leontias, the new Emperor.[13]

The continuing unpleasantness between East and West on the subject of
the ultimate primacy was, paradoxically, eased somewhat by the schism of
1054, for the two churches were then formally divided, and for the ensuing
medieval centuries and beyond could do no more than debate their differences.[14]

The strengthening doctrine – and the increasingly energetic practice of primacy especially in the West – tended to unbalance the more collegial conception of bishops meeting as brothers. The Western pope most instrumental in taking forward the doctrine of primacy in this direction was Gregory VII (d.1085), who elevated the primacy of the Bishop of Rome over his fellow bishops in the West, unbalancing the ancient assumptions about the collegial equality of bishops on which the theory of the second plane of the Church's life depended.

Membership

It should be easy to say who is a Christian and who is not, if it is just a question of membership of the Church, but that was, in itself, not at all a straightforward matter. For much depends on whether the Church is merely an organization with clear rules, one of which allows the identification of its members, or something more, even perhaps a mystery, whose boundaries cannot be seen clearly and may indeed be known only to God. And on this point the Church has never been able to agree.

Augustine's influence on the question of Church membership had been very powerful. In *The City of God* he explains that the true Church is invisible. Only God knows who are his. It is part of the divine plan to allow wheat and tares to grow together until harvest (Matthew 13.30). Some of those who have been baptized are not Christians at all in the sight of God, and God can by grace bring in those who have not been baptized. This left an unresolved contradiction running as a fault-line through the history of Christianity in the Middle Ages and beyond. For Augustine also insisted that baptism was necessary to salvation. He took a hard line on the importance of baptism and the fate of unbaptized infants, who could not, on a strict doctrine of original sin, be deemed to be fit for heaven. It could not be assumed that those who are baptized automatically become Christians in the sense that they are promised a place in heaven, or that the visible Church to which admission is obtained by baptism tidily contains all who are Christians in that sense.

Nevertheless baptism was an important marker of acceptance into medieval society.[15] By the end of the ancient world, from about the end of the fourth century in the West, and in Augustine's lifetime, infant baptism had become the norm, and throughout most of the Middle Ages almost everyone was baptized within days of birth. The Church understood itself to be a community of faith, in which there was a single universal baptism. This intellectual and pastoral standpoint carried on the presumption of Augustine's time, which was that the Church was one, holy, catholic and apostolic and anything which was not 'in' it was 'outside'. The need for baptism had to be taken seriously if the underlying theology was right. It was deemed to be a sacrament approved by Jesus when he allowed himself to be baptized by John the Baptist in the River Jordan (Matthew 3.6; Mark 1.5 and 9). It was insisted from the earliest period that a person's baptism was a unique occasion, a once-and-for-all opportunity to be rid of one's sins. It was believed to wipe out both the punishment due for the original sin in which all humans were held to be born, and the actual sins everyone committed. Those who carried on serious sinning afterwards did not, the rigorists said, deserve a second chance. Even those who thought they could be readmitted to the good graces of God and the Christian community hedged this permission about with provisos and made it difficult, involving periods of public penance. That made the decision when to be baptized momentous and its very momentousness had for a long time in the late antique world encouraged converts to leave baptism until as near their deathbeds as they could safely contrive, because it could not be repeated, if they were baptized too soon and then sinned again.

That same strong doctrine of baptism, paradoxically, seems to have encouraged the swing to infant baptism. In an era of high infant mortality it was a reasonable concern that one's newborn children might spend eternity shut out of heaven for lack of the simple precaution of having them baptized. It was accepted that the sacrament could be carried out in an emergency even by a midwife, so important had it become to ensure that it was done. There was a good deal of hedging of bets. Augustine of Hippo had observed cuttingly that the Pelagians, who said there was no need for baptism, nevertheless brought their infants to be baptized just in case, at the end of the fourth century and the beginning of the fifth.

But the normal expectation was clear and remorseless, for even if the possibility of direct divine intervention to 'save' one of God's secret 'elect' was there, no one could know if it had happened. Hugh of St Victor, in his early twelfth-century *De sacramentis ecclesiae*, begins his discussion of baptism by assembling the texts which show it to be the first among the sacraments because in it lies salvation.[16] Jesus said that no one who is not reborn by water and the Holy Spirit can enter the Kingdom of Heaven (John 3. 5); Mark 16.16 has the promise that he who believes and is baptized will be saved. It is this kind of talk which made it natural to think of baptism as something more than a means of purifying individuals of their sins and the consequences and a route of entry to the Church, not only on earth but in heaven. So in the Middle Ages, almost everyone living in Europe who was not born into a Jewish or Muslim family was baptized, and by virtue of that baptism deemed for practical purposes to be Christians and members of the Church. For order in the Church could best be maintained if everyone was clear who was and who was not a member of the visible Christian community.

The idea of 'ministry'

What doctrine of ministry did all this presuppose, and why was it important? For these structures as they evolved made certain presumptions about ministerial office. The New Testament speaks of a diaconate, whose members are chiefly occupied in looking after people's practical needs and making sure that widows and orphans in the community are not left destitute. 'It is not right that we should neglect the Word of God in order to wait at tables.' Seven men 'of good standing' were to be chosen to see to the needs of the widows and orphans. Acts 6.2–7 thus records the taking of a decision that these 'deacons' should concentrate on such things and leave the leadership of the community and the teaching to others. The others are variously described as 'elders' (presbyters) and 'bishops', though it is never clear in the New Testament whether they were technically distinct or exactly what functions were reserved to them.

The early Church's assumptions about ministry moved on a good deal during the medieval period in the West. Deacon, priest (presbyter) and bishop were now arranged in a ladder, an ascending hierarchy of office, and the expectation was that an individual would be ordained to each 'order' in turn. Below this level were deacons, with their clear New Testament sanction, but a changed remit, since they were no longer senior figures with special practical responsibilities; below them came a lengthening collection of 'minor orders' such as acolytes, of whom it was not quite clear whether they underwent a form of 'ordination' or not, although they were deemed to be in 'minor orders'.

Becoming a priest or better a bishop had considerable worldly attractions. It was a career. It gave influence. There were scandalous examples of the well-born being elevated in extreme youth through all the orders on the same day in order to be appointed to a bishopric in the 'gift' of an influential relative, but though it certainly happened it was recognized as unacceptable. Partly for that reason the rule emerged that no one might be made a priest before a certain maturity had been achieved, or a bishop before he was more mature still. The Third Lateran Council (1179) restates these rules. A bishop must be at least 30 years of age and show by his life and learning that he is worthy. Those in the lower orders which yet have the cure of souls must be at least 25 (Canon 3).[17]

Only bishops could ordain. Part of the underlying theory here was the assumption that the bishop was pastor of a given area, a diocese, and the priests who served there were 'his' priests, his 'vicars', or substitutes. A bishop was thus most fully an ordained minister and a priest lacked the essential additional authority to make priests, though the local priests would participate in ordinations. There also emerged a clearer distinction between the 'order', which was held to be indelible so that once someone was ordained he was for ever a priest or bishop, and the 'title' or local pastoral charge to which he was admitted, which could change as he moved to some other post in the Church.

The letters of commendation given to a priest even in the first Christian centuries if he left one diocese and travelled to another were designed to ensure that the bishop there would know two important things. The first was that he really was a priest and had been validly ordained. The second was that he was in 'good standing' and not leaving his previous diocese under a cloud.

High expectations of good behaviour were not always fulfilled. There were various ways in which a priest could go bad. Those guilty of serious sins, apostasy, murder and adultery, might be restored to the community after a period of public penance, but not to priestly functions, if they had committed them when in orders. Misconduct became at least as important as departure from orthodoxy in the eyes of the medieval Church.

First in the line came sexual misbehaviour. This was not necessarily defined in the same terms in East and West, or in every century. Several early councils in the East asserted that clergy were allowed to be married, and Canon 13 of the Council in Trullo (692) confirmed the position. Thereafter a priest or deacon in the East was allowed to be married but he must have been married before ordination. Bishops must be celibate. Simony was also a recognized problem in the East. The Second Council of Nicaea of 787 decreed that anyone who had obtained ecclesiastical office by paying for it should be suspended, along with whoever ordained him. Even someone who had acted as a go-between should lose his own clerical position or office and if he was a lay person he should be punished by being anathematized.[18]

The West made various attempts to require celibacy, but the real push took place in the eleventh century. It was too commonly found for comfort that if priests had children they would wish to provide for them, especially by procuring for them an 'inheritance' of their father's living. Simony could take the form of cronyism, nepotism, abuse of rights of patronage. The discussion of celibacy was thus linked at least in the public mind to the temptation to simony. Boniface complained of a chaotic breakdown of Church order. Bishops buy their bishoprics and keep mistresses. They behave like the nobles they are, fighting like their secular brothers, shedding blood. This helped to encourage the reforms of the Carolingians, but no reform of that sort was likely to be permanently effective. Each age bred its own challenges. Berengar, Viscount of Narbonne, described how when his uncle, who had been an archbishop, died his parents were approached by Wifred of Cerdana. Wifred wanted to take the office over and offered to buy it from them. At first they were unenthusiastic, but then he made use of the additional incentive that Berengar's wife was Wifred's niece. They capitulated and Wifred bestowed the archbishopric on his son who was still only ten years old. The justification was that such transactions could be seen as selling not the 'holy things' of ecclesiastical office but the mere temporalities attached to holy things, such as lands and buildings.[19] Guibert of Nogent's late-eleventh-century mother was keen to get him a benefice and was prepared to buy it for him. In his autobiography-cum-confessions he discusses contemporary celibacy and simony controversies as they affected his own family. He mentions a priest with a wife who could not bear to be separated from her whatever sanctions he was threatened with. Guibert himself began to become aware of the perils which menaced his soul if he was to pursue this career, and he and his mother then explored the possibility of entry into the religious life, he as a monk, she as a nun.[20]

The First Lateran Council (1123) (Canon 21B)[21] forbade every cleric of the order of subdeacon or above to marry. The Second Lateran Council (Canons 6–8) sought to enforce the new strict rule of clerical celibacy. Any clergy, monks or nuns who have married are to be separated from their partners because no marriage contracted in contravention of the law of the Church can be deemed to be valid.[22] The theory justifying this is that marriage makes them impure and they ought to be vessels of the Lord and sanctuaries of the Holy Spirit. Sexual intercourse, even when it is made legitimate by marriage, is deemed to contaminate the individual's purity. There is also a ban on pretend nuns, women who do not enter reputable houses of Benedictines or Augustinian canons but set up their own private houses where, under the pretence of monastic hospitality, they entertain guests and 'secular persons'(Canon 26), in effect running brothels. It is also forbidden for nuns to sing the divine offices with communities of monks (Canon 27).[23]

The Third Lateran Council (Canon 7) repeated the decree that ministry was not to be sold. There should be no fee charged for installing a priest in a church, for a funeral, for the blessing of a wedding or for other sacraments.[24] By the mid-twelfth century the clerical profession had a number of money-making possibilities, and the Second Lateran Council (Canon 9) made a list of things clerics were not allowed to do. They should not study civil law and medicine so as to make financial gain from the practice of these professions, for example, as priest-advocates. Neglecting psalms and hymns, they are getting so carried away with their fine words in court that they can no longer see the importance of telling the truth. Others make money more directly still, selling cures to the sick. Some sell chrism, holy oil and burials (Canon 23).[25] In the canons of the Second Lateran Council (1139) are included a number of sanctions to be used when something is out of order. If anyone is simoniacally ordained he must forfeit the office he acquired illicitly (Canon 1).[26]

Gerhoch of Reichersberg in the mid-twelfth century refers to 'mad clergy' living lives of 'more than lay and secular luxury' while consuming the goods of the Church.[27] Some medieval bishops expected their 'subjects' to sell church ornaments to pay for a feast for their own episcopal enjoyment. Conspicuous consumption, living in a manner out of keeping with Christ's instruction to his disciples to take nothing with them were matters energetically taken up by some of the anti-establishment groups of dissidents who became prominent in the twelfth century. But there was official disapproval too. The Third Lateran Council reproved those, particularly bishops, who put an unreasonably heavy load on their people (4). St Paul of Tarsus had insisted on earning his own bread by the labour of his own hands, so that he should not be an expense to the people among whom he was preaching.[28]

Sacraments

Augustine had introduced the idea that all the sacraments were 'outward and visible signs of an inward and spiritual grace'. The question remained which signs were sacraments and which were not. The Middle Ages was responsible for a good deal of clarification of the concept of a 'sacrament'. The word really means just 'mystery', but there emerged a much stronger doctrine, that the sacraments are necessary to salvation.

At the end of the twelfth century Peter the Chanter deals with the sacraments one by one in his *De sacramentis*. He is much concerned in his opening remarks with the way the sacraments 'work', the role of merit and the role of 'doing things for love'. The main value of the sacraments he sees as adding to a 'heap of grace' (*cumulus gratie*), with the exception of marriage, which was instituted as a remedy and not *ad augmentum*. He sees this quite mechanically, *ex opere operato*. At the ordination of a priest there is an effusion of grace. At the ordination of a bishop there is a greater effusion. He raises the question whether wishing to receive communion but not being able to because there is no opportunity confers as much grace as actually receiving it.[29]

As the medieval theology of the sacraments developed, the medieval world came to place a higher value on the 'sacramental tasks' of an ordained ministry. The sacraments began to be seen as aids the faithful 'needed' if they were to get to heaven. By the end of the Middle Ages questions of 'powers' were coming to prominence, for if the sacraments could have such important 'effects', those who could make or celebrate them became correspondingly more important to the welfare of the people. Once the sacraments are seen as very powerful, there is an implication that those empowered to administer them are powerful too. Peter the Chanter says that just as they make the good better, so they make the wicked worse. If a priest gives communion to someone who is in mortal sin, that person is polluted by receiving it, even if he did not know he was in mortal sin and did not do it on purpose.[30]

Some important questions had been settled in the early centuries. One of these was that the effect of a sacrament was God's work, not man's. Baptism could be valid and efficacious whoever performed it, whether ordained or not and whether good or wicked. So long as it was done with water and in the name of the Trinity, God would respond with once-and-for-all forgiveness of the person baptized. The other sacrament which could be said to have been 'instituted' by Jesus was the commemoration of his Last Supper with his disciples described in the New Testament. The bread and wine of the Eucharist, it came to be held, could be consecrated only by a validly ordained priest. It was accepted that the act of consecration was not invalidated by any personal unworthiness in the priest, for it too was a work of divine grace, but the channel had to be set up appropriately, and if the priest was not properly ordained there was no sacrament and no 'salvific' effect.

This came to seem even more important with the emergence of the doctrine of transubstantiation, from the late eleventh century and throughout the twelfth, when the term was coined. Transubstantiation is the belief that the bread becomes the actual physical body of Christ and the wine his blood, thus changing in substance (*trans-substantiatio*), yet the appearance and all other impressions the bread and wine make upon the senses do not change. This is the reversal of what happens in nature when bread, while remaining bread in substance, goes mouldy and its appearance, smell and taste all change. It turns on its head the principles of Aristotle's *Categories*. For a priest to be able to 'make Christ' in this way was an enormous power. Bruno the Carthusian, in his deathbed 'Confession of Faith', takes particular care to emphasize the importance of the Eucharist. 'I believe in the sacrament which the Catholic Church believes and venerates, and specifically that it is the true body and blood of our Lord Jesus Christ which is consecrated on the altar.'[31]

During the same period the ancient theology of penance was evolving rapidly. Penance in the early Church had been the public process undertaken when someone had committed one of the 'serious' sins – murder, apostasy, adultery – and it involved a period set apart from the community and the wearing of special penitential garments, at the end of which the local bishop might readmit the penitent. During the Carolingian period this had mutated into a more low-key but general expectation that everyone, even those who committed only the routine minor sins of everyday life, would confess his or her sins to a priest, but privately. These changes threw into prominence the question whether authority to forgive sins, or to declare that God had forgiven them (absolution), was a 'priestly power' conferred by the Holy Spirit at ordination, or whether it was open to all Christians to help one another to forgiveness by hearing one another's confessions, as the Epistle of James (5.6) hinted. The medieval insistence was that the granting of absolution was strictly a priestly function. A minor looseness of practice which had sometimes allowed monks who were not priests to grant absolution to penitents was tightened up. Theologians pointed to Jesus's words when he said that he would give the Keys of the Kingdom of Heaven to his disciples and those they 'loosed' on earth would be 'loosed' in heaven (Matthew 16.19), and argued that the promise applied to those who followed his disciples in the apostolic succession, ordained ministers, but not to the faithful in general.

In the West this process reached a definitive stage with the requirement of the Fourth Lateran Council of 1215 that every person of either sex should make confession to a priest once a year. With this requirement went an elaboration of the requirements of the process and the devising of manuals for confessors so that they would ensure the penance included all the necessary elements. Contrition, says Caesarius of Heisterbach, is heartfelt repentance, true grief for sin, which sometimes arises from the fear of hell and sometimes from the desire for heaven. Whatever prompts it, it must involve genuine bruising. It has to hurt. Contrition is immensely 'powerful', for it is an essential ingredient in confession and reparation. Without it they are useless.[32] With it, amazing quantities of sin may be forgiven. Caesarius tells of a renegade priest and monks who had joined a band of robbers and killed many and plundered much. When the priest finally repented, his confessor did not know how to allocate him a sufficient penance, so he chose for himself a penance of 2,000 years.[33] This penance was commuted by the kind offices of the bishop and the congregation who prayed for his soul after his death, and he appeared to the bishop to tell him so and thank him.

Only priests could declare the repentant sinner absolved and impose the Church's required penances. The idea was that as the Church had authority to impose the penalties for sin, so it had the power to remove those penalties.

So when an 'indulgence' was granted it took away from a penitent sinner
the duty to carry out some of his penances before he could be received into
heaven. It took a bishop or even the Pope to remit those temporal penalties
by granting an 'indulgence', and so great was this power that it was deemed
to reach into the life to come. A plenary indulgence, as offered for the first
time by Pope Urban II when he preached the First Crusade, was a free
pardon of all the penances someone had accumulated. It was taken to mean
a guarantee of heaven.

Purgatory was described (if not invented) during the twelfth century.
Few seemed fit for heaven at their deaths, either to themselves or to their
friends and relations, for few lived to the standards expected of the 'saints'.
Yet it would be discouraging for the majority to believe they had no chance
of heaven. Purgatory was conceived of as a place where for a time after
death people who had penances still to discharge could do so, and when
they had 'served their sentence' would assuredly go on to heaven. Of this
arrangement the Church made itself custodian.

Church and state

When someone in a high position in the Church finds his safety threatened, does he have a duty to stay, or to flee and preserve himself for another
day as Paul did when he was let down in a basket and escaped his pursuers
(Acts 9.25; II Corinthians 11.33)?[34] This is becoming a live question again,
particularly in areas of interfaith tension in the modern world. This question was asked when Anselm, Archbishop of Canterbury, stayed away too
long in 'exile', and again when Thomas Becket, Archbishop of Canterbury,
was in exile between 1164 and 1170, at a period of high tension between
Church and state when his quarrel with the King was becoming dangerous.
The particular medieval complexion of the question derived from a set of
assumptions about the relationship of ruler to ruled, in Church as in state.

Against all the practical evidence to the contrary, it was possible for the
Church in the West to regard society as a unity, a body politic in which the
citizenry all had their roles, which they should not seek to change. 'It would
seem to be pride for anyone to wish to change the condition which has been
given him for good reason by the divine ordinance.'[35] There were considered
to be various standard divisions of function, which corresponded with the
broad social divisions: rulers and fighters, workers and those who prayed on
behalf of everybody else.

In those parts of Western Europe where feudalism emerged, there went
with it a high doctrine of royalty. The making of a king had steps just like
the making of a bishop, for the choosing of the individual to be appointed,
the entrusting of authority to that person and the appointment of a person

to an office in a particular place raised distinct questions for the Church as to the role it and the secular authorities respectively ought to play. Anointing was a new thing for kings in the Carolingian period. It was introduced on an analogy with the anointing of King David (II Samuel 2.4, 5.3; II Kings 11.12, 23.30; I Chronicles 11.2, 29.22; Judges 9.8, 9.15). 'Pippin, according to the custom of the Franks, was elected to be king and anointed by the hand of Boniface of sacred memory and elevated to the throne by the Franks in the city of Soissons.'[36] Is there a sacrament? Is being made king a kind of ordination? It was decided that it was not. A king is not a priest.

There were very senior lay people, such as kings, at the top of the secular hierarchy. The Church had its attitudes to these. They were heroes. They were soldiers of Christ. But they must not intrude upon the sacramental functions of the Church or confuse coronation with ordination. A king was a symbol, but not a sacrament. He was anointed but not ordained. He was a king, not a priest.[37] Nevertheless English kings were commonly buried in full royal regalia, and in some cases their hearts were buried separately, on their own instructions or because it was advantageous to ensure that two or more lucrative streams of intercessory prayer could be expected.[38]

Some rulers set a high moral tone. William of Poitiers wrote a *Life* of the Duke William of Normandy who became William the Conqueror. William is made out to have been notable for his military skill and courage, with great feats described. He is compared with the heroes of ancient Greece and Rome, in particular with Aeneas and Julius Caesar. As a ruler, both in Normandy and in England, he was just and firm. There was no lawlessness where William ruled and the military might of his armies never descended into rape and pillage and attacks on innocent travellers. His attitude to the Church was benevolent and protective. He founded monasteries and made additional gifts to existing religious houses. His motivation was not glory in this world but the hope of heaven, claims his biographer.[39]

These questions of attitude are important because even though kings and nobles may have lacked the personal education which would have enabled them to enter into debate with the leaders of the Church about their respective powers and the balance between them, they were apparently capable of thinking in such terms and ready to see the matter as a problem arising. Gervase of Tilbury's *Otia imperialia*[40] contains a number of references to and discussions of the issues which arose between Church and state. In any case, it is a practical question, which came up at every coronation. If priests are needed to make kings properly, that affects the balance of power between Church and state.[41]

The forged Carolingian document known as the 'Donation of Constantine' was not recognized for many centuries to be a forgery.[42] It appeared to hand over secular power to the Church's keeping. In reliance upon it the West had for centuries struck a working balance of power between Church and state. At the end of the eleventh century there was a feeling in the Church that kings and emperors had begun to trespass into areas which were not properly their province. When a bishop died the see remained vacant until the king or emperor who had the right to nominate his successor fixed on a name. It became customary to keep sees vacant for a year or more so that the patron could take the revenues. Then when a bishop was finally chosen the king or emperor began to intrude on the process of consecration, taking over actions which properly belonged to the ecclesiastical authorities, such as putting the ring on the new bishop's finger or the pastoral staff into his hand, thus 'investing' him as only the Church ought to do. Pope Gregory VII (d.1085) began to press for reform and there ensued an 'Investiture Contest', which rumbled on for some decades while Church and state arm-wrestled their way to a workable power-relationship. The formal resolution came in 1122 with the Concordat of Worms, which distinguished the 'spiritualities' of a see, those parts of the appointment of a bishop which could be regarded as sacramental and were reserved to the Church, and the parts which were 'temporalities', such as the handing over of the lands, which properly belonged to the secular power.

The Investiture Contest of the late eleventh and early twelfth centuries was about the grand question of the balance of power between Church and state and also about small but insistent matters of control over property. The two-way pull of conflicting interests in matters of property was felt at every level in Church and state. Royal officials could be intrusive and proprietary where they had no right to be. *The History of the Church of Abingdon* comments on the way ordinary people living on Church lands could be made to suffer unjust impositions in this way, treating them as 'customs'. The abbey adroitly obtained a charter from King William I stating that no tolls were payable when the abbey's servants bought provisions, and had the royal letters read out in the Berkshire county court.[43]

Gregory VII purposefully set out to elevate the powers of the papacy over the secular power. Gregory wrote to Lanfranc, Archbishop of Canterbury, to explain that the bearer of the letter will make Lanfranc aware of the burdensomeness of Gregory's papal office. He bemoans the way bishops (not of course Lanfranc himself) lust after worldly glory and carnal delights and set a bad example to their fellows.[44] His correspondence includes many such overtures to bishops and archbishops from his vantage-point as primate, and clearly presuming his authority to admonish and encourage them.[45]

Bernard of Clairvaux's *De consideratione* ('On Consideration') was written for the benefit of Pope Eugenius III, who had once been a Cistercian monk and of whose fitness for such high office Bernard does not seem to have been entirely convinced. In a succession of episodes in this book, written as a series of afterthoughts in the light of subsequent events, he first works out a theory of papal duty. In Book I the emphasis is on the need to keep a balance between the active part of the office and the responsibility to make time for a spiritual life. Eugenius had been wasting his own time presiding as a judge in the papal appeal court, where every aspiring advocate was keen to appear because it would benefit his future business. (Appeals to the papal court could prompt misbehaviours of various sorts. In a slightly later episode, one appellant suffered reprisals when members of an archbishop's household pursued and harried the appellant community's abbot.[46]) Bernard then moves on to the question of where in the great scheme of things a pope should see himself as placed. This too has implications for the balance of power between Church and state, but it is also relevant to the balance of powers within the Church, and in particular to the role of a papal monarch in a collegial structure. Bernard encouraged Eugenius to consider everyone to be 'under' him. 'If anyone wants to explore what is not under your care, he will have to leave the world.'[47]

In a sermon on the consecration of a pope, Innocent III (1160/1–1216) cites Matthew 16.18 and goes on to explore the paradox of a service which is also a supreme lordship.[48] Yet when a pope such as Innocent III moved about he took with him a huge retinue, including perhaps a dozen cardinals, each with his own retinue of notaries, scribes, confessors and chaplains. Then there were the domestic servants needed to provide for the creature comforts of all these people, and the litigants with cases in progress reluctant to let the pope out of their sight before their appeals were heard. To those who saw such a progress as it made its way over some weeks or months, the comparison with a royal progress must have been tempting. The peripatetic pope was behaving like a peripatetic feudal king, for whom it was important to keep himself in his people's eyes and minds, and preferably looking as large and impressive as possible. Innocent III had some ground to make up, for some parts of Italy had not had such a visit for half a century by the time he became pope.[49]

The assertion of supremacy might require a little diplomacy. In a letter to the bishops of France, Innocent III is careful to explain that although he does not wish to interfere with the rightful jurisdiction of the King of France he has a duty to rebuke his brother (Matthew 18.15–17) and he is sure that in the circumstances the King should not consider it *iniuriosa* to submit to the apostolic judgement.[50]

Innocent's ideas about secular overlordship went in reality a great deal further than his tact here would imply. At the Fourth Lateran Council of 1515, the Counts of Toulouse and Foix knelt to beg for the restoration of lands of theirs held by the leader of the victorious 'Albigensian' crusaders, Simon de Montfort. Raymond of Toulouse had his lands confiscated by the Council, which handed them over to Simon on the grounds that Raymond had forfeited all right to them by harbouring heretics. Canon 3 of the Council (*Excommunicamus*) decreed that any secular ruler who neglected to take firm action against heretics in his territories after he had been warned should forfeit his lands in the same way. Other canons of the Council also sought to keep lay authority in its place. If a bishop got elected because a lay ruler had improperly used his influence, the appointment would be void (Canon 25). (Conversely a lay ruler must not resist an appointment proposed by the papacy. John King of England had been excommunicated in 1206 and his kingdom placed under interdict for six years because he had not been willing to accept Pope Innocent's recommendation that the next Archbishop of Canterbury should be the Paris theologian Stephen Langton.) Secular rulers who tried to tax the clergy without papal permission or who appropriated ecclesiastical property or intruded on ecclesiastical jurisdiction would be excommunicated (Canons 44 and 46).

Innocent's writings embody a theory of papal monarchy which he sought to put into practice, and the same ideas occur in many of his letters. Significantly two of these set out a position about the primacy of the Western patriarchate. The Patriarch of Constantinople, John X Kamateros, sent a series of challenges on this subject which Innocent answered robustly.[51] He wrote in a similarly determined vein to the Armenians. Innocent saw the pope's power at least as clearly as Bernard of Clairvaux had done, as a *plenitudo potestatis*, a 'fullness of power'.

By the thirteenth century, the papacy had, then, established an ecclesiological primacy and a clear sense of the inherent superiority of the spiritual to the secular realms of rule. The pontificates of Innocent III (1198–1216), Honorius III (1216–27) and Gregory IX (1227–41) were marked by strong controlling moves to advance spiritual hegemony, but there were strong secular monarchs too, who presented a powerful challenge. Within the Church, the emergence of conciliar consultative government became apparent. The Fourth Lateran Council, in which Innocent's controlling hand was significant and deliberation was really mainly approval of a fait accompli, was followed by the First Council of Lyons (1245) and the Second Council of Lyons (1274). These were attended not only by bishops, intended to represent the universal Church, but also by other clerics and representatives of secular powers, and there was active debate. The College of Cardinals was the place to serve an apprenticeship which might lead to election to the papacy. The cardinals advised the Pope, and provided legates and committee members when needed. The papal hegemony of Innocent III remained, however, an active memory and a desideratum of the later thirteenth-century papacy. At the opening of the Council of Lyons in 1274 reform of the Church was one of the chief items on the agenda. Alongside it was a desire to continue to pursue the long-standing central crusading objective of recovering the Holy Land and the holy places within it for Christians, and an aspiration to achieve reunion with the Greeks by an end to the schism of 1054.

The relationship of Church and state in the Eastern half of the old Roman Empire was, in every sense, more Byzantine. There was no Investiture Contest to mark a decisive delineation of boundaries. But, as we shall see again and again, the boundaries were there and patriarch and emperor repeatedly pushed at them in the heat of the politics of the moment.

CHAPTER 5

Church and People

The laity in a top–down society

Medieval society was hierarchical, not merely in social reality but as a matter of principle. Its hierarchical character was understood in cosmological terms. It was taken for granted that the universe was designed in such a way that some of God's creatures were intended to be at the top and some below them. Human beings were a 'higher' form of being than cattle. Cattle were 'higher' than the grass they ate. The grass was 'higher' than the earth it grew in. So thoroughgoing was the sense that this was how the universe worked that the nine orders of angels identified by the fifth-century Greek author Pseudo-Dionysius began to be lined up alongside their human 'counterparts' on the understanding that each person's place in heaven would be related to that of the equivalent angel. So the seraphim and cherubim, the contemplatives among the angels, would be accompanied for eternity by members of the contemplative religious orders, their human equivalents. In modern terms, this was like suggesting that postmen and motor-cycle messengers would spend eternity in the company of ordinary angels, while diplomats and emissaries could expect to find themselves alongside archangels.

Within human society itself no premium was put upon equality. Until late in the Middle Ages, few appear to have seen anything wrong with the idea that there should be rulers and ruled, for hierarchical arrangements of parts within wholes were a normal way of making an organism 'work'. A body needs a head but it also needs feet (I Corinthians 12.20). In fragmentary survivals of the teaching which was given in the cathedral school at Laon at the end of the eleventh and the beginning of the twelfth centuries, there is a discussion of the passage in Ephesians 6.5 where servants are told to obey their masters. 'It is no sin to have a servant or to be a servant.' It was argued at Laon that there are two reasons why 'servitude is given by God'. It may be a punishment for the sins of those who are slaves or servants. Or it may have a purpose of proving or testing them, so that, humbled, they may be better people.[1] This resembles the two-pronged argument found in discussions of leprosy in the cartularies of medieval leper hospitals. The lepers (who were in many cases probably suffering from some form of eczema or dermatitis rather than true leprosy) were encouraged to be patient in their suffering because *either* they deserved it *or* it was a generous gift from God to test them and fit them for heaven if they would only respond to their affliction in the right spirit. In any case the right response was to thank God for the state of their skin and make the best of it.

The Laon discussion makes a fine distinction between the direct involvement of the Church in enslavement and its acquisition of slaves (*servi*), which just happen to 'come with' lands bestowed upon it by lay benefactors. Here the term 'slave' elides with 'serf'; the Latin word is the same (*servus*). The slavery of the ancient world became serfdom in much of medieval northern Europe. A proportion of those at the bottom of the social hierarchy were bound to the land on which they laboured, 'holding' it, ultimately from the king, but in practice usually from a vassal who himself held land from the king. Although he was not a slave, the vassal of the king, however highborn, was 'someone else's man'. He knelt and put his hands between those of his lord when he swore 'fealty', the oath of loyalty. The nobility paid for their holdings in days of war-service each year. The rent which lowlier persons paid for their 'tenements' was work performed for the lord, and the serf was not free to go elsewhere. Even a villein, a little higher in the order of things, was a bondsman. The proposal in this particular discussion at the school of Laon was that although the Church is not allowed to take slaves by violence, it may accept them when they come with gifts of lands (*cum servis suis*). It should then liberate the serfs or slaves in question or ensure that their servitude is as light as possible.[2]

The fundamental assumption that one human being may own another was pervasive in the ancient world and it found its way into Islam too. The Koran accepts the idea that God gives slaves as booty (33.50). The freeing of a slave is a virtuous act, but not because it is good in itself; it means giving up some of one's property in discharge of a penalty incurred for one's wrong actions (4.92, 5.88). It is as legitimate to sleep with one's slave-girl as with one's wife (25.5)

Inseparable from the Western set of ideas about the natural structure of society within the universe were questions about the structure of the Church, which were also most pressing and troublesome in the West. Should it mirror society? Or should it resemble the body, whose parts all work together cooperatively for the common good? We have just seen that it had, by the Middle Ages, acquired well-developed hierarchical structures of its own, with the clergy in ranks, one below the other, bishops, priests, deacons, and, below them, a series of notionally 'clerical' grades such as that of acolyte and sub-deacon, the 'minor orders' which had chiefly liturgical functions without priestly powers.

The question for this chapter is where in such an ecclesiastical hierarchy people who were not clergy could, even in so lowly a way, fit. *Laos* means 'people', and it could be argued that the 'people of God' (*populus*) who made up the Church included both laity in the sense of 'non-clergy' and the clergy themselves. But the tendency was the other way, to exclude the laity or deem them an inferior kind of Christian, of whom less was expected both theologically and in terms of the standard of their Christian behaviour than was expected of clergy and members of religious orders. 'Come, tiptoe as you cautiously lead simple people to the truth' (*Venite, pedetentim et caute inducit illos rudes ad veritatem*).[3]

On closer inspection, however, it is not easy to maintain a sharp distinction between the *rudes* and the experts. Lay people began to crop up in situations where they were teaching or preaching or otherwise 'leading' other Christians. One of the great crises of the later medieval Church was the need to determine categories within the *laos*, the method of placing people within their 'category' and what members of each category were allowed to do and by what authority.

The scope for lay people to express their faith was limited mainly to the personal. They could live good lives, trusting in God and setting a quiet example to their friends and relations. The instructions of Leviticus 19.15–18 set out a number of practical rules for living. One must be impartial when 'judging' one's neighbour, and not judge one's neighbour in the sense of condemning him; one must not hate one's brother but one must reproach him when it is appropriate. Partly upon these Jesus erected his summary of the law: one must love one's neighbour as oneself and love God above all things.

The more highly born might be in a position to do this conspicuously. The wealthy could give generously to support the poor. Everyone, including the very poor and uneducated, could (and mostly did) go to church regularly. Liturgy, in its Christian sense, is literally a 'work' of, or on behalf of, the people of God.[4] The of question what part the people might play in worship beyond being present as spectators was to become important in the later medieval West as dissident groups such as the Waldensians began to ask why they could not lead services, preach, even celebrate the Eucharist without priestly assistance. The Church responded repressively, with ever greater insistence that preaching and the ministry of the sacraments must be reserved to the ordained.

In the Greek East the custom was more participatory for the people, but no less severe about the special roles reserved for priests. Liturgical feasts were frequent in medieval Greek life,[5] adding to Sundays in the twelfth century 66 panegyreis or 'full' feasts and 27 half-feasts. The liturgical texts required reached their settled form from the eleventh century. They carried for the Christian community among which the liturgies were celebrated not merely the theatrical re-enactment of the Christian story but also a theology, and particularly a mystical theology, and a set of assumptions subtly but importantly different from those of the West.[6] Greek had remained the common tongue in the lands of the old Roman Empire, although it was spoken locally in a demotic form. Whereas the populace of the West no longer understood the Latin liturgy and Bible readings in Church for themselves, a Greek congregation might.[7] For the Greeks themselves, the language was perhaps less important than it was for Western worshippers in any case.

Even where the common language was not persuasive, for visitors from the Slav communities might not understand what they heard, the beauty of ceremony and building might well be. At the end of the tenth century a delegation was sent to Constantinople by Prince Vladimir. They took home such a wonderful tale of the brilliance of the celebration of the Eucharist at which they had been present in Hagia Sophia that Vladimir resolved to become a Christian and to adopt Orthodoxy. 'The Greeks led us to the edifices where they worship their God, and we knew not whether we were in heaven or on earth.'[8] The liturgy was a time of joyous elevation of the soul towards the transcendent, of union with God, the celebration of a mystery; it was a merging with the tradition, a memorial (*anamnesis*) and a thanksgiving (which is what *eucharistia* means).

A joyous sense of sharing was to be found in the West too, though it had a different flavour. Even though people were present at the celebration week by week, it was only once a year that they 'received' the consecrated bread or host. This was one of the effects of the establishment of the doctrine of transubstantiation by the end of the twelfth century, for that heightened the sense of the holiness of the bread which was believed to have become the actual body of Christ and the wine his actual blood. Communion in both kinds gave way to an arrangement by which the laity received only the bread, on the pretext that the wine which had become the blood of Christ might get spilt.[9] The focus shifted to seeing the consecration, the lifting up of the bread by the priest before the eyes of the congregation. In some pictures the priest is shown holding up a miniature Christ-child.[10] There is some evidence that the West was particularly fond of hymn-singing. Thomas of Celano, author of the second *Life of Francis of Assisi*, describes how Francis would be irresistibly moved to sing in French, miming the playing of a viol as he did so.[11] (Francis's Canticle of the Sun may be a hymn.)

The debasing of lay devotion

Saint (*hagios, sanctus*) means 'holy'. The New Testament speaks of the faithful as 'saints' without as yet making any distinction between the ordinary believer and the 'specially holy' person who is held up as an example to others. The identification of the especially good was relatively straightforward in the eras when there was persecution of the early Christians, when those prepared to die for their faith marked themselves out at once as heroes of the faith. Stephen (Acts 8.2), Polycarp, Ignatius and the Martyrs of Lyons were the earliest in a growing line. Their deaths were celebrated in local churches and the churches made their calendars available to one another so that cults spread.[12] Less extreme sacrifice consisted in drawing apart from the world to live in ascetic self-denial as a 'confessor' or virgin. To the confessors came the faithful in search of absolution.[13] The cult of saints in the Greek East remained strong and pervaded the life of the Church with a flavour it retains today. In the West it had more clearly identifiable stages of progression.

By the Middle Ages the saint is less likely to die a sacrificial death, though there are plenty of deathbed scenes where that is the metaphor. Bruno the Carthusian (*c.*1030–1101) wrote on the profession of faith which he felt it was appropriate to prepare and to pronounce before the assembled brothers as death approached: *appropinquare sibi horam ut ingrederetur iam omnis carnis.*[14] The dead saint becomes a spiritual hero and an 'example'. The male saint is often seen as a soldier of Christ. Spiritual heroism could be achieved by women too, for saints could be female as well as male. Aebbe was the abbess of a double monastery in Northumbria in the seventh century. She was credited with healing miracles which cured 42 people, more than half of them female. She healed them (chiefly) of paralysis, dumbness, blindness, swellings and madness,[15] with no demonstrable preference for the upper classes or locality.[16] The biographer of Margaret of Scotland in the eleventh century said she had an influence at court and in improving the standards of Christian observance in Scotland.[17]

At the beginning of the account of the *Miracles of St Aethelthryth the Virgin* at the end of the eleventh century Goscelin places a preface in which he sets some of these standards out. Saints are there to form a channel for the reverence the worshipper shows to God by reverencing his saints. They are there to provide us with examples to imitate, so that we may become worthy to be of their company in heaven.[18] Bernard of Clairvaux wrote a *Life* of Malachi, Archbishop of Armagh, who died at Clairvaux in 1148, presenting him as *speculum et exemplum*, a mirror and example to others and 'salt' (*condimentum*) for the life on earth. To write such a life, he suggests, is a way of keeping the dead saint among the living and making it possible for his life to be contemplated as though he was still among them. In order to heighten the effect, he stresses the contrast between the average person and the *raritas sanctitatis* in his own day.[19]

An important example of special sanctity was Mary the mother of Jesus. Devotion to Mary was always profound in the East. She was the God-Bearer (*Theotokos*). In the West the cult of special devotion to her became important in the late eleventh and twelfth centuries, partly as a result of the Mary prayers of Anselm of Bec: 'To Mary when one's mind is heavy', 'To Mary when one's mind is troubled by fear', 'To Mary that she may intercede with her Son',[20] and the encouragement of Bernard of Clairvaux.

In the eleventh and twelfth centuries there was a mounting enthusiasm for canonizations, the official process for making more of the 'approved' saints whose exceptional holiness enabled them to be held up as examples and to encourage aspirations to personal holiness. Official biographies of the holy, or 'hagiographies', were hard currency, because if they could help get their subject canonized there might well be profit to be made from pilgrimages to the shrine where his body or a relic was kept. When an abbot died, the monks might hire a professional hagiographer and seek to get him canonized. Ulrich, Bishop of Augsburg (923–73), led an exemplary life and founded a number of religious houses. His became the first formal or ceremonial ecclesiastical canonization. One way of obtaining a canonization was to cite miraculous cures brought about by relics, portions of the dead man's body or the whole corpse. If the canonization was successful, the saint's shrine became official and the abbey could hope for pilgrimages and a good deal of trade in souvenirs.[21] This could happen at a local level, but there was also an established tradition of the fame of a special saint spreading across oceans. Willibrord, Archbishop of the Frisians, would tell tales of the miracles related by Bede.[22] The twelfth-century cult of Thomas Becket also became international.[23] Local clergy could assist in the spreading of the cult of a local saint by making relics available to their parishioners.[24] The news of a new cult or of cures being achieved at a new shrine could spread by a recommendation spiced with the excitement of novelty.[25]

The saint thus came to have something of the role of the modern 'celebrity' in seeming to stand above the level of common life and to be glossier than normal, an object of emulation and perhaps envy too. Some social prominence, or prominence within an abbey, would be an asset, too. For a saint had functions. Saints were called upon for intercessory prayer, since it seemed only common sense to expect them to have better access to the ear of Mary or Christ than the sinner who was asking for their assistance. The pagan gods had been mercenary. One paid for results. A present (sacrifice, bribe) could be relied upon (up to a point) to produce the appropriate intervention. Popular Christianity had the faithful resorting to the saints with promises of future good behaviour in return for favours. The Council of Trullo (692) issued edicts. Canon 71 instructed bishops to stop students of civil law celebrating pagan rites. Canon 94 forbade the use of oaths to invoke the pagan gods.

The idea of the communion of the saints was already linked in the first centuries with the notion that the just can lend their merits to others. The story of Dives and Lazarus (Luke 16.19–31) was used by Origen and Cyprian as authority for this idea.[26] One mechanism by which they did so was the performance of wonders, supernatural acts. In the Vulgate only the Old Testament uses the word *miraculum* and then it is for a fearful event of some sort.[27] II Kings 13.21 records an episode, unique in the Old Testament and the New, when a dead man was accidentally thrown into the grave of Elisha in a panic, and as the body made contact with the bones of the prophet the dead man came back to life.

The miraculous had a respectable pedigree. Jesus performed miracles. There could be no question to medieval minds that when he did so these were the wonderful works of God. The miracles associated with saints were properly speaking also to be taken to be indications that God was at work, teaching his people. They were signs. The New Testament words for miracle are *signum, virtus, prodigium*.

Ordinary medieval people looked for miraculous help in much the same way and for much the same reasons as had once underpinned the worship of little local gods in Roman times. It gave simple people the encouraging sense that they could enter into transactions with supernatural powers.[28] When Augustine of Canterbury arrived in Kent on his mission to England at the end of the sixth century, the king arranged a meeting with him in the open air, for he feared magical interference if they met in any building; it was suspected that buildings could be enchanted.[29] The worshipping community (including a proportion of the ordained ministry) were under-educated and illiterate, and habits and attitudes persisted over the generations which suggest that paganism never really died out. There are reminders of the continuing vitality of popular superstition and the difficulty Christianity had in eliminating it among peoples when they were converted.

It was disturbing to the ecclesiastical authorities to discover how persistent the instincts of paganism were, even in much later centuries. Local people liked to be able to practise 'devotion' to a local saint as they had once done to a local god, or to a figure who seemed approachable and personal. The devotion focused on objects connected with the saint, which became 'relics'.

In the Christian tradition a number of elements made up a theory of miraculous intervention or assistance. People who were not theologically sophisticated could drive the theology here. Something very like the intensity and character of medieval feeling can still be observed at the shrine at Lourdes and, in the Orthodox world, at the shrine on the island of Tinos. Families sleep outside the church there close to the comfort of the miracle-working power within. Tags are hung from icons bearing picture of eyes, elbows and feet, or any other parts of the body for which a 'cure' is sought.

It was possible to point to a Scriptural foundation for this association of miraculous intervention with relics in which some virtue inheres because of the association with a saint. Acts 19.11–12 describes how God did miracles through Paul, and how cloths he touched could heal the sick even in his absence. This suggested that objects used by saints and parts of their bodies might be powerful healers, and that such objects might also afford protection to churches which had them. Saints' shrines were already to be found throughout the late Roman Empire,[30] and part of their power lay in the very locality and physical particularity of the association with the saint. In the saint's own bones or objects the saint had touched – relics of the saint – power resided.

These patterns persisted into the Middle Ages. Bede describes how King Oswald of Northumbria died in battle at the hands of the heathen, and subsequently many miracles took place as a result of even indirect contact with his corpse. A sick horse rolled on the spot where his body had fallen and was miraculously cured. A man passing the same spot and observing that it was greener and more beautiful than the surrounding soil, collected some of the soil and took it away. That evening the house where he was eating burned down, except for the post on which he had hung the bag containing the miraculous earth. Oswald's niece had his bones transported to Bardney Abbey where they received an uncertain welcome, because this was on territory once conquered by Oswald's kingdom. The bones were left outside the monastery under a canopy all night. Heaven made its feelings on the subject plain by causing a column of light to come down on the bones and stay there all night, visible for miles around. When the bones were eventually honourably received and washed before being placed in their shrine, the very water in which they were washed became holy and so did the earth on which it was poured away. The fame of the healing which emanated from Oswald's relics spread to Ireland in one direction and to the Low Countries in the other.

Miracles engaged the faithful. They were almost interactive. Whether a miracle 'worked' was deemed to depend on the effort the believer put into praying for it, not on the powers or competence of the saint. Failures were not necessarily to be regarded as the saint's fault. In the Prologue to the Life of Margaret of Scotland it is emphasized that it is God, not the saint, who works miracles, but that miracles are performed 'through' the *merita ineffabilia* of the saints. One woman with a swollen arm had toured the shrines of France without finding a cure. Margaret eventually cured the woman with a swollen arm, after she had been sent to her shrine by the prompting of a dream.[31]

Once this power of holy things could be seen as automatic, there was a danger of its being abused. Acts 19.13–20 recognizes this in its description of magician-exorcists trying to use the name of Jesus to cast out devils. The natural antithesis in popular religion lay between demons and saints as well as between demons and angels. Demons were as real to medieval minds as the mischievous minor gods had been to the pagans of late antiquity. Caesarius of Heisterbach gives a convenient list of biblical proof-tests at the beginning of Book V of his *Dialogue on Miracles*: Isaiah 14.12 (the fall of Lucifer); Luke 10.18 (Satan's fall from heaven); Job 1.6 (where Satan comes with the sons of God to present himself in the court of heaven); Psalms 114.5; Habakkuk 3.5; Revelation 12.78, Ezekiel 28.12; John 8.41, 8.44; Job 40.23; I Peter 5.8–9; Matthew 25.41. He tells the story of a knight who did not believe in demons until he saw them with his own eyes.[32] The intimate familiarity such encounters sometimes had is described in another story in which two demons were seen to enter the choir from close to the presbytery, and as they walked towards the abbot's stall and passed a certain corner another demon emerged and joined them, and they passed so close to the observer that he could have touched them and was able to observe that their feet did not need to touch the ground, for they were beings of the air.[33] Demons feature in Caesarius's stories in all sorts of activities, singly and in 'legions', sitting like little dormice on an expensively dressed woman, gathering in large numbers round a deathbed, taking possession of individuals, even a boy whose annoyed father shouted 'go to the Devil' at him.

In ancient paganism supernatural beings could be well disposed or ill disposed. This was roughly translated in popular Christianity into a distinction between the good and the fallen angels, with guardian angels providing support and their counterpart demons doing what they could to impede the footsteps of the believer trying to make his way to heaven. The cult of saints became much more important pastorally than any 'cult' of the angels. Saints had the advantage of being human, so that they had life-stories and left bodies behind, from which 'relics' could be preserved.

Gervase of Tilbury's *Otia imperialia*[34] is the work of an English scholar-nobleman, a lawyer trained at Bologna, for a time a royal civil servant, who spent time at the court of Henry II of England and who wrote a book of amusements for the young prince Henry which does not survive.[35] This larger work, for the Emperor Otto IV, became a huge encyclopaedia of geography and marvels. He describes the marvels in much the same spirit of straightforward acceptance as the authors of saints' lives describe miracles. They serve a similar purpose of heightening excitement and awakening awe. For example, he describes a nut-tree which omits the stage of having flowers, and, four months into the summer, when the feast of John the Baptist (24 June) approaches, it experiences a sudden joy at the advent of the Forerunner (*repentina exultatione nascentis precursoris gaudio congaudet*) and its leaves and nuts sprout forth together.[36]

In Matthew 19.21 Jesus tells his disciples to store up their treasure in heaven, not on earth. By the thirteenth century, a theory of a 'Treasury of Merits' had emerged, with the assistance of Bonaventure. The idea was that when the Church chose, it could make available for the benefit of human beings lacking in sufficient virtue some of the surplus merit of the saints, surplus in the sense that they had had it left over after they had done enough to get into heaven. The saints were real in the popular imagination, patiently ready to listen to people's troubles brought to them in prayer, able to intervene to bring about miraculous cures or to intercede in heaven on behalf of loved ones who had died. Something of the same simple trust is visible today in parts of southern Europe and in the Greek Orthodox world, where the shrine of a popular saint is hung about with tokens, messages and requests. The notion that devotion to these helpful saints might get in the way of the single-minded worship of God became a concern towards the end of the Middle Ages and underpinned some of the concerns which led to the Reformation in the West. In the Greek East those anxieties had their day mainly in the much earlier period of the iconoclastic controversies.

Lay preaching [37]

A Spanish illumination of 1109 shows an angel (messenger) preaching to the faithful represented as a flock of birds of different species.[38] Who was to instruct this credulous community, which seems to have been as hungry for 'celebrities' and dramatic headlines as any in the modern world? The pictures in church, on the walls or in the glass of the windows, also told a story. Worship itself was 'educational' so long as the worshippers understood what was happening. But the natural means of regular teaching was preaching. The early Church expected the bishop to be the principal preacher, and long sequences of sermons which are partly lectures on books of the Bible survive – those of Augustine and Gregory the Great being the outstanding examples. The genre did not survive the end of the ancient world and it was a good many centuries before confidence grew sufficiently to encourage the preaching of new sermons of a comparable type and quality. Nevertheless this material proved invaluable to theologians as well as pastorally. This assumed an audience of some sophistication prepared to listen for perhaps two hours.

Meanwhile local people looked to their local priests for an understanding of their faith and for guidance about the way they should live. There are indications that that need was still being provided for, but in new ways. The Icelandic *Jón's Saga* describes how a local bishop supported popular preaching when it could be seen that the preacher was 'taking his teachings from sacred books and not from his own intuition alone', and an Icelandic homily book survives, written about 1200.[39]

But many priests were of limited education and there were serious questions about their competence in communicating the faith to parishioners. Then as now the local priest was likely to be faced with questions. How can God be one if he is three? The need for a source of information when theological questions presented themselves seems to have been felt even among the better educated. Some of the correspondents of Peter of Blois[40] were quite senior clergy who wanted a theological problem solved and looked to him as a convenient expert. Several lengthy letters survive in which he discusses a series of 'theological questions or rather complaints', in response to the questions of a correspondent who cannot now be identified, a further set of questions sent him by the Abbot of Coggeshall about the Last Judgement and the life to come, and the Abbot of Dorchester about will and action. One of the justifications for the setting up of universities from the twelfth century was that they might serve as schools for those who were to become priests.

Perhaps the main questions for ordinary lay people were likely to concern their own behaviour and that of their families and friends and their chances of reward in the life to come. The priest might be asked not an abstract theological question, but a wistful, 'Is my grandfather in heaven?' The emergence of penitential 'manuals' from the twelfth century was intended to assist priests dealing with people who came to confess their sins and needed guidance about right living as well as an appropriate penance. New manuals of practical preaching also began to appear at the end of the twelfth century, with the works of Peter the Chanter and Alan of Lille concentrating on vices (and how to avoid them) and virtues (and how to cultivate them).

Leo the Great's instruction had been straightforward: 'except for priests of the Lord, let no one dare to preach, whether he be monk or layman, no matter what reputation for learning he might boast'.[41] The problem was to ensure the availability of priests locally. The parish system took some time to emerge in some parts of Europe. In many places it was the local community of Benedictine monks who remained the nearest source of expert assistance to meet local pastoral needs, both intellectual and spiritual. The practice of preaching by monks seems to have been quite widespread – enough, certainly, to ensure that it caused some concern among the ecclesiastical authorities about their entitlement to do so. The pastoral role of monks was not clear and not all monks were priests, so that although in practice monks might be invaluable to their local villagers in providing medical care and general support and help, they remained outside the main structures the Church provided for the spiritual care of the people. Monasteries might be answerable only to the pope and beyond the control of the local bishop.

Rupert of Deutz (c.1075–1129), discussing whether monks are allowed to preach (utrum monachis liceat praedicare), agrees. 'Who is not ordained into the clergy or priesthood, is not sent to preach.' 'It is also written, "How shall they preach, unless they are sent?" To be sent is to be ordained.'[42] Gratian argues that the ministry of preaching is conferred in ordination along with authority to baptize, bless, celebrate the Eucharist, hear confession and give absolution.

Alan of Lille sets out at some length in the second book of 'Against the Heretics' his arguments that the Waldensians are not entitled to preach because they have not been entrusted with the preaching office through the proper channels. He reminds his readers how in the Old Testament Korah with his companions perished by fire because he had taken another's office (Numbers 16.35). It is also read in the fourth book of Kings that because King Azariah usurped the sacrificial office, he was struck by leprosy' (IV Kings 15.5).[43] Yet Walter of St Victor speaks of the 'office of preaching' (officium praedicandi) as something given to John the Baptist, along with the (officium baptizandi),[44] which somewhat undermines the requirement of ordination, for John the Baptist was not ordained and, as we have seen, it was accepted that baptism could be administered by those who were not ordained.

One pretext on which monks who were not ordained were sometimes allowed to preach was that a local bishop was not doing his job well. In 1077 Gregory VII (1073–1085) gave the monastery of Watten in the diocese of Thérouanne 'the power of binding and loosing and of preaching the Word of God everywhere', and so it had both a sacramental and a pastoral role, in the interests of reform and due to the failings of the local bishop. A pope could also intervene by giving special permission to monks to preach if he thought it would forward reform. Gregory VII also gave the monks of Vallombrosa a preaching ministry independent of their bishop in this way. (His campaign against clerical marriage and simony needed enforcing locally.)

The same shortage of territorially based pastors who were also, practically speaking, competent to preach, encouraged popes at the end of the eleventh century and the beginning of the twelfth to give permission to some who were not ordained to be wandering preachers, pressing for these and other reforms wherever they went. Robert of Arbrissel obtained such a permission from Urban II in 1096, Bernard of Thiron got a similar one from Paschal II (1099–1118) and Henry of Lausanne was allowed the same liberty by a bishop, Hildebert of Le Mans, in 1101.

Cistercian preaching against the heretics in the south of France was to become a major effort in the later twelfth century. Bernard of Clairvaux wrote to the citizens of Toulouse (Letter 242), in the consciousness that they are much beset by heretics,[45] urging them not to listen to any 'non-local or unknown preacher' (nullum extraneum vel ignotum praedicatorem recipiatis), unless he should be sent by the supreme pontiff or have permission to preach from the local bishop, for 'How shall they preach unless they are sent?' (Romans 10.15). Not all Cistercians preach because not all are 'sent', notes Alan of Lille. (He, like a number of others of his generation, ended his academic life by retiring to be a Cistercian monk.) Alan suggests in his Contra haereticos that such preaching may be allowed if a monastic superior sends the monk to preach, for, as it was frequently said, 'how shall they preach unless they be sent' (Quomodo vero praedicabunt nisi mittantur)? The Fourth Lateran Council of 1215 insists on a 'sending' which alone ensures that the preacher is not usurping the legitimate ministry of preaching. Anyone who 'sells' his preaching on any other terms will be excommunicated.[46]

The self-assertion of the laity became important to the development and revision of the place of the Church in society,[47] and nowhere so visibly as in the emergence of lay preaching. To allow lay preaching would go further still, for that would be the work of preachers who were not even monks. Yet that was exactly what Jesus seemed to be recommending when he sent his unlettered disciples out to preach the Gospel (Matthew 18.5–23). Bede, writing on the Acts of the Apostles, could still see an argument for preaching by the laity, even though by his time the permitted roles of the ordained ministry were fairly clearly defined. Bede discusses the bishop's need for preachers to help him, for a diocese is much too big for a bishop to do all the work himself. His approved preachers are to preach the Word in different parts of the diocese. Their preaching is to concern itself with the Catholic faith which is contained in the Apostles' Creed and in the Lord's Prayer, which is taught us by Scripture itself. Bede's chief anxiety in this letter seems to be to ensure that the preaching gets done, by anyone, lay, monk or priests, who has the necessary knowledge of Latin, and, if necessary, in translation if there is no one who can manage the original language.[48] He has a number of further recommendations. Preaching by the laity meant that no one would be able to say that the people who had received such teaching had been swayed by improper influences such as rhetorical persuasion, and not by the power of the Word of God itself.[49] Those who do not understand Latin can hear these matters expounded to them in their own language.[50] This may be helpful not only to lay people but also to clergy and monks whose Latin is not very good.[51] Bede has often explained the Apostles' Creed and the Lord's Prayer to simple priests in the English language.[52] Charlemagne's law was that the preacher had a duty to preach so that the people might understand: *ut iuxta quod bene vulgaris populus intelligere possit assidue fiat.*[53]

So the emerging principles became clear. Only monks and canons ordained as priests and who had pastoral care ought to be preaching, except abbots fulfilling their pastoral responsibility for their monks. The question whether preaching was a task reserved in this way became contentious only gradually, when it became apparent that individuals who were not even monks and could not lay claim to any recognized mode of being 'sent' were preaching to the faithful.

The Church became increasingly insistent that local bishops alone had authority to authorize (license) preachers in their own dioceses. There were several reasons for this clamp-down. The most important was uncertainty as to how far lay preachers, poorly educated, could understand what they were saying and avoid leading their listeners into heresy.[54] It was partly a matter of control. In 1228 decretals forbade lay preaching, directing themselves particularly at 'some lay people in Lombardy' who were 'presuming' to preach, with the explanation that there were many members in a body and did not all have the same function, and that preaching requires both education and permission.[55]

Augustine speaks of his sermons 'to the people' (*ad populum*) in the epilogue to *Retractationes* II. The expression did not catch on in the medieval period we are concerned with, when it was more common to call such sermons *vulgares* (common) or *rudes* (simple, plain). Jacques de Vitry's collections of the sermons he preached to ordinary people (*Sermones vulgares*) includes many tales of local life, such as buying meat from a butcher.[56] People would look for plain exhortation, guidance in living lives acceptable to God, illustrated with practical familiar examples, more avidly than they would crowd to listen to an exposition of an abstruse theological point. There seems to have been a distinction in the minds of the ecclesiastical authorities between 'exhortation' to good behaviour, which could be permitted to the laity, and proper preaching, which might involve matters of faith or doctrine, where the preacher was required, certainly expected, to be a priest and to have a licence from the bishop.[57]

Many boundary questions immediately arise. When did exhorting one's household become preaching to the village? When did urging good behaviour become theological? For exhortation to spiritual exercises and daily meditations such as might be offered to the professional religious[58] was also likely to be on too high and demanding a plane for the popular audience. The problem was that a relatively uneducated individual might be more successful in fitting what he said to people's interests, and if he had a touch of the excitement and glamour which could attach to the persons of the renegade monks who had walked away from conventional monastic life to begin ministries of their own, like the notorious Henry (see below), he might appear even more attractive. For popular audiences enjoyed excitement. When Stephen Langton was preaching *ad populum* at St Paul's in August 1213, someone in the congregation shouted out that he was a liar. The protester was thrown out of the cathedral.[59] A renegade might be able to offer even more to enliven a Sunday or a saint's day.

But there was also concern in official circles about the prostitution of the ministry of preaching in the mouths of dissidents and heretics who were alleged to preach for money. Bernard of Clairvaux wrote, after midsummer 1145, to Hildefonsus, *comes* of Toulouse, to express his anxiety about the behaviour of a heretic called Henry, whom he considered to be a follower of Peter of Bruys. This Henry was not unlettered, but when he began to be a wandering preacher, in what he claimed to be the manner of the Gospels, he preached so that he could eat; in other words, he preached for money. And when he had obtained payment from 'the simpler people or some of the matrons', he would spend it on gambling or in even more vicious ways.[60]

The wandering unlicensed preacher might be a solitary and interested in making money, but there was also the danger that if he was successful, a natural demagogue, a sect might form round him. One of the manifestations which caused the Church's authorities most concern was the formation of groups with missionary zeal, whose members were eager to go off preaching, for it would be impossible to ensure that they did not lead the faithful astray. Alan of Lille's *De fide catholica contra haereticos sui temporis*, probably of the 1190s, discusses this problem in connection with the Waldensians. He explains that some heretics believe themselves to be righteous but they are wolves in sheep's clothing. The Waldensians are led by their own 'spirit', not 'sent' in the proper manner and they presume to preach, *sine praelati auctoritate, sine divina inspiratione, sine scientia, sine litteratura.*[61] Alan would 'allow' those sent by a superior to preach. In his view Valdes has offended against this rule because he preached without such authority.

It might be legitimate to claim to be sent directly by God but that would require evidences of the authenticity of the sending in the form of miracles or other works, which are not in evidence in the case of the Waldensians.[62]

Waldensians seem to have had support, or at least an absence of condemnation, from senior clergy at first, for example from Guichard de Pontigny, Archbishop of Lyons from 1165 to 1180/81. Two closely matching accounts of the early Waldensians, Richard of Poitiers's *Vita Alexandri Papae III*, written between 1181 and 1216, and Stephen of Bourbon's *De Septem donis Spiritus Sancti*, written in the 1250s, state that it was the Archbishop of Lyons, Johannes Belles-Mains (a secular cleric), who forbade the Waldensians to preach, and they were expelled from Lyons sometime between 1181/82 and 1184.[63]

Even after the formal condemnation of 1184, some groups of Humiliati still seem to have received support from the senior local clergy. The Humiliati of Vilboldone, a mixed community of priests and those who were not ordained living together under a rule, received a papal bull of protection from Alexander III in about 1179, which was renewed by Urban III in 1186, and they seem to have enjoyed good relations with the higher Milanese clergy. In 1179 Pope Alexander III forbade the Humiliati to preach. They were condemned with the Waldensians in 1184 by Lucius III. But Innocent III (1198–1216) was initially willing to allow the Humiliati and groups of Waldensians (the Poor Catholics and Reconciled Poor) to preach, and he approved of the work of Francis and his followers.

There were, however, other activities in which dangers were perceived, particularly the formation of study groups in private houses, unsupervised by the Church. In July 1199 Pope Innocent III wrote to 'all the faithful of the city of Metz and its dioceses'. The Bishop of Metz had told him that he was concerned about the tendency for a 'multitude' of laymen and women to meet in secret. They were alleged to be preaching to one another, taking as their texts French translations they had had made of the Gospels, the Epistles of Paul, the Psalms, *Moralia in Job* and 'many other such books'. When their parish priest told them to stop they refused and said they had a perfect right to do this.[64] Innocent supported the bishop. It was commendable for his people to wish to understand the Bible; it was not commendable for them to defy their priest and exclude those who did not belong to their group. He made the important distinction that the laity may exhort one another but not preach to one another, for simple and illiterate people cannot fully understand the Scriptures. In 1201 Innocent approved a way of life for married Humiliati living in their own homes. He permitted them to meet on Sundays to hear one of their members expound the Bible to them, provided the local bishop approved and their preacher was of known knowledge and holiness of life and so long as he confined himself to exhortation and did not stray into theology.

The inclusion of women in such communities is worth noting. They seem characteristically to have been surprisingly willing to allow a place to women in their unofficial ministry. A story survives in a Middle High German manuscript of the fourteenth century which describes how Mechthild left home in about 1230 to go to Magdeburg to live as a Beguine. The Beguines were pious lay women mainly in the Low Countries and parts of France and Germany, some of whom lived alone but many of whom formed communities from about 1200. They were not formally under vows but nevertheless dedicated themselves to a life of prayer and the practical assistance of the poor and needy and to simple manual work.

Some of them may have been able to read and write. Lambert de Begue (whose name lent them their label) was a local priest in the diocese of Liège. He was charged with heresy in 1175 and wrote an *apologia* in which he defended himself. He had translated the life and passion of St Agnes for the Beguines and also translated the Acts of the Apostles into verse, adding exhortations. As a consequence he had been accused of opening the Scriptures to the unworthy.[65] God visited Mechthild in visions, she claimed. These she described 20 years later, in an account her confessor had encouraged her to write. She chose the vernacular for this record.[66]

This question of 'papal permission' lingered in the air. Jacques de Vitry comments on the Patarenes (another name for the Humiliati) as flourishing in Milan, a hotbed of heresy (*que fovea est hereticorum*). Hardly anyone there resisted the heretics, he reports, except some holy men and religious women called the Patarenes who had authority to preach from the pope.

> Through the more worthy and instructed in the law of the Lord and in the sentences of the holy Fathers we have judged that the Word of the Lord is to be propounded (*proponendum*) in our school (*schola*) to our brothers and friends, with the licence of and due veneration for prelates, through brothers suitable and instructed in the sacred page, who should be powerful in sound doctrine, to reprove sinful folk and draw them to the faith by every means and recall them into the bosom of the holy Roman Church. We are resolved that we will inviolably preserve unbroken virginity and chastity. ... If indeed any laymen (*qui saecularium*) want to accept our guidance, we shall take care that apart from those qualified to exhort and dispute against the heretics, the rest will remain in the houses religiously and living in due order.[67]

The Cistercian Order had made a distinction from an early stage between choir monks and lay brothers, providing an avenue by which those who were born into the lower strata of society and could not aspire to mix as equals with the well-born recruits to the monastic life could live in the community and serve it with humble manual work. The sense of vocation some lay people felt began to encourage new experiments which would allow people of a wide range of social classes to live a specially dedicated religious life while remaining lay people. The Templars and Hospitallers, foundations of the twelfth century, had been early examples of this kind of thing, in which knights could live somewhat like monks and defend the Holy Land or tend the sick.

The thirteenth century saw a new manifestation of lay piety. The novel idea of the thirteenth century was the establishment of fraternities. Groups of lay people from a particular place or involved in a particular trade or activity, natural brotherhoods or sisterhoods, united with a shared purpose of living the Christian life better and sometimes of helping the poor, underprivileged and outcasts of society. In some parts of Europe, especially in Italy, where orders of penitents were popular, they processed as penitents and beat themselves in public displays of flagellation to show the world the sincerity of their repentance and the seriousness of their purpose in the amendment of their lives.

Some of the Beguines came to the special notice of leading figures who were impressed by their desire to suffer and live in voluntary extreme deprivation for Christ. Jacques de Vitry wrote the life of Marie d'Oignies, who died in 1213 and who interceded with the pope to obtain at least an oral approval of this way of life, although it never achieved formal recognition.

As a rule, all such groups of the 'do-it-yourself' pious lay religious ran their own affairs and this commonly caused anxiety to the local and wider clerical hierarchy because it was perceived to be only too easy for them to go astray theologically and to mislead the faithful in various ways, especially in attracting new members and prompting further independent experiments.

Even in the early Church there were stirrings of rivalry among the followers of Jesus. Indeed his disciples had recorded moments of jealousy, for instance about who was to sit next to him in the Kingdom of Heaven (Matthew 20.21). The model on which the Church was to be formed was, inevitably, dependent in part on the assumptions of the age and the political and institutional patterns familiar to people in their ordinary lives. The medieval developments in this area of ecclesiology were particularly significant and took their colour and form from the age in just the same way. It was never easy for contemporaries to realize that their contemporary norms were not perpetual, not laws of the universe.

CHAPTER 6

The Church Divided:
East and West

Many kinds of Christian

At the end of the old Roman Empire Christians themselves were divided. In North Africa the 'schismatic' Donatists were opposed to the Catholics, each claiming to be the one true Church but divided not in doctrine but on a point of order. The disputed point was whether episcopal succession could validly run from a 'traitor' (*traditor*) who had 'handed over' the Bible under the threat of state persecution. More widely in Europe, mainly as a result of the great Christological controversies of the fourth and fifth centuries, there was a division into 'Arians' and 'Catholics', where the dispute was on a matter of faith and therefore technically a heresy and not a schism. Legend had it that Constantine, the first Christian emperor, had been baptized by Pope Sylvester, which would have been convenient for those who later sought to establish the primacy of the Roman see. In reality, however, it was probably Eusebius of Nicomedia, who had become Patriarch of Constantinople, who baptized him. Eusebius was an Arian.[1] Perhaps ironically, it was the Nicene Council which Constantine called to deal with the Arian controversy, that defined the faith in terms which outlawed Arian Christology.

The Arians were so called after the followers of Arius (d.336), a priest in Alexandria who questioned the eternity of the Son of God and his equality with the Father, arguing that he was a creation of God the Father, who used him in his work of creation, but merely as an instrument. These were views which owed something to the Platonists, but they may also have been inspired in part by a wish to get a clearer understanding of what it meant to say that God became incarnate in the Son.[2] The theological questions involved are some of the most difficult in Christianity and it is not surprising that subtle differences of opinion gave rise to a proliferation of versions of Arianism. More surprising perhaps is the appeal Arius's teaching had to the mass of the Christian faithful in Alexandria, where he became such a threat that his bishops' condemnation at a local synod in 320 did not calm things down, and the threat Arianism posed to Christian orthodoxy made it necessary for the Emperor to summon an ecumenical Council at Nicaea in 325 to pronounce upon the matter.

It is hard to know how clearly the generality of the population understood what it meant to be Arian at any given stage in the controversy, for the theologians themselves struggled with definitions for more than a century. The reality was probably that a people 'went with' the labels adopted by or attached to its leaders. So the division of opinion between Catholics and Arians coincided with some of the tribal divisions. For example, from Christian captives who had lived among the Goths beyond the Danube for several generations sprang Ulfilas. His beliefs happened to be of an Arian cast, and when he was made a bishop in 341 and sent to exercise his ministry among the Goths, the Christianity he encouraged was naturally also Arian. The Bible was translated into the Gothic language and Arian Christian ideas spread to the Visigoths in the east, the Ostrogoths in the west, and the Burgundians and the Vandals, so that when these various tribes came down upon the Empire and destroyed it, they imposed their own version of Christianity, importing their own clergy and building their own churches.

This state of affairs in which a number of distinguishable versions of Christianity were disseminated across Europe with the baggage of conquest was itself transient, with the Catholics gradually getting the upper hand. The barbarians were culturally and linguistically assimilated. They learned Latin from their new servants among the conquered. The Catholic Franks conquered the Arian Burgundians, who abandoned Arian for Catholic Christianity in 517. In 589 the Visigoths became Catholics. On the Byzantine wing of the Empire, the Vandals of North Africa were conquered in 534 and the Italian Ostrogoths in 554. Gregory the Great was preaching on Ezekiel in 593 when the Lombards were pressing upon Rome. He opens his revised text of the sermons with the explanation that it has taken him eight years to prepare them for publication because 'many pressing concerns have got in the way' (*multis curis irruentibus*).[3]

One category of dissidents from the emerging Catholic position on Christology remained unreconciled. The Council of Chalcedon (451) decided that only those who accepted that the incarnate Christ was one Person in two Natures, divine and human, were true Christians. This effectively outlawed the 'Non-Chalcedonian' churches, the Nestorians, Armenians and Copts and the Syriac Christians of the Middle East and Egypt, who would not accept this version.

These communities, geographically remote from their political concerns, faded a little from Western recollection for some centuries. Despite the fact that between 687 and 751 11 popes out of 13 came from the Eastern Empire or from Sicily and were Greek speakers, and that Pope Theodore I (642–49) was a Greek from Jerusalem, the evidence is that it was not widely understood in the West how important, politically speaking, the division was proving to be in the Eastern half of the old Empire. This left the Church in the Greek East with an uneasy sense that the Armenians and others who could not agree to the Chalcedonian doctrine were potential enemies. For it made the region vulnerable to the invasions of the Arabs and the Persians if it could not present a united front to fight them off.

Two poles of empire

The Roman Empire had had two 'poles', two centres of government, in Rome and in Constantinople (Byzantium) for some time before the Western end of the Empire began to lose control under the repeated assault of the barbarian invasions. The Byzantine half of the old Roman Empire was under considerable political and geographical stress during the seventh century. It lost provinces to the east and south – Syria, Palestine, Egypt and the northern coast of Africa – as Islamic Arabs took them over. The Slavs came down from Central Europe into the Balkans and the Byzantines lost control there too. Even the remaining area around the city of Constantinople and Asia Minor was under repeated threat, with regular annual invasions to be driven off.

The crying need for military cooperation encouraged attempts to splice the theological differences. The Monothelite ('one-will') movement was in part a device to tempt the Non-Chalcedonians more or less back into the fold by suggesting that even if they could not accept that there was only one Person in Christ perhaps they could accept that there was a single 'will' (or perhaps a single driving force). On the other hand, in order to get Western military cooperation, it might be politic for the Byzantine Church to reject any such solution. The Muslim conquests of the seventh century got as far as Alexandria and the situation began to look more desperate still. At the Sixth Council of Constantinople (680–81) the Emperor coaxed the bishops to reject 'one will' so that Byzantium could put itself in a position to get military aid.

The Easter controversy

Easter is a moveable feast which has to have its date calculated and agreed each year. In the early Church different communities sometimes arrived at different dates. On the face of it, a mere difference of dates ought to be no more than an inconvenience, but it was seen as representing something much more profound, a failure of common rhythm in the lives of the local churches. The idea of the whole Church celebrating the resurrection of Christ together on the same day had a strong resonance.

Opinion on this subject was itself divided. In about 190 Pope Victor decreed that those who refused to accept the Roman date for Easter were separating themselves from communion with the Roman see. Constantine, the first Christian emperor, had thought a difference over the date of Easter was Church-dividing and that view is reflected in the record of the Council of Nicaea (325).

It was still seen in that way in Bede's England. The Synod of Whitby, held in 664, was held to try to resolve this and other questions, and Bede says that it was opened by King Oswiu:

> declaring that it was fitting that those who served one God should observe one rule of life and not differ in the celebration of the heavenly sacraments, seeing that they all hoped for one kingdom in heaven; they ought therefore to enquire as to which was the truer tradition and then all follow it together.[4]

Being 'out of communion' in the sense of being unable to celebrate the Eucharist 'with' another community of Christians could come about for various reasons. The differences could be small but acquire a powerful significance. For example, there was a custom of keeping a fast on Saturday at Rome, but not elsewhere, which became a bone of contention.

Differences of calendar had pastoral and practical consequences too. Bede describes a royal marriage where the couple came from the two different communities of Christians in the British Isles, one converted by Irish missionaries and the other by the mission of Augustine of Canterbury, which had been sent from Rome by Gregory the Great in 597, so that one was still fasting for Lent while the other was celebrating the Easter feast. This made for marital as well as political disharmony:

> In these days it sometimes happened that Easter was celebrated twice in the same year, so that the King had finished the fast and was keeping Easter Sunday, while the Queen and her people were still in Lent and observing Palm Sunday.[5]

The next great controversy to divide East and West concerned icons. This will be explored in the chapter, 'Arts to the Glory of God'.

Photius and the Bulgarian question

In this uneasy balancing of political advantage and theological position, the Frankish rulers of Western Europe were eager for alliances, and they were not too fussy about where they found them. The Holy See would do as well as Byzantium, so long as there was political benefit. There were a number of exchanges in the Carolingian period and afterwards which indicate a mistrustful reluctance on the part of either side to take its eyes off the other. Charlemagne had after all set himself up as a rival emperor to the emperor of the East.

Photius, Patriarch of Constantinople from 858, seems to have known no Latin, although he was a learned and cultured man who wrote book reviews. He had been a highly placed layman until his election to the see and his rapid ordination and consecration, which were necessary to allow him to occupy high ecclesiastical office. (This practice was disapproved of in the West, though it was not unknown.) Photius's appointment was achieved only by deposing his predecessor, Ignatius, whose supporters were not willing to let the matter go. Photius was not an iconoclast and was not active in the controversy which had torn the community in the East in preceding generations. His own interests lay further eastwards. He had made his name as ambassador to the Arabs.

There were areas in dispute between East and West, partly because they lay geographically between. Photius encouraged missionary efforts to convert the Slavs and Bulgars to the Greek Church. He was nervous of the Russians who had made raids on the Empire in 860. But the Bulgarians had their own ideas. They began negotiations with Pope Nicholas I in the hope of getting the Greek missionaries expelled from their territories.

Nicholas was made aware that Ignatius and his supporters were still active and he let it be known that he favoured Ignatius's reinstatement. In the end relations broke down irretrievably between Pope Nicholas and Photius and the business of the missionaries in Bulgaria proved equally divisive within the West. Frankish missionaries were told to leave too, so as to give full scope to the Roman missions to Bulgaria. Photius informed the German Emperor that he had leave from him as Patriarch of Constantinople to call himself King of the Romans.

The *Filioque*

The desire for unity of order and life expressed in the search for a commonly agreed date for Easter was important, but most important of all in the Greek-speaking part of the Church was the preservation of unity of faith. Theologically speaking, of the key issues which were to be crystallized as Church-dividing in the schism of 1054, and which were already rumbling some centuries earlier, the most important was the *Filioque* ('and the Son'), the clause which had been added to the Nicene Creed.

The date and provenance of the Nicene Creed was easily established. It was the declaration of the faith made by the Council of Nicaea in 325 in an effort to resolve the Christological disputes which were the subject of the

Arian controversy:

> I believe in one God the Father Almighty, Maker of heaven and earth, and
> of all things visible and invisible. And in one Lord Jesus Christ, the only-
> begotten Son of God, Begotten of his Father before all worlds, God of God,
> Light of Light, Very God of very God, Begotten not made, being of one
> substance with the Father, by whom all things were made; who for us men
> and for our salvation came down from heaven; and was incarnate by the Holy
> Ghost of the Virgin Mary, and was made man; and was crucified also for us
> under Pontius Pilate. He suffered and was buried, and the third day he rose
> again according to the Scriptures, and ascended into heaven, and sits on the
> right hand of the Father. And he shall come again with glory to judge both
> the quick and the dead: whose kingdom shall have no end. And I believe in
> the Holy Ghost, the Lord and giver of life, who proceeds from the Father,
> who with the Father and the Son together is worshipped and glorified, who
> spoke by the prophets. And I believe in one catholic and apostolic Church.
> I acknowledge one baptism for the remissions of sins. And I look for the
> resurrection of the dead and the life of the world to come.

The Apostles' Creed was another matter. It emerged from ancient liturgical usage and the legend grew up that it was the work of the Apostles.
The word *symbolum* for 'creed' was taken literally in its Greek meaning,
as though the Apostles had actually sat together round a table and put it
together by contributing a clause each:

> I believe in one God, the Father Almighty, Maker of heaven and earth,
> and in one Lord Jesus Christ, his only-begotten Son, who was conceived
> by the Holy Ghost, born of the Virgin Mary, suffered under Pontius Pilate,
> was crucified, dead and buried. He descended into Hell. The third day he
> rose again from the dead. He ascended into heaven, and sitteth on the right
> hand of God the Father. From thence he shall come again to judge the quick
> and the dead. I believe in the Holy Ghost, the Holy Catholic Church, the
> Communion of saints, the remission of sins, the resurrection of the body and
> the life everlasting.

In Carolingian times in the West it became customary to add the
phrase 'and the Son' to the text of the Nicene Creed at the point where it
asserts that the Holy Spirit proceeds from the Father, so that it reads 'who
proceeds from the Father and the Son'. Probably this addition was intended
merely for clarification. Certainly there was no idea of altering the underlying theology of the Trinity. But to the Greeks, who had not done the
same thing themselves, it appeared unacceptable both as an innovation or
addition to the tradition (which they believed would be a serious wrong in
itself even if the substance of the decision had been 'right'), and because it
seemed to them that this would radically alter the doctrine of the Trinity,

creating 'two origins' or first principles. It was a fundamental insistence of the Greek Church that the faith had been deposited complete and correct and that nothing could legitimately be decided after the period of the early ecumenical Councils (ending with the Council of Chalcedon), which could alter that 'deposit' in any way. This attitude of resistance to 'development' may have derived partly from the autocephalous structure of the Church in the Greek world. The Patriarchates of Jerusalem, Antioch, Alexandria and Constantinople had a degree of independence, but that worked only if they met in council and affirmed the 'one faith' absolutely consistently.

The second problem was the concern that the unity of God was somehow diminished if the Western addition was accepted. The Holy Spirit would then be seen as coming from two first principles and not one. This was a Neoplatonic worry, gaining its force from the philosophical purity of the idea that God is One. Photius made a case against the Latins from the Greek point of view. His *Mystagogia*[6] contends that the Western addition of the *Filioque* clause is mere Sabellianism, the heresy that God is Three only in human thinking and not in his actual self. It seems to have been Photius who first articulated the objection that to say that the Holy Spirit proceeds from the Son as well as from the Father is to introduce two first principles into the universe.

Up to a point, the Western apologists understood how the Greeks felt about this, though not necessarily in exactly the same terms. Alcuin identified the 'two principles' problem in a commentary on John's Gospel.[7] Heiric of Auxerre (841–876/7) also comments on the two principles, insisting that 'Just as the Father is the beginning so is the Son the beginning, but there are not two beginnings, Father and Son, but one.'[8] The debate on this crucial point continued into the later Middle Ages and beyond, culminating in the near miss of the resolutions arrived at at the Council of Florence (1438–45) and the lifting of the mutual anathemas in the twentieth century.

The Franks had a monastery on the Mount of Olives which provided accommodation for pilgrims to the Holy Land travelling from the West. Local Greek monks regarded the Frankish community with some suspicion and one, from St Sabas, accused the Franks of holding heretical views on the Trinity. The affair reached the desk of Thomas, the Patriarch of Jerusalem, and he communicated some concerns to Pope Leo III, who referred it to Charlemagne: 'It is essential for us to communicate to your imperial power everything which occurs in our parts. This year the monks on the Mount of Olives sent us a letter about a dispute concerning a matter of faith.' This letter he encloses for the Emperor to read. He also sent to the Eastern Churches 'Pope Leo's Creed of the Orthodox Faith', 'so that you and all the world may hold the correct faith according to the Holy and

Apostolic Roman Church'. The creed includes the phrase: 'the Holy Spirit, fully God, proceeding from the Father and the Son'.[9] The monks called on the Pope to support them. They asked to be provided with reference material in the form of quotations from the Greek and Latin Fathers which would endorse their position. Leo gave this task of compilation to Alcuin (c.740–804), Charlemagne's reliable educational adviser.

The Carolingian Church began to be firm on the *Filioque*. *Quicunque Vult*, the 'Athanasian' Creed, says that the *Filioque* is necessary to salvation. Theodulf produced a treatise, which was given formal approval by a Council held at Asachen in 809. Rabanus Maurus (c.776–856) composed a hymn (*Veni Creator Spiritus*) whose last stanza includes the lines:

> Teach us to know the Father, Son
> And thee of both to be but one

Nevertheless Pope Leo III seems to have been determined at least at the beginning of the ninth century not to allow the *Filioque* to divide East and West.

Schism

The great schism of the medieval period took place in 1054 between 'Greeks' and 'Latins' at the end of a long period during which tension had been building up. The schism of 1054 was in large part political, and its theological dimensions were spelt out more fully after the event, but that does not mean that the theological disagreements were trumped up. They had been rumbling for some generations.

The bitterness was extreme and in part justified by the events, and that entitles us to ask now whether the medieval Church in East and West after 1054 regarded one another as henceforth of different 'faiths'. Guibert of Nogent, writing about the First Crusade,[10] remarks on the 'perpetual changeability' of the 'faith of the Easterners', who, he says, wander constantly from the rule of true belief. Giraldus Cambrensis explains the bad feeling that exists between Greeks and Latins. The Greeks have removed themselves from the jurisdiction of Rome and that continues 'to our own day'. The Greeks, for their part, maintain that it is the Romans who have separated themselves from the Greeks, for that is the spirit in which they reply to overtures from the Vatican inviting them to return to unity (*et ecclesiae unitatem invitare volentibus*).[11] The Greeks came to hate the Latins so much that they disinfected altars on which Latin priests had celebrated the Eucharist and rebaptized those baptized by Latins. Offenders are to be excommunicated and deprived of their livings, instructed the Fourth Lateran Council. It offered a welcome to those who wished to return to communion with the

Latins: 'We wish to respect (*reverentes*) the Greeks who are returning to obedience to the Apostolic See.' They could be allowed to continue in their own rites (*mores ac ritus eorum ... sustinendo*) as far as possible, but they must not be deferred to in matters which might endanger souls.[12]

The events which led up to the schism were not edifying. By the eleventh century, the Normans, who had originally settled in northern France, now Normandy, as Viking invaders from Scandinavia ('Northmen'), were becoming greedy for further expansion. They invaded southern Italy and Sicily. In those lands there was already a struggle for dominance between Greek- and Latin-speaking Christians, for these were the areas where the old language division between the two halves of the ancient Empire cut through. The differences were not merely linguistic. Christians were allowed differences of rite, and the communities became deeply attached to the practices of their own familiar liturgies. And liturgy carries a theology within it. Worshippers who may not have much formal knowledge of theology understand their faith partly in terms of the pattern of worship they know best.

The battle of the mid-eleventh century over the use of leavened bread in the Eucharist resembled the Easter Controversy in that what may seem a minor matter in other ages can become a Church-dividing issue at a particular time. It was also not obvious in either case whether the difference of practice was a matter of rite or of theology, for variations of rite were not supposed be Church-dividing. From the point of view of the East this was also a complicating factor in their attempts to achieve reunion with the Armenians, where the Church-dividing issues were the Chalcedonian definition and this same question of leaven.

The difference in the kind of bread which was to be consecrated in the Eucharist became a matter of strong contention. Increasingly dramatic and polarized positions were struck. The Greeks used leavened bread, claiming that bread without leaven was not bread, and that it was essential to the true Eucharist that bread be consecrated. The Latins had moved, probably after the fourth century, to the use of unleavened bread. Rabanus Maurus had argued in the ninth century that the bread used in the Eucharist should be unleavened (*infermentatum*). He cited Leviticus 2.4 and pointed out that Christ himself must certainly have used unleavened bread at the Last Supper because it was Passover time and no one was allowed to have yeast in the house. The question is why it was controversial enough for Rabanus even to mention it. A correspondence began in 1053 in an attempt to get bishops of the Greek rite to take an uncompromising position. Churches in Constantinople using the Latin rite were closed to ensure that no celebration using unleavened bread went on in the city.

The Normans, apparently without recognizing the potential political important of these sensitivities, sought to take control of ecclesiastical
affairs and to impose the Latin rite. When the news reached Constantinople that Greek services were no longer to be held in the lands the Normans
had conquered, it caused considerable anger.

The two halves of the old Empire had been trying to make arrangements at the highest diplomatic level to ensure that the Normans were kept
in check, for that was in the interests of both communities. There was a
reluctance on both sides to admit that there might be an undercurrent of
commercial speculation in the overtures either made, for there were important trading considerations between the two communities. An alliance of
the two imperial powers seemed desirable, but it involved delicate diplomacy which was thrown into confusion by this new ecclesiastical dispute.

Cardinal Humbert unwisely tried to take a hard line when he wrote on
behalf of Pope Leo IX. He knew the scene in Sicily well, having been archbishop there. He made threatening noises and tried to brush away the theological considerations which were presenting themselves. The burden of his
letter was that the Bishop of Rome, as successor to St Peter, was universal
primate, and Constantinople should not get above itself by resisting the will
of Rome. He relied on the Donation of Constantine as authority.

The Donation of Constantine, whose authenticity was scarcely questioned until the late Middle Ages, purported to be a gift from the Emperor
Constantine to the Pope and all his successors, until the end of the world,
of an authority greater than that of the Patriarchs of the East. It appeared
to leave to the Pope authority to determine all that affected the Christian
faith and Christian worship. The Pope was to have his Lateran Palace in
Rome, the Emperor his imperial palace in Constantinople. They were not
to interfere with one another's jurisdiction. The Donation did not form part
of the earliest debates about papal primacy; no Pope relied on it as authority for a claim of papal primacy over the East during the eighth or ninth
centuries. It was only with the division of 1054 that it came to prominence
in this regard.

The question where universal primacy lay was not in itself new. There
had been five great patriarchates since ancient times, Rome in the West
and four in the East (Jerusalem, Antioch, Alexandria and Constantinople), with the last seizing the hegemony in the East with the conversion of
Constantine and the establishment of the city as the capital of the Eastern
Empire in the early fourth century. In the time of Gregory the Great there
had been the stirring of active hostilities. He had spent time in Constantinople himself and there was not much love lost between him and the
Greeks. He did not like the Greeks' use of the title 'ecumenical patriarch'.

He called it a novel form of pride which was disturbing the bowels of the whole Church. He said that if one primate is called 'universal' the honour of the title is diminished for others. Nevertheless, if there was to be a single supreme primatial office, Gregory believed it should lie with the Bishop of Rome.

The entangling of the question about the use of leaven with the question about the leadership of the Church heightened political controversy. Once a serious dispute was in the air, the subject of yeast became a problem inseparable from the question of who had primatial authority. It was argued by the Latins that submission to Rome was essential for the preservation of unity. Rome had made its rulings and could not have been in error all these years. The apologists of the East counter-attacked, pointing disapprovingly to other differences of rite and practice. Nicetas Stethatos, monk of Studios, mounted accusations about Rome's requirements for priestly celibacy, which the Greeks thought unnecessary, and criticized Rome's custom of fasting on Saturdays before the Sunday Eucharist.

Pope Leo IX sent a legation to Constantinople in the persons of Cardinal Humbert (who had some knowledge of Greek from his time in the very territories where ecclesiastical preeminence was now in dispute) and Peter, Archbishop of Amalfi, who was also conversant with the ways of Greek Christians in Sicily. As the legation was arriving in Constantinople, Leo IX died.

The already precarious remaining mutual trust rapidly broke down, with additional heat deriving from divisions at the highest level among the Greeks. The personal dislike for one another of Patriarch and Eastern Emperor was strong enough to get in the way. The letter Humbert and his team were bringing from the Pope had gone first to the Emperor, Constantine IX Monomachos, who had not had the courtesy to inform the Patriarch that the legation was on its way. When it was put before him, Michael Cerularius, the Patriarch, suggested that the Pope's letter had been opened and tampered with, for that could be the only explanation for its abusive tone. Humbert, in possession of a copy of the writings of Nicetas Stethatos, had matter for an angry rejoinder.

It was the Western legation which precipitated the schism. On 16 July 1054 the Roman legates went to Santa Sophia and laid upon the altar there a papal bull of excommunication of the Patriarch of Constantinople and all under his authority. The Patriarch refrained from a reciprocal excommunication, though anathemas flew. Both sides set about publishing lists of the other's errors.

The problem was that once the East and the West fell out of touch with the collapse of the Roman Empire and the loss of the habit of educating

people to be bilingual in Greek and Latin, the Greeks – with some justification – had begun to think of the Latins as barbarians. The schism became
entrenched as the leaders of Church and state in East and West 'escalated'
the seriousness with which they claimed to take the justifications for their
division. The Emperor Alexios received a letter in 1089 in which Urban
II complained that his name was not being included in the diptychs in
Constantinople, which was as much as to say that Constantinople was deny-
ing that he was Bishop of Rome at all, and that Latins who had attended
a Latin Mass were being excluded from Greek Eucharists after they were
known to have done so. The Emperor asserted coolly that there was no
schism as far as the East was concerned. Nevertheless the Patriarch's Synod
invited the Pope to send in a document listing his beliefs, so that they could
ensure that he was truly orthodox before putting up his name.

Anselm of Canterbury was brought into the debate partly because of
his opportune presence at the Council of Bari in 1098. He was there as an
exile, seeking papal backing in his quarrel with the King of England. Bari,
indeed the whole area of southern Italy and Sicily, had become an interface
between the Greek and Latin worlds. The Pope, Urban II, invited Anselm
to explain to the Greek representatives who were present why the West was
right and they were wrong about the procession of the Holy Spirit. Anselm
asked for a few days to prepare and then gave an explanation, of which we
have a polished version published about four years later.[13]

This seems to have awakened his interest in other questions on which
the Greeks and the Latins were in dispute, and he was soon writing a series
of 'letters' on the sacraments, exploring the question of the use of leaven in
the bread which the priest consecrated as the Body of Christ in the celebration of the Eucharist. The Greeks used leavened bread, the Latins unleavened bread, because they argued that yeast symbolized sinfulness. Anselm's
conclusions on this were startling. Indeed there is a difference of practice
but it is not Church-dividing, he maintained. The opinion of the Greeks
does not go against the faith of the Church. Leavened and unleavened are
both bread. There is no disagreement on anything that matters. Anselm's
only real sensitivity is on the divisiveness of the difference of opinion. It
disturbs him to hear the Greeks accuse the Latins of 'judaizing'. It troubles
him that the Greeks do not 'accept' (*nec recipiunt*) and rely on the same
patristic authorities as the Latins.[14]

The problem was at least in part one of mutual incomprehension. When
Anselm of Havelberg went to talk to Greek Christians a generation later, in
an effort to mend the schism, he found that not merely a language barrier
stood in the way. Translators were found, but it turned out that the translation of the ideas was not so easy as the translation of the words which

conveyed them. 'When I was posted in the city and often took up various questions with the Greeks', it pleased the authorities, both ecclesiastical and lay, to arrange a colloquy; they all met on 10 April, with secretaries to take notes. A good few Latins were present, including three who were fluent in Greek: Burgundius of Pisa, James of Venice and Moses of Pergamum, all known for their activities as scholarly translators. A large, keenly interested crowd gathered. Anselm began with a speech in which he said that it was Christian to discuss differences peaceably rather than to dispute. Nichites, Archbishop of Nicomedia, agreed, and it was decided that an attempt should be made by both sides to clarify positions so that the differences, if any, might be properly understood. Most of the discussion was about the problem of the *duo principia*. There was a serious attempt to examine the Greek terminology.

There was a near-success in mending the schism at the Council of Florence in the early fourteenth century but it was not until the mid-twentieth century that the mutual anathemas were lifted. And the schism is still not mended.

CHAPTER 7

Bringing the Outsiders In

Interfaith relations

It was difficult if not impossible for the Church's apologists to think in terms of 'interfaith dialogue' in the Middle Ages, or of 'ecumenical dialogue' either. The sixteenth-century Erastian theory that whoever rules a state should determine its faith (*cuius regio eius religio*) was in part a pragmatic response to the political problems which were being caused by the divisions of the Reformation at the time. But it went back much further, into the period of the Roman Empire, when it was already the assumption that when territory was conquered, the conquered people could reasonably be expected to adopt the faith of their conquerors. The Middle Ages saw things differently because the Church was not geographically co-extensive with the numerous states which came into being and changed into other states after the end of the Roman Empire.

So a key question for the medieval Church was whether there is a duty to capture territory for one's faith, a duty to 'convert the unbeliever' to the truth, overturning a 'wrong' view whether held collectively or individually, and, if necessary, by the use of force.

An important exception to the rule that in medieval Christian Europe almost everyone was baptized as a baby, was the adult convert from another faith, who had seen the error of his beliefs. One of the principal tools of intellectual conversion was the fictional dialogue in which those who held different faiths debated their differences. Where such a dialogue is designed for Western Latin readers it is routinely also an *apologia* for the Christian faith, in which the argument is lost by the non-Christian in the debate. But it is of course only the exceptional individual who writes a book about his change of opinion.

The evidence for real changes of heart and mind in the masses is harder to assess. Enforced conversions and political conversions might be insincere conversions. Augustine of Hippo experienced something of the sort in his dealing with the Pelagians, who claimed there was no need for sacraments and being good was just a matter of trying hard, but who quietly came to him to have their babies baptized just in case. The Second Council of Nicaea (787) complains that some of those who claim to have converted from Judaism secretly continue to observe the Sabbath and maintain other practices of the Jews. Thus they deny Christ in private. If they are behaving like that they should not be received.[1] The Albigensian Cathars of the late twelfth century would go to church as well as attending meetings of their own sect. The motivation for hedging bets in this way could be a genuine uncertainty as to where the truth lay. But there could also be fearfulness about exposure as heretics.

Crusading

Augustine's idea of a just war was that it must in some sense be restorative. Christians ought not to start wars to capture others' property, though they could justly use force to retrieve their own if it had been taken from them, or to repel invaders.[2] This depended of course on a theory of property and a theory of the state which belong to the ancient world, but it was not difficult to adapt it for medieval use. This was a warlike society, whose upper classes, especially in feudal states, had a choice of only two professions, the Church or soldiery. It needed to make war respectable by setting its parameters. Guibert of Nogent, in his account of the First Crusade, *Gesta Dei per Francos* ('Deeds of God through the Franks'), suggests that a war to protect liberty or to defend the property of the state would fulfil the requirements. So would a war to repel invasion. The soldier who fights in such a war ought to have no doubt that it is the right thing to do. Indeed, not to fight when one's country needs one would be wrong. Everyone should be required to go to war, except those in 'protected occupations', that is, those occupations which are essential to the safety of the Church.[3]

A holy war is different. A holy war is God's war, and those who fought in such wars saw themselves as simply serving him. They were 'soldiers of Christ'. God is seen as actively behind such a war, prompting it, at least in the sense of permitting it, and determining its outcome. Guibert of Nogent goes so far as to say that God 'instituted' certain 'wars of our time' (*nostro tempore prelia*). He meant the Crusades.[4] 'It was a divine work to destroy the Turks,' cries a later chronicler.[5] Such a holy war is an evil turned to good, analogous with the *felix culpa*, the 'fortunate' sin of Adam, out of which God has made such good things come. The Church will approve.[6]

In a holy war the *patria* or homeland which is God's chosen dwelling-place becomes a holy place. This could be taken both literally and spiritually. Crusaders saw themselves as defending the actual lands where Jesus lived and died and also as going to the 'spiritual Jerusalem'. The *croisade* took the cross (*croix*) as its banner and it went to the place where Jesus's Cross was really set up for him to die on. This metaphorical or figurative dimension became important as the term 'crusade' was extended to embrace 'holy' war against heretics such as the Albigensians as well as against the Muslim invaders of the Holy Land. There was a good deal of metaphor in the writing on the Crusades. The earthly Jerusalem became fused in people's minds with the heavenly Jerusalem. William of Malmesbury wrote such a long digression on crusading in his 'Deeds of the Kings of the English' (*Gesta regum Anglorum*) that it almost amounts to a treatise in its own right. He saw the crusade as a 'pilgrimage' and the account as one which needed the weight of the authority of ancient authors if it was to be truly edifying. He passed in his own mind from ordinary history to sacred history in writing on this sacred theme.[7]

The background to the First Crusade

Jerusalem had been conquered by the Arabs in 636. They allowed Christian pilgrims to visit the holy places for a fee. Damascus and later Baghdad were their capitals in the Abbasid period (seventh to eighth centuries). Liutprand describes wars with the Saracens in the *Antapodosis*, an account written while he was himself a mere deacon of Pavia. This tense (but working) balance was disrupted towards the end of the eleventh century by the arrival of the Turks from central Asia, who overran the lands of the Sunni caliphate and in 1076 captured Jerusalem. These 'Seljuks', as the West called them, set up a sultan in Baghdad who exercised military control, but they allowed the caliphate to continue as supreme religious authority, many Turks converting to Islam themselves, with intermarriage between the populations. Access to Jerusalem became more difficult for would-be Christian pilgrims, for the Turkish conquerors lacked the polish and sophistication of the Arabs.

Some First Crusade literature was quite literary in its aspirations. Gilo of Paris wrote an account about 1119, though he had not been on crusade himself, featuring scraps of Ovid, brought in to help make the claim that Jerusalem had been dominated by pagans, that the pagans had polluted the holy places with their idols (a striking misstatement of Muslim views on idolatry) and that the Arabs were bearing arms against heaven and had to be stopped.[8]

Yet this supernatural dimension and high-mindedness sat uncomfortably with the political and social realities. Crusading tended to be seasoned with self-interest. From the Western point of view the driving force, especially of the First Crusade, involved much more than a 'pure' desire to recapture the holy places of Christendom from Muslim invaders. Some of the leaders of the First Crusade wanted land for themselves in the reconquered territories. There were also trading interests, which became much more obvious when the Venetians funded the Fourth Crusade on condition that the Crusaders would first capture Constantinople for them. This was expressly and tellingly denied by Guibert of Nogent in his *Gesta Dei per Francos*. He celebrates the novel and incomparable victory of the expedition to Jerusalem, which was undertaken 'not for vainglory, nor for money, nor for enlargement of territory'.[9] He protests too much.

From the Eastern point of view, both Greek Christian and Muslim, the Crusades appeared an intrusion, even an invasion of their sovereign territories, involving a bid for 'regime change' they had not asked for. A comparison with the resentment in the modern Middle East about what is perceived as interference on the part of the USA may not be inappropriate. Mutual suspicion and rancour poisoned the mutual perceptions of all the parties. The 'Deeds of the Franks' (*Gesta Francorum*) says that the Emperor was willing to receive Bohemond only at a secret meeting, and that he lodged him outside the city of Constantinople. The Emperor was very angry and was plotting, the chronicler says, how he could cheat these Christian soldiers.[10] These 'allies' were as full of ill feeling as the enemies the Crusade was directed against, and it would be difficult to say who hated whom most.

The Muslims themselves were demonized in the propaganda literature. The *Gesta Francorum* describes the Turks as howling like demons in their unknown language (*stridentes et clamantes demoniaca voce*).[11] It calls them 'a barbarous nation' and 'enemies of God' (*inimici dei*).[12] There was strutting and posturing. Colourful accusations were apparently made against Muslims by Urban II preaching the First Crusade, that they practised magic, were given to sexual excesses, to defecation on Christian altars, to brutal cruelty to captives. Some of these are testified to in manuscript pictures.[13] The Eastern Church's leaders, although they had an understandable wish to recapture Asia Minor and Syria from the Muslims, had learned to respect them as civilized adversaries. The *Gesta Francorum* contains a description of an encounter between the Turks and the Arabs in which the Turks tell the Arabs how fearful the Franks are and they run away.[14]

Under the mutual dislike throbbed the politics. Urban II was anxious to foster a crusading movement in which the Eastern Empire could collaborate, partly, no doubt, to strengthen support for his candidature, since he was in dispute with the antipope, Clement III, as to who should be accepted as pope. For his part, the Emperor Alexius I (1081–1118) saw the Eastern Empire as an opportunity not only to get Islamic territorial ambitions curbed, but also to assert himself against the West. He attempted to get all the leaders of the Crusade who were arriving from the West to swear an oath of fealty or to be his mercenaries. With some he succeeded.[15]

Anna Comnena (d.1153), daughter of the Emperor Alexius and born to him in 1083 when he was already reigning, wrote an account of her father's reign in which the flavour of Byzantine Greece may be observed – its decadence and cruelty, an over-ripeness already in evidence in the last days of imperial Rome, but brought to new heights in Byzantium. Anna herself had attempted to procure the assassination of a brother of whom she was jealous. Rather than fearing the Westerners who came East on crusade, she despised them. In Book X she describes how the crusading armies appeared to the Byzantines as they approached. Her father, she says, dreaded their arrival, knowing what he did of their 'uncontrollable passion', their 'erratic character' and their 'greed for money, which always led them, it seemed, to break their own agreements without scruple for any chance reason'.

Complex motivations stirred among the Muslims too. Shi'ites could see advantages for themselves in the First Crusade, which threatened Sunni control of the region. Emboldened, they moved against Jerusalem themselves, and captured it in 1098. So the entrance of the Crusaders on the scene had the effect of further complicating the already tense and intricate relationships within the Middle East.

Urban II called for the Crusade, and thus gave it the Western Church's ultimate stamp of respectability. He took the unprecedented step of promising a 'plenary' indulgence to all those who undertook the Crusade and either reached Jerusalem or died in the attempt. We have seen how the theology of ministry located the power of the Keys, the authority to let people into heaven or keep them out, in the ordained ministry, and, *a fortiori*, in the papacy. A plenary indulgence was well worth obtaining, for it freed the Crusader at a stroke from all the penances he owed. It was believed that it would give him immediate entry to heaven. 'I advise that we all let ourselves be killed for then we shall go to heaven,' suggested Joinville (1224–1317).

Taking the cross could be an exciting experience in a crowd of fellow enthusiasts egged on by rousing speeches, as happened at Clermont when Urban II made his promise of heaven (and probably confused many into thinking that when they reached the earthly Jerusalem it would turn out that they had actually travelled to the heavenly one) and when Bernard of Clairvaux preached the Second Crusade. How far the excitement of the crowd endured through the months of marching to the East and the grim realities of battles of a kind Western soldiers were not used to is another question. For the pitched battles, foot-soldiery, heavy horses and two-handed swords of the West faced nippy Arab horses and curved one-handed scimitars, a quite different set of battle rules and an unfamiliar etiquette. It was like setting out to play football and finding that the other side was playing polo.

Some had reservations. Young monks were sometimes fired with excitement and asked to be released from their vows so that they could join the crusading armies. Anselm of Canterbury wrote to Lanzo, a novice at Bec, to encourage him in his novitiate. 'You have entered and are professed as Christ's soldier,' he reminds him. It is important for him to persevere where he is, for if a newly planted tree is dug up and moved it does not put down roots properly and then it does not bear fruit well.[16] Anselm saw in crusading the temptations of worldly ambition. It is wicked to be insatiable for false honours and avid for false riches, he writes. The monk should follow Christ at home in the monastery where he is professed.[17] In effect he is saying that the journey to heaven may be undertaken anywhere and that it is for the individual to look to his own soul. Guibert of Nogent, who knew Anselm and was consciously influenced by him, says much the same. The monk who does not go to war 'gives himself' in one way in his monastic profession; the soldier who does go to war 'gives' himself in another way. He also 'gives up' at least temporarily his castles and lands.[18]

The First Crusade

The 'Deeds of the Franks' (*Gesta Francorum*) is an anonymous account of the First Crusade, written by someone who was present and a witness of at least some of the events he describes, and who appears to have belonged to the Norman contingent, led by Bohemond, from southern Italy and Sicily. His descriptions show no detailed personal knowledge of the dangerous journeys of those who came from northern Europe, such as he would have had if he had been in one of those groups. He was himself a fighter, he says, which raises the interesting question of the literacy of someone who, we must take it on this evidence, was not himself a cleric. He may have had to dictate his tale to a clerk, but it is possible he was capable of writing it down for himself. There were a few *milites literati* who had been intended for a clerical career by their families and had the beginnings of an education until family fortunes changed and they had found themselves in the military life instead.[19]

The *Gesta Francorum* links the call to crusade with Jesus's words, 'If anyone will come after me, let him deny himself, and take up his cross and follow me' (Matthew 16.24).[20] Tudebod does the same, describing the active recruitment for the Crusade by the Holy See as an opportunity to preach a way of salvation, for to join the Crusade and fight on to the end was to be sure of saving one's soul.[21] Raymond of Agiles is sensitive to the idea that God could use the Crusade as an object lesson in more than one way. He could show his strong right arm in action and demonstrate his power through the victories of the Crusaders. And he could remind the Crusaders of their own unworthiness and need of his help.[22] It is alleged by the author of the *Gesta Francorum*, in evidence that God had indeed had a hand in the outcomes, that the Amir himself remarked on the way in which so small a force of Christians had been able to defeat the great armies of his own people.[23]

The later Crusades

Bernard of Clairvaux, at first reluctant, became a passionate preacher of the Second Crusade with the encouragement of the Abbot of Cluny, Peter the Venerable.[24] He wrote to the Abbot, 'I believe the groans of the wretched Church of the East have come to your ears, penetrating even to the depths of your heart.' But even when there was a sincere belief that the way was holy and those who fought it were doing God's will, the outcome might be unexpected. The second time the West went crusading, the venture did not succeed. Bernard of Clairvaux, required to explain how this could have happened if the Crusade was God's will, resorted to a device much like that used by Augustine when educated upper-class pagans arrived in North Africa in exile and complained that the Christians must be wrong about the omnipotence of their God. Otherwise, how could a Christian empire be collapsing before the barbarians in this way? The 'reasoning' was that it was more important to God that his people should learn the error of their ways and become truly faithful than that political security should endure. So he 'allows' failure as a lesson to his people.

The Third Crusade (1189–92) involved a good deal of posturing by the French and English kings and was the occasion of some live encounters with the Crusaders' Muslim opponents in which a little was learnt about the high degree of sophistication in matters of manners that Islam expected. Saladin, of Kurdish origin, was the ambitious son of the governor of Baalbek under the then caliph. He established himself as governor of Egypt and began to consolidate his position in Syria too until it became politically necessary for him to make a serious attempt to overthrow the Crusader kingdoms which had been set up after the First Crusade. There had been a good deal of sniping and guerrilla warfare and a series of attempts to seize key cities, and now Saladin needed to consolidate his position. In 1187 he attacked the kingdom of Jerusalem. The local crusading forces were unable to put up an effective resistance and he recaptured most of the lands they held. The threat was perceived in the West as sufficiently serious to require the mounting of a further Crusade. First the Emperor, Frederick Barbarossa, set off with a huge army, taking the cross at Mainz Cathedral in the spring of 1188. Richard I, the new King of England, followed in 1190 and Philip Augustus, King of France, also left for the Holy Land. Both had imposed a 'Saladin tithe' on their respective kingdoms to raise the money, and the matter was important enough to encourage them to pause (mistrustfully) in their war with one another to enable them to deal with the crisis in the Middle East. Richard the 'Lionheart' and Saladin, once face to face, were able to treat one another with a courtesy which respected the formal etiquette of warfare as both communities of faith understood them. The Eastern Emperor was, in his way, arguably more perfidious that the formal enemy of the Crusaders, Saladin himself, for, Christian monarch though he was, he had agreed a deal with Saladin to make it difficult for the Crusaders to reach the Holy Land by going through his territory, in return for the assurance that Saladin would leave his Empire alone.

In 1198–99 Pope Innocent III was corresponding with Alexios III and the Patriarch of Constantinople in the context of continuing military needs and commercial imperatives. This time it was the German Empire, in the persons of the Hohenstaufens, rather than the Normans, who were the threat. Alexios writes with words of respect on the subject of Roman primacy and thoughts on the reconquest of the Holy Land.[25] A letter from John, Patriarch of Constantinople, chastises Innocent III about the claims which are made for the primacy of Rome, a reminder that schism continued. The Pope's reply is to insist that the primacy of the Apostolic See was not a human invention but the work of God, indeed of the God-Man.[26] Innocent required the Latin clergy in Constantinople to recognize his jurisdiction and to obey him.[27] The papal Curia was vigilant and was interfering in the East in a number of ways. Innocent III writes to the Patriarch of Jerusalem about crusading projects and the affairs of the Holy Land.[28] He writes again asking the Patriarch of Jerusalem to get the Patriarch of Antioch to satisfy him about certain disputes, with the threat that if he does not, the case will have to come before him in Rome.[29] He writes to the Hospitallers[30] and to the Templars.[31]

During the period of these major crusades a new experiment had begun. Walter Map's *De nugis curialium* describes the origins of the Templars. Paganus, seeing the need for a military force to protect pilgrims to the Holy Land, founded an order both sober and chaste.[32] There is also an account of the Hospitallers,[33] who made a good beginning taking in poor pilgrims and other guests and who attracted many recruits, but as they became rich they grew covetous. Bernard of Clairvaux wrote a treatise 'In Praise of the New Military Life' (*De laude novae militiae*),[34] in which he proposes the view that whether someone dies in bed or not, the death of his 'saints' is precious in the sight of God. If God does not approve of wielding the sword, why did Jesus say that soldiers ought to be content with their pay (Luke 3.14)? He paints for the reader pictures of the soldier-monk living in the community in a joyous but sober common life, polishing his armour while he keeps his soul bright.[35] He conducts a 'virtual tour' of the holy places.[36] 'Let us stand, then, with our loins girded with truth and our feet shod in preparation for the peace of the Gospel, bearing the shield of faith in everything we do.' In that way, suggests Guigo the Carthusian, no weapons will be effective against us. He cites St Paul: 'We do not fight as though raining blows on the air' (I Corinthians 9.26–7).[37]

Constantinople was sacked in 1204. The chronicler Villehardouin stresses the greed of the conquerors. When they are given their share of what has been captured they run their prize lands oppressively and cause the conquered Greeks to hate them.[38] The sack of Constantinople was intended by the papacy to achieve by military force that restoration of unity which theologians had so far failed to achieve. Terms were made with the Emperor Isaac, who had been blinded and kept in prison until the 'usurper' Alexios fled. The Greek Empire was to be placed under the jurisdiction of Rome. The Greeks were to bestow money and provisions on the Latin army, in gratitude for their 'liberation'. It failed in its objective, for the Greeks responded by refusing to celebrate the Eucharist at any altar where the Latin rite had been used unless it had been washed and disinfected.[39]

The conquest of Constantinople during the Fourth Crusade in 1204 had been invigorating. Crusading persisted as an ideal, and intermittently actual expeditions took place. The setbacks of repeated failures did not diminish ardour for the idea. They were put down to failure on the part of the Crusaders to achieve a sufficiently high standard of commitment for God to allow the Crusade to succeed.

There are indications that Pope Innocent III envisaged something close to the modern 'war on terrorism' in his arrangements for the institutionalized continuance of the *negotium crucis*. He established the principle that only the pope could call for a crusade and legitimize it for the purposes of the granting of indulgences. He tightened up the rules for taking crusading vows, and on the liturgical and taxation aspects of crusading.[40] All this was taken forward by Innocent's successor, Honorius III,[41] and by his successor, Gregory IX. Innocent III himself called the Fifth Crusade in 1213 and Jacques de Vitry preached it so energetically that he was made Bishop of Acre as a reward (from 1216). While the crusading armies were in Acre between 1218 and 1221 he continued to preach to them. He reported to Pope Honorius on the Siege of Damietta (Letter III) and mentions the arrival of the Templars and Hospitallers and how cooperative they have proved (Letter IV).[42]

Papal propaganda preaching and inquisition

One of the great needs was for the commissioning of approved preachers and here the new mendicant orders were invaluable. Perhaps the most memorable preaching of the Crusade in the twelfth century had been that of Bernard of Clairvaux, but the Dominicans had now largely taken over the preaching role of the Cistercians 'against the unbelievers', and 'crusade-preaching' clearly came into that broad category. Dominicans went on trying to convert the Albigensians by preaching while military methods were being tried during the Albigensian crusade. The attitude of the Franciscans at the time of their inception also seems equivocal. Francis of Assisi visited Damietta during the Fifth Crusade and it seems that he may have gone on a peace mission, rather than with any intention of furthering the military intervention of the Crusade itself. When there was a momentary pause in the fighting he crossed the battlelines to preach before the sultan.

If preaching of the Crusade was to be effective it required organization, and as the thirteenth century proceeded, potential groups of Crusaders were identified and 'targeted' for recruitment. For example, in 1240 the Dominican province of Francia was commissioned by the Pope to remind *crucesignati* that they were expected to redeem their vows by actually going on crusade. By 1290 the Pope expected between half a dozen and 40 preachers to be provided by each Dominican province to concentrate on crusading.[43] There was even a thirteenth-century list of crusading sermons for the hard-working preacher to draw on, including some directed at Albigensian crusading.[44]

Crusading pressure was directed against Muslims not only in the Holy Land but also in North Africa. Raymond of Penyaforte preached the projected conquest of Majorca by King James of Aragon in 1229, and the Dominicans were expected to encourage Christians to go there and settle to consolidate the achievement and secure the island once and for all for Christians. In the mid-thirteenth century Alfonso X, King of Castile, tried over several decades from the 1250s to defeat Islam in parts of North Africa.[45] North African crusading was still high enough on the agenda in the 1270s for Innocent V to give the Archbishop of Seville powers to use Dominican resources to provide for preaching. This was propaganda preaching, as became apparent in Germany when the friars were used to preach the Baltic crusade.[46] And the mendicants did not long preserve the clarity of their respective first idealistic vision. They became institutionalized, powerfully influential in high places through their role as confessors to the mighty and the mighty's wives.

The thirteenth century saw the emergence of the Inquisition as a regular instrument for rooting out heretics, organized and carried out on orders from the highest level in the Church. Some 'professional' preachers of the Crusades among the friars seem to have been recruited as inquisitors later.[47]

The techniques of the inquisitors included a number of modern tactics familiar from the 'war on terrorism'. They made return visits to villages so that individuals under suspicion were never free from anxiety, they encouraged neighbours to report one another as heretics, they formulated stock questions along the lines of the famous 'have you stopped beating your wife', which made it difficult for a simple villager to give any answer which did not show him in a bad light. An important example was the question whether the accused was willing to swear to the orthodoxy of his beliefs. A reluctance to swear an oath was common to many kinds of dissenter, who took Jesus seriously when he told his followers not to swear oaths but simply say yes and no.

CHAPTER 8

Extreme Lives:
The Religious Orders

An apostolic life

Jesus himself set an example by living a shared life among his disciples, a life of poverty and simplicity. When he sent them out to preach the Gospel, he instructed them to rely upon the charity of those they went among and to travel very light in material terms (Matthew 10.14; Mark 6.11; Luke 9.5). An ideal of the 'apostolic life' had emerged during the early Christian centuries modelled on a selective reading of the Gospel, but with additional emphases derived from the asceticism contemporary philosophers so highly valued. This was particularly suspicious of the body and its enjoyment and regarded them as temptations as well as distractions, thus amending Jesus's message and departing from his example. Jesus did not apparently insist on fasting. It was even complained that the Son of Man came 'eating and drinking' (Luke 7.34).

In the ancient world it was possible to live a life of special devotion in one's own home. A number of the high-born Roman women who corresponded with Jerome at the end of the fourth century were doing that. But from the fifth and sixth centuries the fashion changed and it became the custom to separate oneself from ordinary society and go apart, either to live as a hermit – favoured in the Greek East – or to join a community, as was more usual in the Latin West. Communities of individuals who had committed themselves to live a particularly demanding form of the 'religious' life became a significant feature of medieval society. Their lives were, at least in intention, marked by self-denial. Monastic asceticism was always a doubled-edged sword, in East and West, because embedded in it was a profound mistrust of the body and of matter, which easily tipped over into dualism.

In the Middle Ages many chose to give up the ordinary pleasures of life and live stripped of anything which might distract them from the concentrated endeavour to love God 'most', in the belief that they thus greatly improved their chances of heaven. The acceptance that giving up pleasures and satisfactions in this life improved one's prospects for eternity led to the undertaking of extreme lives, lived so as to reach out into eternity, albeit at some immediate cost to the individual in comfort and opportunities in life. The popular expectation that this was to be an accepted requirement raises the difficult question of the right place for simplicity of life and how it is to be distinguished from puritanism. Caesarius of Heisterbach suggests that the very life of a monk is an exercise in resisting temptation, for while the ordinary Christian will experience a temptation and either give in to it or resist it, the monk is 'always fighting against vices and lusts, by watching, by fasting, by prayer, by obedience in prosperity and adversity, by having no possessions in this world for the sake of Christ … this temptation itself is a satisfaction for their sins', and the monk does not have to do penance for his former sins when he joins the religious order,[1] for being a monk is penance enough.

The underlying belief of the Middle Ages was that it was worth enduring some voluntary discomfort, or accepting involuntary discomfort cheerfully, in order to improve one's hopes of heaven. There are biblical encouragements supporting that view. Matthew 19.12 speaks of those who make themselves eunuchs for the Kingdom of Heaven's sake; Matthew 19.29 of leaving brothers and sisters, father and mother, in the assurance that one will be repaid abundantly; Matthew 19.21 of selling what one has and keeping one's treasure in heaven; Matthew 10.38 of taking up one's cross and following Christ, of losing one's life and finding it.

The theology of 'faith and works' which may seem to hover here was not to be developed fully until the Reformation, when Luther objected that the idea that it was possible to 'work one's way to heaven' was fundamentally incompatible with wholehearted acceptance that Christ had 'done' all that was necessary by dying on the Cross. More congenial to medieval preoccupations was the attempt to determine a balance between the value of human good behaviour in God's eyes and the free generosity of God acting through *grace* to make the good behaviour possible in the first place – for Augustine was adamant that the effect of Adam's sin had been to disable the human will to the point where it could not do anything right of its own volition.

The monk or hermit was expected to despise the world for his own ultimate good, but also for the good of others. Such lives were not regarded as selfish. On the contrary, those who 'prayed for a living' were regarded as doing so for the benefit of others, people who were too busy to lift up before God even their own troubles, let alone the troubles of the world. The reli-

gious were professionals at prayer and their job was to pray for others, both
in the sense of remembering them before God and of putting the time into
praying that those they mentioned in their prayers could not do for themselves. There was an acceptance in medieval society that this was discharg-
ing a valuable function on behalf of others who were occupied in tilling the
soil or fighting the wars or ruling the country and could not spare the time.
Members of the religious orders were the Marys to the Marthas of the ordinary working population. The religious orders thus became a recognized
part of the body politic. In one characteristic image, Noah, Daniel and Job
signify the three 'orders' in the Church (*ordines Ecclesiae*). The way Bernard
of Clairvaux explains it, Noah is the ruler, just as Noah captained the Ark
to save it from sinking. Daniel is the man whose life is led in extreme denial
of his natural desires, for he is given to abstinence and chastity, and he
stands for the monk. Job is the family man who dispenses earthly goods in a
sensible way and he stands for the ordinary people who legitimately possess
the earth.[2] Bernard of Clairvaux says that the Church as a whole, in which
there are so many different 'orders', is like the queen in the Psalms clad in a
garment of many colours (Psalm 44.14).[3]

The range of available jobs monks could do for society could extend
beyond this primary function of praying on its behalf. Monastic houses
could provide medical care for their local village. One of the converts
described by Caesarius of Heisterbach, Henry, once a rich and powerful
noble, was appointed interpreter to Bernard of Clairvaux at the time when
he was preaching the Second Crusade because he was skilled in both French
and German.[4] Friars became important as confessors to the great.

These themes of maintaining a balance in the body politic and contributing to the needs of others did not, however, encourage monastic life in
the direction of 'social work', except of the spiritual sort. Monasteries did
not make themselves responsible for the support of the local widows and
orphans.

Becoming a monk was often, until the late eleventh century in the West,
a family not a personal choice. The recruits to Benedictine abbeys were
often child oblates. Guibert of Nogent describes a change in his own generation when a number of mature adults felt a vocation and left their careers
as knights and farmers, and also their wives, to spend their last years as
monks. One example he gives was in the full flower of his age (*aetate positus
florulenta*), wealthy and successful.[5] Guibert describes dramatic changes in
such persons when they became monks. Éverard of Bretcuil had formerly
been seen in the most fancy and luxurious garments and was well known
for his ill temper. But once he was a monk he ceased to care in the slightest about his clothing, dressed like a peasant and became mild-mannered.[6]

Anselm wrote while he was still Abbot at Bec to beg a wife to allow her husband to become a monk. 'What can compel you, reverend lady, lady of proven chastity, to prevent your husband from seeking his soul's salvation to the uttermost (*perfecte*), for you love his soul no less than your own?' 'It is not to be imagined that you do so out for the vile pleasure of the flesh.' He urges her not only to allow her husband to go but to urge him to do so, and he suggests that she might do well to consider a parallel course for herself.[7]

A trend emerged in which these new interested adults began to make conscious choices, not only to enter the religious life but about which branch of it they preferred, and an age of experimentation began. In the Latin-speaking West in the Middle Ages the term conversion (*conversio*) was commonly used to refer to the decision to become a monk.[8] A series of examples of conversions suggests that it was recognized that the triggering event which causes someone to discover a vocation could come in many different ways: from hearing a sermon, from seeing a vision or even hearing a vision described, or from the example of others. The desire to be received as a monk might be so strong as to lead one to conceal the fact that he was already a priest and another the fact that she was a woman. One 'woman monk' fooled her brothers, though as she was carried to her deathbed one was heard to remark that she was either a woman or a devil, for he had never been able to look at her without temptation.[9]

Caesarius of Heisterbach wrote his *Dialogue on Miracles* in his capacity of novice-master to instruct recruits to his Cistercian house. He chose the form of a dialogue between the novice and his instructor.[10] Caesarius explains to his novices that 'conversion is a turning of the heart, either from bad to good, or from good to better, or from better to best'. He tells a story which nicely underlines the distinction between 'becoming a monk' and the inward 'conversion' which ought to prompt it. A 'convert' decided to become a monk because he thought that it would give him a good opportunity to steal the precious vessels from the monastery. But the moment he made his profession, promised obedience and put on the habit he was truly converted and became known for his sanctity of life.[11] He tells other stories, too, of the difficulty young men have in holding to their profession if they enter in youth or early manhood, unless they come in with a strong sense of sin. Otherwise they are at best lukewarm monks and at worst give up and leave.[12]

What were these converts turning *to*? To God, they might have answered, but also to a way of life which, although it turned its back on society, was held to be useful. But from the end of the eleventh century in the West some were thinking afresh about the purposes of the religious life. A few individuals had begun to question the existing assumptions of the religious life and to experiment with living as hermits or setting up their own communities with their own variations on the conventional rules. It was still possible for individuals to begin movements or to found religious houses of their own. Lanfranc came upon Herluin, the founder of Bec, in a field trying to construct an oven for his new house at Bec. Guibert of Nogent describes the growing number of mature individuals who were tempted to give up their lives as knights and to make arrangements with their wives and to enter monastic life in their declining years, where they might better prepare themselves for heaven. This was an age of high consciousness that there were questions to be debated about how best to live the religious life.

A 'Little Book on the Different Orders' (*Libellus de diversis ordinibus*), written in the twelfth century, allows us to glimpse the assumptions of this age of experimental monasticism in the West. The question the author addresses is whether the proliferation of different orders in recent times is pleasing to God.[13] His arrangement is thematic, beginning with hermits and working his way to communities who live close to human habitations and then to those who live far away. His idea is that there are significant differences in strictness, 'self-denial and removal from the world'. On one level the proliferating varieties, the hermits, monks, canons, the orders of women as well as of men, could be distinguished by their external differences of form and conduct. At another they could be taken to exemplify to a greater of lesser degree the strict or the casual approach to the living of the religious life, or something in between.

A quite different kind of account of the diversity of the religious life is to be found in Walter Map's anecdotal and gossipy *De nugis curialium*. The Carthusians, he explains, are severe on themselves. No one but the prior is allowed to have both feet outside his cell at the same time. On three days a week they have only bread and water. They wear hairshirts at all times. All their time is spent in prayer and reading. They exclude all contact with women. But alas their daughter-houses are going to the devil (*diabolum sequens*), urged by greed and the love of luxury. The Grandmontines keep only bees, no other creatures. They live on charity. When they run out of food they fast for a day, then send out a single brother to beg. All their business is done for them by lay brothers who are their Marthas, while the monks themselves live the life of Mary without worldly cares.[14] This idea of distinction or expectation between social 'classes' may be met again in the Cistercians, and we have noted its possible relevance to the emergence in the thirteenth century of a number of experimental do-it-yourself lay religious movements.

Eastern monasticism

In contrast with the rule-led community life of Benedictine and most other
Western monks, the style of Eastern monastic life favoured the idiorhyth-
mic. Monks might live in loose associations, meeting only occasionally for
worship or to eat together, with each monk pursuing his private path of
prayer. Hermits were held in high respect. There was merit in lowering
down a basket of figs on a rope to solitaries of the sort who may still be
observed living on ledges half-way down a cliff, gazing out over the sea
to eternity, in everlasting prayerful colloquy with his God. Such eremitical perches can still be seen from the sea on the coasts of Mount Athos.
The history of Mount Athos, the Holy Mountain, a peninsula in northern Greece from which all females are excluded, probably began with the
foundation of the Lavra monastery by Athanasius the Athonite in 961;
subsequently the mountain became an icon of the religious life in Greek
Christianity.

Going to extremes in the religious life became a strong feature of Eastern monasticism from patristic times. It sent Daniel the Stylite (409–93)[15]
to live upon a column, and the desert fathers out into the wilderness. The
pious would come to these totemic figures for advice and perhaps be sent
away with an uncomfortably demanding requirement to amend their ways.
They had less high-minded visitors too. As Gregory the Great describes it
in his *Dialogues*, the naughty populace, curious to see what they were up to,
would creep up to their windows and peer in; beautiful girls would arrive
to see whether they could tempt them from their vows of chastity.[16] Various
collections of sayings (*sententiae*) such as the *Apophthegmata patrum* and the
Sentences of Sextus,[17] preserve examples of the tales told about such saintly
eremitical figures, in the West as well as in the East.

Asceticism also tended to lead to excessiveness in the subjugation of
the flesh on the part of the monks themselves The early seventh-century
Patriarch of Constantinople, St John the Almsgiver, had two biographers,
Sophronius and John Moschus.[18] John the Almsgiver reflected the concerns
of his time and place in his work for the poor. His kindness to the poor was
imaginative. He arranged for his stewards to distribute food to the needy
When it came to his attention that women who had just given birth were
coming for food when they had had no time to recover, so great was their
hunger, he arranged for the building of seven 'nursing homes' about the
city, in which such women could rest and recover after childbirth.[19]

John was vigilant about propriety. He would take no money for ordinations himself, and when a priest or bishop sought ordination or consecration from him, he made him produce a written declaration that he was not
contaminated by simony. Yet he lived to the extremes which win approval

on every side in Byzantine accounts of the heroes of the Church. He had been married, but his wife and children died, and this is celebrated as a release from worldly ties which allowed him to give himself entirely up to the love of God. It is emphasized that he had married in the first place only to please his father and would not consummate the marriage until his father-in-law insisted. When he learned that the invading Persians had taken control of Jerusalem and destroyed holy things, he lamented so long and loudly that he outdid the lamenting prophet Jeremiah, and in order that his laments might not go unrecorded or unnoticed, he committed them to writing.[20]

St Theodore of Sykeon, contemporary of John the Almsgiver, is another holy hero of the seventh-century East. His biographer mingles hagiographical convention with insights into the religious life of contemporary society. For example, Theodore's pregnant mother has exactly the sort of dream which is so frequently reported of the mothers of Western saints, in which a bright star comes down from heaven and enters her womb. The child was accordingly baptized 'Theodore', Gift of God. His mother was ambitious that he should have a career at court, but again she had a dream in which she was told that the King of Heaven needed him. She then handed him over to be educated, and he proved himself cleverer than his fellow pupils. He was attracted to self-denial and prayer and refused to eat with his family so that he could go and pray at the local shrine of St George instead. When they remonstrated with him he ran away from home and comfort. These were the actions, his biographer suggests, of one who understood that the friend of the world is the enemy of God (James 4.4) and that no one can serve God and Mammon (Luke 16.13).

As he grew up his resolve strengthened and he took up residence in a pit, and later in a cave in the mountain, and continued to refuse food. Such athletic spiritual exercises were a wonder to the population, and like other ascetics he began to make a reputation. Extremes of mortification thus won extravagant admiration in contemporary Greek society. Forcibly brought out of his cave at last by his family, he was covered in sores and pus, his hair was matted and full of worms, his bones stuck out all over him and he smelt so strongly that no one could bear to stand near him. 'In short, people saw him an another Job,' comments his biographer. A father brought his son, who had an unclean spirit, and told Theodore to beat him and call upon the devil to come out of him. Theodore is vouchsafed visions of angels and troubled with the visits of devils.[21]

Symeon the New Theologian was born about 949 in Asia Minor into a good family with some political connections. He was removed to Constantinople by his father at the age of 11 to begin his studies in the schools there.

But he refused to take up the post his family were arranging for him at court and he refused to go on to higher studies, preferring a life of juvenile dissipation about the town, until, finding all this very unsatisfying, he came to his senses, and his conversion, like those of many others held up as examples, swung him to the other extreme. By the time he was in his mid-20s he had entered the monastery of Studios, from where he soon moved to the monastery of St Mamas and became a priest and in due course its abbot.[22] His writings on the theology of the spiritual life place a characteristically Byzantine emphasis on the importance of 'compunction' (with tears), or abstinence and endurance and silence and self-denial of all kinds and in their most extreme form. In Catechesis V he explains that although repentance is essential, it is not sufficient to purify one's soul merely to give away all one's worldly goods. It is necessary to go to the point where one suffers affliction. Some Old Testament Patriarchs are offered as examples. It is stressed that lay people as well as monks are capable of true repentance, and it is even possible to achieve it with a wife and children and a successful career punctuated with tears.

Western monasticism

There had been experiments in the monastic and eremitical life during the patristic period in West as well as East which suggest that the 'social usefulness' theories were developments of the later Middle Ages. It was not uncommon for enthusiasts in the late patristic period in the West to do the kind of thing Jerome did more than once, and set off into desert places to live lives of extreme self-denial, alone or in company with others.

Monastic life seems to have been encouraged in Ireland from the fifth or sixth centuries, with a strong emphasis on the ascetic life. Gildas's *De excidio* cites Columbanus's letter to Gregory the Great as an authority on discipline.[23] Early Irish monasticism was as extreme as anything Byzantium afforded. It encouraged vigils and beatings. Bede describes the extreme practices of an Irishman called Adamnan. He would spend whole nights in vigils and ate only on Thursdays and Sundays. He had adopted this way of life on the advice of a priest who had suggested to him that the more he made himself suffer now the more likely he was to find divine mercy being exercised at his death.[24]

The distinctive Western trend was set in the sixth century by the *Regula magistri* and the *Rule* of St Benedict. In Genesis 12.1–3 God tells Abraham to leave his country and kindred and go where God prompts him. Four kinds of monk are distinguished in the *Rule*: cenobites, who live in a community; hermits or anchorites, who ought to have long experience of community life before they attempt the difficult life of solitude; those who remain attached to the world and merely pretend to live a dedicated life; and the gyrovagi, who do not settle anywhere but spend their lives wandering about, enjoying the hospitality of others.

From the sixth century Irish monks set off in this spirit and in coracles to see where God would lead them, letting the sea take them where it would. Cuthbert, Bishop of Lindisfarne, became a monk at Melrose in 651, and is the subject of two *Lives*, one anonymous, the other by Bede. It is explained that his personal desire for the life of a hermit eventually grew so strong that he set off for the island of Farne, where no one had previously been able to settle by reason of the diabolical illusions which beset everyone there. But Cuthbert drove the demons out and built himself a cell in the hard and rocky ground, so enclosed that his only view was upwards towards the heavens.[25] Yet the anonymous *Life* (III.1) describes how he composed a Rule for his own community.

The more stable and enduring communities which lived under a Rule were the preference in the West. Cassiodorus established a monastery on his estates at Squillace in 554 and began to gather together a substantial library there, getting Greek texts copied for it. The community died in the seventh century. The *Regula magistri* ('Rule of the Master') was composed by an unknown author at the beginning of the sixth century and portions of it, particularly the prologue, were imported by Benedict of Nursia into the Benedict *Rule*, which laid the foundations of monastic life in the West. (The Benedictines were known in the Middle Ages as the Black Monks because of the colour of their habits.)

Benedict was drawing quite widely on the monastic customs which were already being experimented with, for the house of monks he founded at Monte Cassino. His *Life* was written by Gregory I, who inserted it as the second book of his *Dialogues*.[26] Benedict was of good family and sent to school in Rome, but Gregory emphasizes that he was repelled by the evil living he found there. He turned his back on the fleshpots of secular life and went to dwell in a cave at Subiaco. He spent three years living as a hermit, where he made a name for holiness until he was invited to be an abbot. When he began the community at Monte Cassino he first had to burn the grove where the pagans worshipped and take possession of the temple and citadel.

The *Rule* was designed to foster the community life. The brothers are to choose one from among themselves to be their abbot and then they are to regard him as their father. So at the head of the Benedictine community is the abbot, who must always remember that he occupies Christ's place and is his representative in the community and should behave accordingly. The brothers are to have everything in common. They are to live lives of poverty, chastity and, above all, obedience. Their daily round is to have regularity, being composed of periods of worship (the *opus dei* or 'work of God') and manual labour, as well as reading and reflection.

The religious life was attractive to women as well as men. Some of the earliest experiments in the living of dedicated celibate religious lives were made by the well-born women (virgins and widows) of Rome in Jerome's day at the end of the fourth century. Bede describes twin houses in which communities of the male and female religious lived side by side. Eorcenwold, before he was made Bishop of London in 675, founded such a double community with his sister Aethelburh presiding as abbess of the community of nuns, though in this case the two houses were geographically separate, his at Chertsey, hers at Barking.[27] Those double monasteries, where the communities were next door, mostly seem to have remained remarkably scandal-free, though Bede mentions the 'wickedness' of the community at Coldingham in Berwickshire.[28] It cannot have been easy to maintain standards of chastity. Bede describes a house in which it was observed that most of the monks and nuns were to be found in bed, either together, or, if alone, slothfully idling their time away. Their cells, which were built to pray in, have become venues for feasting, drinking and gossip, and the nuns use their leisure to make themselves fashionable garments.[29]

The full-time commitment to a life of retirement from the world was of its essence something of a luxury. It was available in practice mainly to those of noble birth. There is no way of knowing whether peasants felt vocations in the same numbers as the nobility, but it is obvious that they do not appear among professed monks in any numbers. If peasants had vocations in the same numbers as the nobility they do not appear in proportionate numbers as professed monks. In reality, in the high Middle Ages, the monastic life was reserved for those who could afford it. It had a distinct class bias.

Cycles of reform and decay

Because of their essentially institutional character and their comparative permanence in the places where they were established, monastic communities in the West acquired property and sometimes considerable wealth, and a 'place' in society. Patrons could have a variety of sometimes very personal reasons for encouraging the foundation of a new monastery. William de Warenne founded a priory of the Holy Sepulchre at Thetford in the middle of the twelfth century apparently because he was himself drawn to crusading. The priory belonged to an independent order of Augustinian canons which had been founded to care for the Holy Sepulchre in Jerusalem. He also made yearly gifts to the Templars out of the rents he drew from Lewes in Sussex. He took the cross in 1146.[30] Patrons of such foundations could expect the prayers of the community for their families for generations, while retaining a degree of control because with each generation charters granting them might need to be renewed.[31] Good neighbours and benefactors might prove to be a mixed blessing for several reasons. Disputes could arise out of land grants, especially if no proper provision was made for confirmation and protection of the gift.[32]

Once the Benedictine monasteries of Europe were established they became a 'draw' for gifts of lands in this way, and by virtue of such endowments they became financially independent and some very wealthy. Wealthiness in a monastery repeatedly led to corruption, and corruption to the need for reform. Wealthier and nobler families provided not only financial support but a good proportion of the recruits, and in effect a benefactor might be able to buy an abbacy for a relative. If bishops were barons, so, often, were abbots in the high Middle Ages. Political influence was as important here as was the selection of bishops from noble families who chose to wield their influence in that way. Caesarius of Heisterbach gives examples of two well-connected women who became abbesses, Matilda of Fusinnich and Helswindis of Burscheid, both of whom, he relates, had to argue hard with their parents from an early age to be allowed to become nuns, when their parents had destined them for worldly and advantageous marriages.[33] The advantage would have been as much to the family as to the girl, for such marriages were likely to be property deals and involve dynastic arrangements.

The Cluniac houses were particularly notable in their reforming period for the stamp they left on traditional Benedictinism. Cluny was founded in 909, and its first abbot set a very high standard of observance of the *Rule*, but one which put a premium on worship and greatly elaborated the detail of the rules by which the monks lived, with some loss of the balance Benedict had intended between prayer, study and labour. Cluny drew the children of important people and was consequently even more influential. Anselm was tempted to go to Cluny when he realized he had a vocation. Cluny he knew would impose upon him a severe discipline (*districto ordine*).[34]

The founding of the Cistercians was partly a response to this cyclically recurring awareness of the need for reform. Stephen Harding (d.1134) was of a generation inspired by revolutionary ideas in monasticism, and was himself a member of the founding community at the Abbey of Citeaux, where he was made abbot in 1109. The arrival of Bernard three years later, accompanied by 30 friends and relatives, ensured that the community, hitherto precarious, became a success and an attraction. Its distinctive character lay in the austerity of the lives the monks led.

The Cistercians followed the Benedictine *Rule*, but, conscious of the danger of decadence and the bad example of some Benedictine houses, they built their own houses in remote places, avoided farmland which was rich and productive and tried to avoid material prosperity with its seductive inherent dangers to the purity of their way of life.

It could be argued that those whose work was to pray should not be expected to have to attend to the practicalities of life. The Cistercians arranged for such matters to be looked after by *conversi*, thus making a distinction between 'choir monks' and others, though it had been and remained a core principle of mainstream Benedictinism that labour, manual labour, should be expected of the professed monk as part of a balanced life. 'If anyone should object that there are many [among the canons of certain orders] who do not know how to proclaim the Gospel, as for example the unlearned ones of the *conversi*, I reply that whoever lives well and ... follows his calling as best he can may have it said of him that he evangelises, that is he announces good things. It seems to me that he who lives well proclaims it better than he who speaks well.'[35]

The Cistercians had their 'cycles' of reform and decay too. Walter Map's *De nugis curialium* is disparaging about the Cistercians,[36] for many seekers after pleasure joined them and they lost their first severity and rigour.

Bernard of Clairvaux and Peter the Venerable, Abbot of Cluny, corresponded about differences of practice in the light of the embarrassing loss of Benedictine monks to the Cistercian experiment. For example, Peter defends the Cluniac's elaborate variety of permitted clothing with a reference to the principle stated in Benedict's *Rule*. Benedict thought it appropriate for clothing to be adapted to the climate.[37] Caesarius of Heisterbach includes for the edification of his Cistercian novices an account of the founding of their order in which he brings out the differences. He emphasizes that Cistercians and Cluniacs (as 'reformed' Benedictines) follow the same Rule, that of Benedict; the difference is in the 'ways of observance'. 'They say that the rigour of the Rules was modified by certain holy fathers, in order that a greater number of souls might find salvation in the Order.' But he wants the novice above all to keep it firmly fixed in his mind 'that the author of our Order is the Holy Ghost, S. Benedict its founder, and its reformer the venerable abbot Robert [of Molesme]'.[38]

The religious in the world: canons and friars

Since the time of Charlemagne cathedrals had been required to maintain schools and ensure that their canons had a reasonable standard of education. Canons were priests who might be called upon to discharge parish duties in the diocese. New orders of 'regular canons', that is, canons living under a Rule, were founded in the twelfth century. Twelfth-century orders such as the Victorines in Paris and the Premonstratensians tended to follow the Rule which was believed to have been devised by Augustine of Hippo.[39] Canons did not lead the inward and cloistered lives of monks. They got out into the world and could have considerable impact.

Norbert (c.1080–1134), the founder of the Premonstratensian Order and eventually Archbishop of Magdeberg, was of a noble family. In his mid-20s he was caught in a thunderstorm and, suddenly terrified of death, he experienced a conversion. He became an energetic reformer. He was accused at the Synod of Fritzlar in 1118 of unlicensed preaching (and of preaching 'novelties' at that). He sought papal approval for what he and his followers were doing. In 1120, with the support of the Bishop of Laon, he founded the Premonstratensian Order of canons, so called after the valley (Prémontré) in which their first house was built. Pope Honorius II gave the order recognition in 1126 and Norbert himself was made Archbishop of Magdeburg in the same year. Premonstratensians were not necessarily outsiders in the great affairs of Church and state; they gained considerable respectability. Anselm of Havelberg was one of Norbert's first disciples, and Norbert consecrated him as Bishop of Havelberg in 1129. He travelled as an ecclesiastical ambassador to Constantinople in 1135 and held ecumenical dialogues with leading Greek Christians about the schism. He was also influential in court circles.

Next emerged the friars or mendicants, professional travelling preachers. At the beginning of the thirteenth century Francis of Assisi founded the Friars Minor or Franciscans, and Dominic founded the Friars Preacher or Dominicans. Francis's direct inspiration was the teaching of Jesus, especially his instructions to his disciples. He wanted to live in his own lifetime the apostolic life of mission, wandering without possessions, simply preaching the Gospel wherever he found himself. Dominic, more focused, identified for his order of preachers the task of bringing back to the fold heretical lost sheep, first and foremost the Albigensians of northern Spain and southern France, against whom the Cistercian preachers had had limited success. The Waldensian heretics, too, presented an intellectual challenge, with their mastery of biblical quotations and their willingness to counter arguments with reasonings of their own.

The friars settled in towns and these new orders, particularly the Dominicans, placed a heavy emphasis on the intellectual as well as the spiritual training of those who joined them. If they were to be effective preachers against the heretics they needed to know what they were doing, so as not to replace one unorthodoxy with another in the minds of the faithful. Every priory of Dominicans had a school. Intellectual rivalry between the Dominicans and Franciscans became intense at an early stage, sharing an ideal which included the constant travelling preaching which really needed towns for its success, if the preachers were to be heard by sufficiently large audiences to be successful. The Franciscans produced some of the most enterprising scholars of their era. Early in the thirteenth century Robert Grosseteste was the first lector for the Franciscans in Oxford,[40] a pioneering scholar, studying Greek and the modern sciences,[41] and not long after, Roger Bacon, whom he influenced, also became a linguist and challenger of received ideas.

The advent of the friars also inadvertently prompted the explosion of the great thirteenth-century controversy about poverty. When Francis died his former followers were faced with the classic dilemma of such movements. How were they to continue? A proportion of them opted for institutionalization. Others resisted any change which might threaten them with the burdens of wealth and interfere with their freedom to go where the Holy Spirit led, and live as Francis himself had done. The Church took the side of the 'safe' and its apologists increasingly found themselves having to argue that Jesus had not seriously meant that his disciples were to lead such lives, and that in any case there were significant differences between 'owning' things and merely 'using' them. (We shall meet both these orders again in the next chapter.)

There were other thirteenth-century flowerings of experiments with the idea of a mendicant way of life. The primary inspiration of the Augustinian friars, like that of the Carmelites, lay not in preaching but in the hermit life. The Carmelites first came into being in the late twelfth century as the Order of the Brothers of Our Lady of Mount Carmel. Their original inspiration was eremitical and they lived in the deserts of the Middle East. In 1247 the Pope granted approval for them to live in towns and cities and preach, and also for them to live in communities and eat together. A series of papal directives brought orders of hermits under the Rule of Augustine in the thirteen century and various congregations were united in 1256 by Pope Alexander IV.

The balance of action and contemplation

Christianity has always placed a high value on personal asceticism and withdrawal from worldly advantage, even in periods when the Church was extremely wealthy and some of its higher clergy enjoyed a lifestyle which caused shocked comment and revolutionary criticism. But it has always done so with an uneasy consciousness that there is a choice to be made. The preservation of the balance has taken up a good deal of the Church's intellectual energy. In the Gospel, Mary and Martha, sisters of the Lazarus that Jesus raised from the dead, showed Jesus hospitality, but while Martha busied herself with the practical preparations, Mary sat at his feet and listened. Martha expressed her resentment (Luke 10.38–42). The bishop or priest, busy with administrative duties, was liable to see himself as Martha to the Mary of the monk who had chosen the contemplative life. Among the more hostile accusations of base motivations was the contention that both black and white monks recognized their prey (the knightly classes) and coaxed those who had used up their inheritance or were in debt to join them to make up their numbers, though this accusation hardly accords with complaints that those who ran abbeys were interested only in their houses getting rich.[42]

Two treatises, written 600 years apart, and each immensely influential in its time and after, address this dilemma. The first was the *Regula pastoralis* of Gregory the Great. The *pastorale magisterium* involves learning the *ars artium*, which is the 'rule of souls' or others (*regimen animarum*).[43] This is a heavy responsibility and no one should treat it lightly. No one should presume to teach, says Gregory the Great, until he has first learned to meditate[44] and his own life is matured by meditation and the way he lives matches the words he says as he preaches.[45] Gregory the Great's own experience prompted him to gloomy reflections about the difficulty those in high office are likely to find in maintaining an inner quiet in which to meditate, even if they are able to live in public view in such a way as to set a good example to their subordinates.[46]

The second was Bernard of Clairvaux's *De consideratione*. Like Gregory, who certainly influenced his thinking, he was primarily concerned with the balancing trick required of those exercising pastoral office, indeed the highest pastoral office, that of the Pope. But the fundamental principle was the same. Bernard sympathizes from his own experience as an abbot and monk. 'Where should I begin? Perhaps from your occupations, for in that I fully sympathise with you.'[47] There is a danger in being too busy, he continues. It upsets one's priorities and takes one's attention from what really matters.

CHAPTER 9

The Church and the Intellectuals

From 'culture' to 'learning'

The modern reader coming new to the Middle Ages has to make an effort to enter into a world of thought which does not always begin from our contemporary assumptions. It was just the same for medieval readers of the literature which had come down to them, but they did not take it for granted, as we tend to, that the objective was to understand earlier writing as the authors intended. It was not even always realized that writers of another age and another culture might have had different ideas about what they were doing. The medieval reader tended to regarded the work of earlier writers with awed respect, as 'authority'.

Medieval writers were expected to affect an elaborate if sometimes slightly disingenuous timidity (for many of them were as vain as any modern author). They made much use of the 'modesty topos', the convention of expressing the writer's unworthiness. They described themselves as near-illiterates, mere beginners when it came to matters of style. They were apologetic. They bowed before the superiority of those who had gone before them. In the famous image Bernard of Chartres used in the twelfth century, they were 'dwarfs sitting on the shoulders of giants', and if they could see a little further it was only because they were lifted so high on the giants' shoulders.

There was no question of discarding earlier authors as out of date, or superseded or simply wrong. When the 'authorities' disagreed, the only question was which authority trumped which. A very great deal of medieval intellectual endeavour was devoted to weighing against one another the thoughts of earlier ages. The emerging rule was relatively clear. The Bible was the directly inspired word of God and had a higher authority than anything else. Then came the writings of early Christians who were gradually classified as 'Fathers', figures such as Augustine, Jerome, Gregory the Great and Bede in the West and Origen and the Cappadocian Fathers in the East. The secular writers of classical antiquity had a place, too, especially Cicero and Seneca, who wrote on theological and moral subjects and who were rated highly as figures who had done very well to come as close as they had to Christian principles. Jerome's personal concerns about the difficulty of resisting the delicious temptations of secular literature were memorably recorded in his story of the dream in which he was accused of being more of a Ciceronian than a Christian. We can already see here a tension and a bifurcation between the secular and the Christian, which would roll on through the Middle Ages. The two never quite parted company.

The commentator who began at the beginning of the Bible in its Vulgate version would first read a letter which Jerome had written to Paulinus. This is in reality a separate work, a commentary on Jerome's Letter 53 to Paulinus, in which Jerome defends his Vulgate translation. Grosseteste, however, takes it at face value as a kind of preface to the whole. The interest for our present purposes lies in his remarks as he tries to assess the intellectual qualities of the relationship between them. This man, we learn from another letter of St Jerome's to him, was of great intelligence and limitless linguistic ability, who spoke with ease and purity; and the ease and purity of his speech were combined with practical wisdom. So Paulinus was a person of high culture. As yet, however, he was not well versed in the Scriptures. Jerome advises him to learn from masters rather than trying to master the text on his own. That was how this struck Robert Grosseteste. He was unusual among his early thirteen-century contemporaries in a number of respects. He thought it important to learn Greek and took a lively interest in natural science. In his commentary on the passage at the beginning of Genesis which describes the six days of creation, he took the opportunity to explore a number of the scientific questions which arise. But here we see him busy with exactly the task which faced all medieval readers, that of trying to strike the right balance in 'appreciating' the range of earlier authorities which had to be taken into account as one read.[1]

The ancient world took it for granted that a man of consequence would cultivate his mind in the service of the state. Education (Greek *paideia*) 'formed' and stocked the minds of cultured citizens. They were going to need well-stocked minds to play a full part as citizens in Roman society. The late Romans in particular taught their boys to argue elegantly and persuasively, which was a practical skill they would need in public life. In the study of rhetoric with a specialist master boys were entering a higher stage of education, which could be obtained only in the major cities. Students of rhetoric were expected to grasp the formal skills of argumentation (logic or dialectic) and to get sufficient practice in the presentation of those arguments persuasively to enable them to perform as advocates in courts, as political orators, and, on the rare occasions when it might be necessary, as panegyrists capable of flattering an emperor as he would wish to be flattered.

All this is a sharp contrast with the world of medieval politics, in which, with the exception perhaps of some of the Italian city states, there was little call for such sophisticated public performances for the best part of a millennium, and, in most of Western Europe, a limited possibility of enjoying citizenship of that sort either. Even in the Byzantine Empire, where something of the flavour of the late Roman Empire persisted, a decadence and brutality in the behaviour of the imperial family and their hangers-on, and even that of the senior figures in the Church, undermined refinement and made citizenship very different in reality from the urbane political life of ancient Rome. A new style of urban life developed across Western Europe but driven by trade. The rising bourgeoisie lacked the culture of their ancient counterparts, even where they had some degree of literacy.

This was partly a matter of changing educational patterns. In the ancient world, the necessary subject matter for arguments, the illustrations and examples and *bons mots* and amusing anecdotes, were acquired through the study of literature. The student first mastered the use of his native language (grammar), which, in late antiquity, needed upgrading to classical standards from the norms of a later age, when both Greek and Latin were living languages and actively changing. This was achieved principally through close study of a limited range of authors designed to improve the students' command of the language and their stylistic skills (Virgil, Terence, Sallust, Cicero, Homer, some Greek dramatists, both tragic and comic, Thucydides, Demosthenes, with anthologies to represent other authors). 'Quintilian's' Declamations[2] are a useful indicator of the way books were 'used' by the classical orator. They were a source of quotation and of illustrative stories and examples.

As a 'finish', a young man from a wealthy family might be sent to Athens, Rome, Constantinople or Alexandria to acquire some philosophy to lend depth to his arguments, or to become expert in mathematics, medicine or law (a speciality of Berytus). There were no universities in the ancient world, but academies offering teaching at a sophisticated level existed in these important cities, where leading teachers offered instruction. The students obtained no 'qualification', except in legal studies at Berytus (legal studies always seem to have had a strong vocational element). As to career opportunities, in major centres of population there was considerable demand for men competent to enter the civil service, especially perhaps in Constantinople, whose remnants of housing suggest that there was a higher proportion of middle-class dwellings there than in Rome (which was full of tenements for the poor). The kind of 'career' – especially in public life – which required such preliminary education ceased to exist with the fall of the Empire, but something like it was to reappear from the eleventh century with the growth of a class of clerks and civil servants serving both the Church (staffing the Curia in Rome and the secretariats of local bishops) and the state, as the correspondence of kings and emperors expanded. This was marked by the appearance of a series of manuals on letter writing, based on the formal principles of composition of a speech, and forming a new medieval branch of the classical art of rhetoric, with the addition of rules for composing salutations (greetings) and for ensuring that the prose was elegant, with each sentence ending in one of a range of accepted dying falls or cadences.

The recreations of adults of the middle and upper classes of the ancient and late antique world, as described in their memoirs and reflections, set a high value on intellectually stimulating conversation. Groups would meet for a weekend to debate a particular topic. That was still happening in Augustine's lifetime, as Macrobius's *Saturnalia* records.[3] Or friends would assemble to listen to a draft speech one of them was working on and wished to try out on a sympathetic audience. With the end of the Empire the kind of community in which this was an attractive pattern of recreation largely disappeared, though something like it may have lingered where Arabic civilization still read and discussed Greek books and ideas.

It is possible to see the shift of cultural expectation which took place with the end of the Empire in the reflections of Boethius's contemporary, Cassiodorus. He was a senior civil servant with the same Ostrogothic regime as was responsible for Boethius's house arrest and execution. Cassiodorus left a collection of model letters, the *Variarum* (about 537–38),[4] a strong indication that he believed they might have value, in both their style and their content, for posterity. He lived at the wrong moment, for the civil-service world he worked in was soon to vanish. And eventually he himself turned from such work in distaste. He describes how 'one day in Ravenna' he had put from him the cares of state and his worldly responsibilities which suddenly had a nasty taste for him (*noxio sapore conditis*), and savoured the sweetness of the Psalms instead. 'Trusting God's commandment, let us push at the door of the heavenly mystery, that it may open to our senses on a world full of flowers,' he cries.[5] This had him writing a commentary on the Psalms. He looked for a model and found in Augustine's *Enarrationes* on the Psalms just what he needed for the purpose. Here was a highly educated later Roman, in whom all the traditional cultured taste for fine language was well developed, who found himself attracted by a different style of beauty, a spirituality for which late antiquity had no exact counterpart.

John of Salisbury is an example of the medieval civil servant whose intellectual tastes were painfully frustrated by the crude preferences of the courtiers around him. He was like a modern aesthete surrounded by sports enthusiasts, the medieval equivalent of drunken football fans, as he describes them in his *Policraticus*.

That is not to suggest that the pleasures of this sort of elevated conversation ceased to appeal with the Christianization of the Empire, but the opportunities to enjoy them diminished and changed. Adults discoursing as equals and for pleasure gave way to a teacher-and-taught paradigm, with a purpose of 'edification' replacing the exchange of views among equals. From the bishop's seat (*cathedra*) in the principal church of the diocese, the bishop taught the people. Sermons and lectures were almost indistinguishable in the lengthy exegetical series preached by Augustine or Gregory the Great.

The pleasures of shared mental stimulation or something like them appear in the colloquies or *Collationes* on matters of spiritual education Cassian records from conversations in his monastic community.[6] Gregory the Great's *Moralia* on the book of Job was the product of similar conversations with monks in the late sixth century. Anselm is said to have drawn about him circles of eager apprentice-philosophers at the monastery of Bec in the late eleventh century. In all these debates and discussions within the context of monastic life there is a presiding figure, with a teaching role, focusing the colloquy. But now – with rare exceptions known to us – tastes in subject matter and approach were changing. The objective had become not the shared exploration of philosophical and theological questions of common interest, but the earnest pursuit of a 'Christian' edification. When Anselm encouraged his monks to think like reasoning beings be was confident that the use of reason could lead them to only one set of conclusions, the orthodoxies of the Christian faith.

It is not that ancient conversationalists had not been serious. Ancient philosophy was strongly interested in the way of life which went with the metaphysics. Nevertheless the ancient world scarcely knew what we should now recognize as 'academic research'. Medieval people with lively minds began to see learning as a serious business in a new light, as a way to heaven. The question is what happened to bring about so radical a change of tastes and expectations in these two directions, and how far was it a product of the intellectual and social dominance of the Christian Church?

The first changes seem to have come about as a consequence of the breakdown of the 'school' system which had provided a high-class education for the governing classes since the days of the Republic and for many centuries in the city states of Greece. In late antiquity elementary school-masters taught the basics of reading, writing and arithmetic. These were not publicly funded posts and such masters were to be found even in small towns and villages. Well-born youths often had private tutors at this stage. Paid five times as much in the reign of the Emperor Diocletian (284–305) were the grammar and rhetoric masters. The children of the middle and upper classes went to a public teacher of grammar in one of the cities, where they often held official posts, appointed and salaried by the civil authorities. In the ancient world the citizen left school and joined a collegial body of citizens. In the early Middle Ages in the West the monasteries became the natural place to acquire the elements, but the quality of the teaching and the content depended on the availability within a given community of someone competent and willing to teach, and an adequate library.

There was also a dying away of the expectation that educated Romans would be able to read Greek as well as Latin, which is first noticeable in Augustine's complaint that he found the second language difficult to master, and more apparent still in the case of Gregory the Great, who does not seem to have learned Greek even though he spent some time in the Eastern Empire. Conversely, with the fall of the Empire, the Greek-speaking East had far fewer who could also read Latin. A significant consequence for the Church of this linguistic divide was to be the coming into being of two largely distinct streams of 'authorities', the Greek and Latin Fathers. It is not that there was no reading 'across the divide', but it was limited in extent. For example, the Greeks were aware of some of Augustine's ideas, and Rufinus translated some of the work of the controversial Greek Father Origen into Latin at the end of the fourth century.

More important for the history of the Church was the way the styles of the 'two cultures' diverged profoundly. The Greek speakers developed a Christian Platonism with a strong streak of mysticism. This could lead to some ways of expressing the faith which seemed of dubious orthodoxy as far as the Latins could understand what was being said. Yet the Greeks were more determined than the Latins to allow no change in or development of the original 'deposit' of the faith as it had been stated by the ecumenical Councils of the first five centuries.

Thanks to Boethius, the Latins were not completely cut off from Greek philosophical thought as it was to be read in the original texts of the philosophers. Boethius's idea was to transmit the ancient culture he feared would be lost to the Latin-speaking world by means of translations from the Greek of the works of Aristotle and Plato. He explains in his commentary on Aristotle's *De interpretatione* how he had planned to translate every work of Aristotle he could lay hands on, *in Romanum stilum*, and to provide each with a commentary in Latin: *eorum omnium commenta latina oratione perscribam.*[7] He was executed before he had got very far with this project, but he made some of the textbooks of Aristotelian logic available from the end of the ancient world.

Cassiodorus saw the same need that his contemporary Boethius identified, which was to try to salvage as much as possible from the culture which was disappearing. Cassiodorus, however, had a different solution, inspired by the needs he perceived within the monastic community he had newly founded on his own estate, at Vivarium (554), for resources to enable them to get the essentials of learning. When the 'soldiers of Christ (*milites Christi*) have filled their minds with holy reading (*divina lectione*) and consolidated their understanding with frequent meditation (*frequenti meditatione*) they can, he hopes, move on to his own little book (*verbum abbreviatum*) (Romans 9.28), where the things which need to be read are set out briefly in their most fitting places. Cassiodorus hopes that this will assist the reader in attaining salvation (*quae sunt salubriter tractata*). As a practical study-aid, he favoured the creation of a convenient digest, an 'encyclopaedia'. His *Institutiones* are divided into two parts, in the first of which he summarizes the essentials of the preliminary studies, the 'liberal arts', and in the second he holds out the importance of 'public masters' giving equal attention to the teaching of Christian writings and in particular the Scriptures. *Cum studia saecularium litterarum magno desiderio fervere cognoscerem, ... dolore permotus ut Scripturis divinis magistri publici deessent* (when they are so quick to teach secular authors).[8]

The other great change lay in the almost complete disappearance of the laity from the educational scene for many centuries. It is no coincidence that the English words 'clerk', 'clergy' and 'cleric' come from the same root, for education in reading and writing leading on to 'further' or 'higher' education now became largely the prerogative of those who were to become clergy. Broadly speaking the royal heads of early medieval and feudal Europe were not learned men, though a number had leanings in that direction, often expressed mainly through patronage. Some wealthy noblemen and royal persons had intellectual interests, however. The story of Charlemagne's touchingly ineffectual attempts to learn to read should not mislead anyone into thinking that his wits were not sharp and his policy-making compass not well positioned. Alfred the Great, King in England in the ninth century, has been credited with various translations into English, done by him or commissioned. Among them are Augustine's *Soliloquies*, Bede's *Historica Ecclesiastica*, Boethius's *Consolation of Philosophy*, the *Dialogues* of Gregory the Great, and Orosius's *History*.[9] This is a striking selection if it is to be supposed that even the most elevated of the

laity wished to read such works or hear such works read to them. But even
if there is exaggeration, this is evidence of a benevolent and encouraging
attitude to the importance of things of the mind. William of Aquitaine
(993–1030) kept 'plenty of books' in his palace, and if he chanced to have a
moment of leisure he would apply himself personally to reading, going on
late into the night until he was overcome by sleep, *Librorum copiam in pala-
tio suo servavit, et si forte a tumultu vacaret, lectioni per se ipsum operam dabat,
longioribus noctibus elucubrans in libris, donec somno vinceretur.*[10]

Nevertheless these seem to have been exceptional individuals. Walter
Map in his *De nugis curialium* remarks that the *generosi parcium nostrarum*,
the better-off of the land, are too idle or arrogant to put their children
to study (*aut dedignantur aut pigri sunt applicare literis liberos suos*). This is
important because it is the right of free men to learn the liberal arts (*cum
solis liberis de iure liceat artes addiscere, nam et inde liberales dicuntur*). Those
who have no such right, the *rustici*, on the other hand, *suos ignominiosos et
degeneres in artibus eis indebitis enutrire contendunt, non ut exeant a viciis sed
ut habundent diviciis, qui quanto fiunt periciores tanto perniciores.*[11] This states
the principle that the purpose of learning is to make the student virtuous.

Guibert of Nogent's mother was widowed and she wanted to do her
best for her son so she found him a grammar master through the media-
tion of the local clergy. His schoolroom of the end of the eleventh century
became the *studium generale* of the town. The master's previous pupil had
been a liar and badly behaved and kept running away and hiding, as he had
had no taste for literature. Guibert was a delight to teach by contrast and
was treated affectionately, although he was also frequently beaten because
his master was so determined that he should learn. Guibert says he studied every day and had scarcely a single holiday for six years.[12] Boys of 12
to 14 in London in about 1170 are described by William Fitzstephen as
holding informal matches in which the pupils of different schools tried to
outdo one another in linguistic games. The schools included St Paul's, St
Mary Arches and St Martin-le-Grand, all 'Church' schools, that is schools
attached to ecclesiastical institutions. This is elementary schooling, but
something more advanced was already available. It was already apparent
in the twelfth century that there were career-ladders for ambitious young
men to climb from a good education to influential positions in Church
and state. Students increasingly wanted the kind of advanced study which
was provided in the emerging universities, for career reasons. Well before
there was a university in the town, wandering teachers are known to have
taught in Oxford. Theobald of Étampes was there for four years around
1117, with as many as 50 pupils, which would have made a sizeable school.[13]
Robert Pullen (who is thought to have taught in Paris too) and the lawyer

Vacarius taught in Oxford in the 1130s and 1140s. Englishmen as well as scholars from abroad were teaching there: Robert Crickslade and Walter, Archdeacon of Oxford.[14] Even those who had left looked back nostalgically. The Bishop of Hereford, claims John of Salisbury, used to be avid for praise when he was in the schools (*laudi avarus erat*) and as much a lover of glory (*amator gloriae*) as he was a despiser of money. The present Bishop of Worcester, he suggests, may be won in much the same way, by letters from masters in the schools.

This was the era in which universities invented themselves in Western Europe. The study of Christian theology became an academic discipline and the 'canon' law of the Church also became the subject of systematic academic study. A civil service came into being which could write sophisticated letters for secular and ecclesiastical employers, citing earlier 'authorities' and reflecting contemporary academic opinions. When the Church held a council, academic consultants might be present, with all the difficulties that could create for the ecclesiastical authorities in determining their role. Controversial academics could gain a popular following and seem to be leading the faithful astray, and here too the ecclesiastical authorities might find themselves having to field a team at a council to rebut their arguments.

The universities of the north of Europe, led by Paris and Oxford, quickly became institutionalized, evolving on the model of a craft guild (*universitas* is another word for guild). A medieval guild combined features of the modern professional association and trade union. It had apprentices (the undergraduates) and journeymen, or qualified craftsmen who had not yet proceeded quite so far as to become masters of their craft (Bachelors of Arts), and Masters (Masters of Arts). The graduate who obtained his degree by examination was doing nothing essentially different from the master fishmonger who had to demonstrate an appropriate mastery of his craft in order to become a member of the Fishmongers' Guild. The masters in the craft of scholarship set and monitored the standards to be attained, not so much by requiring a level of attainment in students as in setting the content of the courses to be taught, their length and the number of series of lectures a student must have attended before he could graduate.

Oxford was referred to as a *universitas* before it is certain that it was yet a true corporation (with the royal grant of privilege to it as a corporation in 1231, the chancellor acting as the recipient, so that the grant was made to the university in his 'person').[15] Being a 'corporation' meant that the body of masters could be regarded as a legal person. Legally, it was a 'body' which could act like a human person in law, suing and being sued as a litigant.[16] The university *was* the free association of the established scholars in a guild (*universitas*) or corporation. It *was* the people who made it up, and they chose who to admit to membership of their 'body'.

The internal rules of the community or guild of scholars were largely of their own devising, but they were keen to seek the additional authority and protection of grants of privileges by state and Church. Ecclesiastical and secular authorities could be powerful allies for a university. A different model emerged at the Italian University of Bologna, where graduate student lawyers ran the University for their own convenience, hiring their lecturers and making the rules.

It would not be true to say that minds trained in one way never applied themselves to the mental exercises needed to live life in a different way, or that the new career of the professional academic was the only direction in which university study led. The twelfth century in particular is notable for the stories of academic retirements and movements between one way of life and another. Peter Abelard, for example, was alternately a monk and a lecturer in the schools, retiring at last to Cluny to a disappointed death. Gilbert, who made his name as a lecturer of extreme intellectual daring (although he was so obscure that it proved difficult to be sure what his challenge actually was), became Bishop of Poitiers. John of Salisbury became a senior civil servant after a dozen years as a student and ended his life as a bishop. He left the schools for the papal civil service and then moved on to the civil service of the King of England, Henry II. Eventually he became Bishop of Chartres.[17] Alan of Lille was one of a number of academics who favoured the Cistercian life in retirement.

So we can see the Church's control of clerisy slipping from its grasp as the universities of northern Europe became the first truly independent schools and discovered that they could both accept privilege and protection from the Church and defy it in the independence of their work.

An agreed syllabus of respectable authors

Part of the problem for the authors of the early medieval world was to get hold of books, to know where information was to be found. The modern reader can find a note on almost anything on the internet. But not everything to be found on the internet is reliable. It is necessary to possess a reasonable level of education and to know where to look for confirmation and alternative opinions in order to be able to judge. The modern reader shares with the early medieval enquirer the difficulty of knowing what trust is to be placed in the books he reads unless he can 'place them' in the scheme of knowledge.

The task which faced early medieval Christians who had a taste for the intellectual life, had questions in their heads about the faith, how to live the

Christian life and what they should believe, was how to find an authoritative ruling. We have already seen hints of the way they answered this question. Could classical moralists still be relied on, though they did not know Christ? Yes, on the basis of Romans 1.19, which says that everything which can be known about men and women has been revealed to them in the world which lies around them. Philosophers could therefore find out about God by studying his creation. Could the old skills of rhetoric have a place in Christian exegesis? Augustine had discussed that at length in the *De doctrina Christiana*, displaying much ingenuity in arriving at the answer yes.

The patristic period produced a number of authors who gradually attained a special status as 'Fathers'. We see Cassiodorus, some generations after Augustine and Jerome, viewing these Christian authorities as already respected. 'Let us ascend to Holy Scripture by way of the interpretations of the Fathers, as if by Jacob's Ladder' is Cassiodorus's call.[18] It is a cry which assumes that it is already possible to identify the 'Fathers', or at least some reliable writers whom Christians could trust, for the label 'Fathers' took time to become established.[19] That remained the practice in the Middle Ages but it now mattered not merely whether a text conveniently made a point but whether what it said was safe for the soul.

Jerome's 'On Notable Men'[20] became an influential list of 'safe' or reliable authors, prompting others to follow his example. Gennadius of Marseilles (fl.470) begins his own list[21] by referring to 'Our Jerome', ' outstanding in his learning in both Greek and Latin literature', *litteris Graecis ac Latinis Romae apprime eruditus*. Sigebert of Gembloux took the opportunity, while extending the list through the eleventh century, to add an extensive entry for himself in which he describes in some detail what he has written and the way he has approached the author's task: 'I have written many things for the instruction of the young', 'I have improved the style' in revising existing biographies of saints.[22] For the quality of the writing, looked at from a stylistic or literary point of view, remained important.

The beginning of theology as an academic study

In the West, the study of theology remained primarily the study of texts, with formal debate about disputed points of interpretation gradually being added as a forum for instruction from the twelfth century. The principal text was the Bible, and for a long time theology was known simply as 'the study of Holy Scripture', with the word *theologia* being restricted to those topics which had been studied by the philosophers of the ancient world with the aid of reason alone, and not relying on an 'inspired text'. (These were such questions as whether God exists, whether there is one God or many, how the world came into being.)

Clarembald of Arras, a student of Hugh of St Victor in Paris and Thierry of Chartres, was one of a group of scholars of the mid-twelfth century, teaching in northern France, who became interested in Boethius's 'theological tractates'.[23] This little group of short treatises deals mainly with questions which lie at the borderline between philosophy and theology. It was fashionable for a time to lecture on them; they presented interesting technical difficulties and they lay tantalizingly at the boundary between the classical secular authors and the Christian ones. They were the only real evidence that Boethius himself had been a Christian.

Clarembald commented on Boethius's book on the Trinity. He sent his interpretation to Master Odo, a student of Peter Lombard. Odo had been an academic but gave up the life to become a Cistercian at Ourscamp, where he was abbot from 1167 to 1170. Clarembald describes in his prefatory letter how, 'taking a few friends with me', he had gone to look at the *archivum* in the Church of St Vincent. On this visit a question was put to him. How exactly did the Creator breathe into the face of the first man (Genesis 2.7)? 'If only,' it was said reproachfully, 'you were as keen on such questions as on reading the secular authors such as Boethius and Aristotle.' Clarembald explains that while Aristotle was indeed a pagan, Boethius was not. The abbot was delighted to hear this and asked him to write his commentary on Boethius.[24]

But central to Christianity are other events which can be known only from history, as recorded in the text of the Gospels and Acts of the Apostles and the Epistles and so on, which could not be worked out by reason alone; they had to be 'revealed'. A full systematic 'theology' would need to explore these aspects of the faith and place them in the scheme of Christian belief, and that required assiduous study of the Bible. Theology was therefore dependent on reading. Reading for oneself or 'with' one's students therefore became the core process of 'doing theology', as 'doing theology' became increasingly sophisticated and turned itself into a recognizable academic discipline.

Quintilian comments on the contrast between listening, which is over in a flash, and reading to oneself, where it is possible to go back over what one is reading and work on it (*repetamus autem et tractemus*). Quintilian goes on to say something about the value of careful reading of the best models, for that alone will enable the student to understand how a good speech is constructed. This involves a mental mastication. In the late antique world it was quite usual for the individual to read aloud to himself.[25] (Gregory Nazianzus took a vow of silence for Lent in 382, but he spent the time writing about his silence and its implications.[26])

This foreshadows the method of reading encouraged in monastic life, where the individual reads slowly and reflectively, and also the custom of reading to the community at mealtimes, where mental and actual chewing went on simultaneously. For Quintilian's imagery of chewing and rumination is to be found much developed in the monastic practice of the Middle Ages. Benedict's Rule 42 says that whenever the brothers eat, they should sit down together and one of them should read improving matter such as the Lives of the Fathers, but nothing too testing, for there is a more appropriate time for the serious study of Scripture. The contemporary Rule of the Master (*Regula magistri*), whose precepts strongly influenced Benedict, has a similar idea, though it envisages that the monks will want to ask questions about the reading and that the abbot may need to say a few words of comment or clarification. Bede wrote a prefatory letter to Acca, Bishop of Hexham, who, he says, has stirred him from his torpor to compose the 'exposition' of the Acts of the Apostles which accompanies it. This has involved the very reverse of torpor – daily thought and study of the Scriptures (*meditandis scrutinandisque cotidie scriptures*), tireless and sleepless (*vigil atque indefessus*). He explains what he has tried to do, which is mainly to clarify and explain. 'Wherever anything seemed to be done mystically or said rather obscurely, I have tried to throw light on it.' He also mentions the conscious need to make a fair copy of the definitive version.[27]

The phrase 'holy reading', *lectio divina*, seems to refer at first to the holiness of what was read, Holy Scripture. But Caesarius of Arles describes in a sermon how the Christian ceases to spend much of his time in playing board games and begins to occupy himself in 'holy reading'. Such masticatory reading, properly digested, would both nourish the soul and direct the believer's activities. The Carthusians adopted the imagery of chewing and digestion. Their librarian was to regard the library as a table for the soul to eat at (*liberarium nostram esse mensam ... de qua sacre lectionis et sancti studii cibum sumimus*).

Hugh of St Victor's *Didascalicon* (which also bears the title *De studio legendi*, 'On the Study of Reading') explains that three things are needed in reading: to know what to read, what order to read things in, and how to read. For Hugh, reading and meditation are the two complementary routes to learning, of which *lectio* stands first (*priorem in doctrina obtinet locum*). 'The method of reading consists in division. Every division begins from finite things and goes on to infinity.' Finite things are better known and more easily understood. So learning starts with those and through knowledge of such things the learner progresses to knowledge of things which are hidden. Meditate about what you have read, he advises, and the meditation he has in mind is purposeful, even analytical. It will involve frequently and assiduously examining the cause and origin and 'method' and 'use' of each thing.

This style of reading changed again with the transformation of medieval cathedral and monastic 'school' into universities. From the time of Charlemagne there was strong encouragement to cathedrals to ensure that priests attached to them as canons had an adequate level of learning. There was formal 'lecturing'. 'Lecturing' (*lectio*) developed from 'reading' a text with a teacher. The process involved discussion and explanation and was quite different from monastic 'community reading' at mealtimes, though it seems to have been used in some form in monastic teaching, at least of the elements of grammar. In the late eleventh century, Anselm of Canterbury writes in a letter to a young monk about reading with, or literally 'from', a master called Arnulf (*a Arnulfo legere*).

The lecturer acted as commentator and critic, as he expounded and explained the text he was 'reading with' his students. This habit of commentary was central to medieval study. It could be extremely thorough, leaving no word unturned. A ninth-century commentary on Boethius's *De consolatione philosophiae* promises after the first *lemma* to expound this *per singula*, a bit at a time. The commentator patiently clarifies, defining words, giving some longer explanations, occasionally offering a paraphrase ('the sense is like this' (*sensus est talis*), or 'it is as though he had said' (*quasi diceret*)). It was apparently the custom of Gilbert of Poitiers not to omit a single word in explaining or commenting on a text, though there were complaints that his painstaking gloss was more obscure than the text. This almost literally 'pedestrian', certainly 'step-by-step' character, proceeding pace by pace, makes it all but impossible for the medieval critic to take a view of a work as a whole, except in the short standardized preliminary *accessus*. The process is essentially piecemeal.

Among the practical study aids to emerge at the end of the twelfth century to meet the needs of the growing crowds of students in a hurry to complete their courses, *Distinctiones* took the form of roughly alphabetical lists of occurrences of words in Scripture.[28] They greatly assisted the preacher to find parallel passages to cite as he expounded the themes suggested by his text for the day. Among the earliest, late-twelfth century examples are Peter the Chanter's *Summa Abel*, Peter of Poitiers's *Distinctiones super Psalterium* and Prepositinus of Cremona's *Summa super Psalterium*.[29] Alan of Lille's *Distinctiones* begins with a prologue in which he stresses how dangerous it is for the reader to remain ignorant of the force of theological terms in the Bible: *in sacra pagina periculosum est theologicorum nominum ignorare virtutes*. He promises more than to list them; he is to distinguish (*distinguere*) significations, metaphors and tropes, so that the way into the text may be laid open to the reader. Alan's work as a lexicographer was quite sophisticated. *Currere* (to run), for example, as used *proprie*, as in the Gospel, has John running faster than Peter (John 20.4); or it signifies the passage down the racecourse of this life, as in I Corinthians 9.24; or it can refer to anxiety about behaving badly (Psalms 49.18).

Teaching manuals began to appear on a wide range of subjects – some going far beyond the obvious academic areas – such as the *Dialogue on the Exchequer* (*Dialogus de scaccario*) of Richard FitzNigel.[30] And these signs that those engaging in reading for study and the obtaining of degrees now stood in need of a great deal of apparatus of many kinds if they were to swim purposefully in what had by now become a veritable sea of knowledge are not confined to the early generations of university study. Wyclif's work at the end of the fourteenth century was still attracting summaries to help readers along and also attempts to provide indexation and helpful lists of the biblical passages he had cited. These examples of a pedagogic response to a newly felt need to be able to 'find' texts or words, and 'place' them in a scheme of knowledge, gave rise to such practical improvements as the notion of the index and the idea of using alphabetical order, but its implications for the theory of interpretation and the understanding of what a text is are far more profound.

Given a text to study, the medieval way was to begin by 'accessing' it.[31] The lecturer read the text with his students. *Accessus* were very hard-wearing and adaptable ways of 'approaching' a text. There seems to have been more than one type. Eriugena (*c*.810–*c*.877), whom the Emperor appointed to be head of the Palace School at Laon, is credited with using the classical *circumstantiae* of forensic rhetoric. So the lecturer told his students who the author was, what book he had written, where he wrote it, with what aids, why, in what manner, and when. A simpler three-part system had evolved out of this by later Carolingian times. The seven had been boiled down to person, place and time ('who wrote this, where and when').

Alternatively the lecturer might use a different series of key points and talk about the life of the writer, the title of the piece of writing, what kind of writing it was, the intention of the author, the number and order of the sections in the work. The twelfth-century preference seems to have been for a somewhat hybrid sequence. First came the title, then the author's name (*nomen auctoris*), then the *intentio* of the writer, then the *materia libri*, its subject matter. This was followed by the way the subject matter has been handled (*modus scribendi* or *modus tractandi*), the parts of the book (*ordo libri*), the *utilitas*, or usefulness, and the branch of study to which it belongs (*cui parte philosophiae supponitur*).

John of Salisbury comments in one of his letters on the way one of the

Fathers (*patrum*) would approach the exposition of a text by setting out at the beginning the name of the author and his subject, the purpose for which the book was written, the *causa*, or reason for writing it, the title, what kind of book it is (*qualitas*), the intention of the author, and anything else which would assist the reader to understand it. This was a form of 'prologue' based on the Aristotelian quartet of the types or modes of causation: *causa finalis, formalis, efficens* and *materialis*. Here the interesting question for medieval Christian 'lecturers' was whether these types of causation could be identified with the Father, the Son, the Holy Spirit and the 'matter' of which the world is made. Henry of Ghent addresses the question 'Whether God is the author of Holy Scripture'. The same issue is raised by Richard Fishacre, Guerric of St Quentin and others, in their commentaries on sentences, for it had an attractive philosophical complexity.

The development of the academic lecture needs to be seen alongside another strand which is of importance because it shows a direct line of theological endeavour by the Church as distinct from the schools (although once there were universities they soon started having 'university sermons' and taking over the training of preachers). The main vehicle for the interpretation of Holy Scripture in the early Church was not lecturing but preaching, though a listener might have been hard put to tell the difference until he noticed that the preacher was exhorting and persuading as well as explaining and analysing. This multiple exegetical task was conceived of as the bishop's special responsibility in the first centuries, part of his task of maintenance of the faith, and he might engage in long series of sermons on a particular book of the Bible. Not all bishops preached in this way, but examples survive in Augustine's preaching on the Psalms and John's Gospel when he was Bishop of Hippo. Pope Gregory the Great's series on Ezekiel and I Kings are of the same kind. It is hard to say whether such sermons are homiletic or lecturing, for the distinction did not yet exist.

Early medieval preaching seems to have lost this habit. With a few notable exceptions, such as Bernard of Clairvaux's lengthy unfinished series on the Song of Songs, extended serial exegesis disappeared from the pulpit. The bishop's role subtly changed, until in the twelfth and thirteenth centuries they were rarely to be heard as preachers; the friars took over and an academic training taught a method of exposition of a 'text' for a sermon which was thematic rather than an extended exegesis.

But it did not disappear from the lecture room and as the universities developed their syllabus, theology students routinely studied the Bible by *lectio*, that is reading phrase by phrase with a lecturer explaining it to them. The medieval Church continued to regard God as Scripture's author, in the literal sense that he chose the words which were written down by the human authors of Scripture at his dictation. Pictures of the Evangelists placed at the beginning of the Gospels show the Holy Spirit in the form of a dove dictating the words with his beak in the ear of Matthew, Mark, Luke or John as he writes. East and West differed radically here, in that the medieval West could not read the New Testament in the original Greek text or the Old Testament in the Greek Septuagint. They used a Latin translation, indeed several, until Jerome produced a version which became known as the 'common' text or Vulgate. Although he did not pretend to have been inspired in this work, the Middle Ages in the West forgot or ignored him and studied the text with a care which could have been no more minute if each Latin word had dropped directly from the lips of God. The early exegetical preachers had expounded the Bible. Medieval Bible study was increasingly characterized by a need to explain the fact that God appeared to have chosen words whose sense was not always clear; they were even, quite often, seemingly contradictory. This was more of a worry in the West than the East, for the late Platonic mysticism of the Greek Church made such paradoxes mere indications of the profundity of the text. The West was more anxious for rational explanations. When the Apostle wrote to the faithful that they should believe and say the same thing, so that there might be no division among them, how was it that there was difference of opinion about the mystery of the Eucharist and the meaning of Jesus's words, 'Let this cup pass from me', asks the Carolingian Ratramnus of Corbie.[32] It was not that this did not strike Greek readers in the East, too, but they preferred to respond to it by celebrating the mystery rather than by attempting to explain it away.

The explanation devised and highly developed in the West was that this seeming contradictoriness is in fact a benevolent disposition of a God who knows that our sinfulness prevents our seeing things clearly.[33] Peter of Poitiers describes a number of advantages of the fact that the text of Scripture displays these characteristics. It mocks the conceit of the proud (*ut eorum altitudine superbos irrideret*), stirs up the lazy (*desidiosos excitaret*) and keeps the energetic on their toes by challenging them with its profundity (*strenuos profunditate acutos teneret*); the less highly educated are drawn onwards from the obvious to what is immediately apparent (*rudes per visibilia ad invisibilium notitiam exercitatos promoveret*). In all these ways this secrecy makes what is said more precious (*quo magis essent occulta pretiosiora faceret*).[34]

The expectation of both East and West was that the study of the Bible would endlessly repay care and thoroughness. Its riches are inexhaustible. No human insight into the meaning of Scripture which is in accordance with the truth can ever go beyond what God has already put there to be found.

It is, literally, all there for the seeking, for those with the patience and faith. But it proved necessary to devise a system for interpreting it which would deal with the problem of reading it as though it was entirely self-consistent. The Jewish exegetical tradition favoured keeping to the literal sense. It was the Christians who saw the advantages of figurative interpretation, for that was most helpful with the contradictions and anomalies. Augustine was still sufficiently impressed by the list of seven Rules of Tichonius the Donatist that in his essay on the interpretation of Scripture (the *De doctrina Christiana*) he was prepared to overlook the fact that Tichonius was a schismatic. Gregory the Great fixed on four levels of meaning, and those became the accepted set in the West throughout the Middle Ages.

In Gregory's system, the first, the literal or historical sense, remained the plain meaning of the text. It included 'historical' passages, but it was not confined to those. The literal meaning could be thought of as the author's plain intention. Paradoxically, if the 'intention' was to be figurative, to tell a story with a meaning, the figurative sense could become the literal sense. When Jesus told a parable he was using a metaphor. The sower who went forth to sow the seed, some of which fell on stony ground, was not a real person.

'Above' the literal sense were ranged 'higher' senses, which were also finer, spiritually more edifying. The Western medieval interpreter was sure they were higher. This architectural image of the relationship of the sense is rather strikingly described by Hugh of St Victor. He sees the literal sense as resembling the rough-hewn blocks and rubble which form the solid foundation of a building. Upon them are placed the higher senses which are like stones or blocks cut to fit, keyed into the rough pieces below, but much more elegantly fashioned.[35]

The three figurative senses recognized in the medieval West could be described collectively as 'allegorical'. Every figurative sense 'transfers' the meaning of a word or sentence from a 'proper' to a figurative meaning. 'Allegorical' can also be used to refer to a single one of those meanings, where nothing is involved beyond this transference. The anagogical or prophetic sense points to the future. The tropological or moral sense contains lessons for the living of a good Christian life, for example, the man who 'going down' from Jerusalem to Jericho falls among thieves: *descendebat ab Ierusalem in Iericho et incidit in latrones* (Luke 10.30). This was the sinner who 'goes down' from the Church into the sin of this world: *ab ecclesia in defectum huius mundi*, suggests Thomas of Chobham.[36]

Disputations and the emergence of a systematic theology

Out of this studium *sacrae scripturae* the West gradually fashioned a systematic theology, contemporaneously with the emergence of the universities, in which theology became uncontested queen of the sciences. Peter Abelard, having made his reputation as a logician, described how he went to listen to the lectures on the Bible of the most famous theologian of the day, Anselm of Laon. He had expected to see a tree full of leaves but he saw only bare branches, he claims in his autobiographical 'letter' describing all this. As a challenge he said he would himself lecture on Ezekiel, famously the most difficult of the prophets to interpret, and he would do it the very next day. Naturally Anselm's students flocked to hear him. And he complains that Anselm was jealous and that he became the subject of his resentment.[37] So the stirrings of academic rivalry among the theologian masters were noticeable from the very beginning, before universities formally existed at all. Examples survive of one master telling his students that another's opinions should be ignored and of students teasing masters with quotations from their rivals.

Abelard's own commentary, particularly that on Romans, illustrates the pressures which led to the next development. It is clear that as lecturing evolved during the twelfth century from the simple explanations of the meanings of words and cross-references which had been considered enough in earlier generations, a considerable body of disputed questions began to cluster round certain key passages. Peter Abelard breaks the flow in his commentary on Romans with a long digression into a very great question (*maxima ... quaestio*) which arises at this point (Romans 3.25). What can Paul mean when he speaks of justification in these terms? Abelard goes through a series of views on this point which can be shown to have been the subject of active contemporary debate. He mentions, only to dismiss it, the theory that the Devil had acquired some rights in humanity when Eve ate the apple. This was an idea being discussed at Laon, too, as he expected his readers to be aware. Abelard has a pedagogic principle in mind here, which is that being uncertain prompts one to enquire, and that by enquiring one learns the truth: *dubitando quippe ad inquisitionem venimus; inquirendo veritatem percipimus*.

With this kind of thing, *lectio* has become debate and it needed conscious justification as such. Dialogue had been used for teaching purposes in the ancient world. The 'Socratic' type of dialogue purported to be a conversation between a teacher and his pupils, in which a genuine exploration of an issue took place. It was the convention that this was polished up, and thus appeared far more purposeful than a conversation could be in real life; for in it the teacher succeeded in leading his pupils to the discoveries and conclusions he wished them to reach. Augustine made use of the genre in his *Cassiciacum* dialogues, which were 'records' of informal conversations with friends, and in the *De magistro*, a discussion with his son Adeodatus. Anselm of Canterbury did the same in a fair proportion of his monographs of the late eleventh and early twelfth centuries, undoubtedly in imitation of Augustine, though this was a method of teaching he himself found it natural to use in any case. Anselm's pupil Honorius says he chose the dialogue form because it had been used to good effect by respectable authorities before him. 'I turned my pen to the dialogue because it seemed good to the greatest philosophers, Socrates and Plato and Cicero and our own Augustine and Boethius. They have proved its usefulness as a method of introducing beginners to a subject.'

In the mid-twelfth century, William of Conches provides a useful sketch which recognizes three kinds of dialogue. *Collocutio* is of three kinds, he suggests, between teacher and learner (*inter docentem et discentem*), between equals who are engaged in a sequence of question and response in which neither is the pupil (*inter interrogantem et respondentem*), and where the speaker or writer is simply addressing the listener or reader in *continua oratione*, such as a narrative (*enarrativum*) or a commentary (*hermeneuticum id est interpretativum*).

The academic disputation took the form of a session set aside to deal with major questions arising in the course of a lecture on a text, on which there was a good deal to say for and against, with reference to the authorities. Early examples are the mid-twelfth century *Disputationes* of Simon of Tournai. Disputation XXXV, for example, presents 'five questions for today: whether God always wills what he once wills, whether prophecies necessarily have to be fulfilled, whether a prophecy already fulfilled is still true, whether God loves every creature equally, whether man ought to love every good thing. Each of these is dealt with by putting the arguments on either side and proposing one or more solutions, citing a series of *auctoritates* in support of each, wherever possible (*ait enim auctoritas*). There is also reasoning. Not all prophecies once fulfilled can remain true; otherwise the statement in the future tense, 'the Virgin will conceive', would still be true. The disputation became an established teaching method and as a genre it eventually got something of a stranglehold on medieval scholarly debate. For Thomas Aquinas it had become difficult to preserve the proportionality which could keep a minor matter in a subordinate place and allow a major matter to take prominence. The *Summa theologiae* was a *tour de force* of treating everything at the same level of detail and as though its topics were all equally important.

One of the early 'disputations' considered by Simon of Tournai and his mid-twelfth-century pupils concerned whether every petition of Christ was 'heard' by the Father. Christ asked that the 'cup' of his crucifixion should pass from him (Matthew 26.39). It did not. So it seems that the Father did not hear this petition. *Ergo non in hoc exauditus est.* Can this be so?[38] Simon's contemporary, Robert of Melun, asks the same question, which tells us that it had become fashionable. Robert relays points from what was evidently a considerable debate here. If Christ asked for something he ought not to have, his *petitio* was *iniusta*, and to say that of Christ is wicked (*nefas*). If he expressed a will which was not that of the Father, Jesus's will was contrary to the divine will. These things cannot be possible. Some say that his request was conditional (that he should have what he asked for if it was his father's will). Some say that he spoke as he did *quia nulla necessitate, sed voluntate spontanea passus est Christus.* Robert's own view is that those who see into this more penetratingly (*acutius*), say that in speaking these words Christ made no petition. He simply showed his true humanity in the fear of death.[39]

From the early thirteenth century, Peter Lombard's *Sentences* became the standard textbook for theologians alongside the Bible. In it he assembled a systematic theology, under topic headings, with reference to the body of authoritative opinions, so that students could take stock of the areas of dispute and disagreement. He included extracts from patristic authorities so that students could compare points of disagreement. The book had an uncertain reception at first because it became embroiled in controversy about the position Peter Lombard appeared to have taken on the doctrine of the Trinity. But within a generation it had established a key position in the syllabus of theological studies. For several centuries every budding theologian commented on it.

Robert Grosseteste served his period of regency in theology in about 1230–35. Peter Lombard's *Sentences* had not yet fully established themselves as the basic textbook of the systematic theology course and it was historically too soon for him to think of writing a *summa.* Grosseteste's writings reflect the resulting lack of system, but they also suggest that he felt it. He made some experimental ventures into tabulation, indexing and referencing, in which his arrangement of themes foreshadows that of future *summa* literature. The extremely important point is made that the development of a systematic approach, which relies on rational argument, was not in itself a departure from the twelfth-century tradition that theology is the study of Scripture. The two methods are complementary, as Grosseteste's commentary on the *Hexaemeron* makes plain. The second section of the book takes three main areas of theological debate in turn: the Trinity and infinity of

God, the necessity of the Incarnation and the work of the Church in the 'deification' of humanity. Ginther shows how Grosseteste is able to maintain conservative positions in novel ways. Is God the form of created things?, he is asked in a letter. God is both the maker who shapes created things and the presence within which they are maintained in their shapes.[40]

Academics and controversy

Polemic was not an invention of the twelfth century. It sprang up much earlier than that, from debates about points of doctrine, such as the one which occupied the early Church for so long in the Arian controversy.[41] It continued in the Middle Ages, for instance in quarters where there was indignation at the worldliness and corruption displayed by some of the higher clergy. But polemic was a natural concomitant of the rise of academe. Waspishness and rivalry arrived with the first beginnings of the universities. Peter Abelard speaks with feeling of those who are envious of him and therefore his detractors.[42] Gerhoch of Reichersberg was one of the more turbulent bishops of the mid-twelfth century, and he fell out with a number of leading academics and fellow ecclesiastics, especially on matters of Christology which were controversial in the 1140s in the environs of Peter Abelard. But he also quarrelled with Eberhard II, Bishop of Bamberg, and Peter of Vienna, a disciple of Gilbert's.[43] Walter of St Victor, successor of Richard of St Victor, wrote a polemic against the 'four labyrinths of France', Peter Abelard, Gilbert of Poitiers, Peter Lombard and Peter of Poitiers, probably in 1177–78. The treatise on the 'four labyrinths' is an acknowledgement of the power of writing and teaching to influence minds and affect events. That is why the work of the individuals labelled the 'four labyrinths' is causing so much alarm. Walter's contention is that these are the *novi heretici*. The book, heated and perhaps consequently often confused in structure, nevertheless sets out to be a *summa contra gentiles*. This indicates the presence of passionate divisions of opinion among scholars. 'Whoever reads them will not doubt that the "four labyrinths"… puffed up with an Aristotelian spirit [*Aristotelico spiritu afflatus*] … write about the ineffable subjects of the Holy Trinity and the Incarnation with scholastic levity [*scolastica levitate*].' The debates drew in the Church, for when it came to theological topics, the justification for attack on the opinions of others was commonly that the 'others' were guilty of heresy. Lanfranc condemned his former pupil Anselm for presuming to write a book, the *Monologion*, which, however faithful it was to Augustine's teaching, neglected to quote him in support of its arguments. Peter Abelard was tried twice for his opinions, because he seemed to the ecclesiastical authorities to be a danger to the faithful. The pope told Gilbert of Poitiers to correct certain statements made in his commentary on Boethius's *De Trinitate*.[44] Gilbert, too, was tried, at the Council of Rheims in 1148.

By these processes, the Middle Ages turned theology into an academic discipline, in which all the points which had been the subject of dispute were drawn together into a systematic structure. It was recognized that this had happened before. Hugutio of Ferrara, in his commentary on the Apostles' Creed, explains how the Apostles, about to disperse to obey the command to go forth and preach the Gospel to all peoples, met to agree what they were to say about the faith, 'lest any discord or dissonance be discovered in their preaching, and so that none would differ from another in the holding, preaching and teaching of the faith'.[45] But the medieval achievement was on an altogether grander scale.

CHAPTER 10

Arts to the Glory of God

Honour or idolatry?

Christian artistic endeavour in the Middle Ages made no real separation between craft and what modern generations treat as 'fine art'. The making of pictures, statues, buildings and the 'performance' of worship shared two main conscious purposes. One was to do honour to or 'glorify' God, and for that purpose things that were made had to be dressed in their best. The other was to instruct the faithful. Sense-perceptions had an accepted place in the 'educational' use of things. As Augustine put it in the *De doctrina Christiana*, 'In the sacrament of his body and blood [the Lord] signified his wishes through the sense of taste.'[1]

Nevertheless awkward questions bristled everywhere. Even the use of light relief, the small visual witticisms of medieval art such as gargoyles, was not unproblematic. Bernard of Clairvaux famously asked 'What is that ridiculous monstrosity doing?' His chief criticism is reserved for the depiction of creatures which do not really exist, beasts with many heads, and so on. The problem is, he suggests, that people find them distracting and spend their time puzzling over them instead of meditating on the law of God.[2] He recognized that the faithful could be led astray by representational art rather than being helped by it to a more profound devotion.

The first concern was that creating representational images of anything which could be mistaken for a god (saints, the Virgin Mary), particularly if it was done well enough to 'compel' by the beauty of the likeness, might lead to idolatry. There appears to be a perfectly clear commandment that the worshippers of the true God are not to make 'graven images' of anything at all (Exodus 20.4; Deuteronomy 5.8). This anxiety was already a commonplace in the Old Testament, which meant that Christian writers were repeatedly reminded of it. They understood how easy it was to slip into idolatry, the picture or statue – even the bread and wine – becoming confused with the holy thing it represented, so that people worshipped the externals their senses perceived rather than the mystery or holy thing they stood for. Here the theologians of the Western Church broadly adopted the approach to signs and sign-theory which had been worked out by Augustine of Hippo in the first part of his book *De doctrina Christiana*. 'Things are learned through signs,' he begins.[3] He makes a distinction between signs used in ways 'instituted by humans',[4] which leads to 'worshipping the created order or part of it as if it were God' – or even the making of compacts with demons – and the signs God himself has provided as means of learning about him. 'What the apostle says about idols and the sacrifices made in their honour must guide our attitude to all these fanciful signs which draw people to the worship of idols or to the worship of the created order or any parts of it as though they were God.'[5] By contrast the right use of signs makes them edifying. 'Instead of many signs there are now but a few signs, simple when performed, inspiring when understood, and holy when practised, given to us by the teaching of our lord himself and the apostles, such as the sacrament of baptism and the celebration of the lord's body and blood.'[6]

The danger of idolatry was heightened where the object was seductive to the senses. For artistic representation of holy things in the Middle Ages made a number of tacit or conscious assumptions about what was appropriate if the image was to do honour to its subject. Holy things were thought to deserve representation in appropriately precious substances. For the Virgin, for example, crystal and ivory were fitting. This expectation extended beyond pictures and statutes to buildings and hangings. Books were treasures too, and Bibles might be bound with gold and gems.[7] In the records of archives and libraries which survive from the late eleventh and twelfth centuries (for Lanfranc, Archbishop of Canterbury, encouraged the bishops he appointed to attend to such list-making), it becomes clear that they were often kept with the relics and precious objects of a monastery or cathedral.

The paradox was that the more beautiful something was made – the more it delighted the senses – the more likely it was that people might stop in awestruck contemplation of the image and worship that instead of the thing it represented.

> A man that looks on glass,
> On it may stay his eye,
> Or if he pleases through it pass,
> And then the heaven espy.[8]

That reverence, or even respect, could readily mutate into a worship which treats the thing revered as a god was only too well known to the early Church. One of the anxieties of the monotheistic religions which emerged from antiquity was to ensure that there was no relapsing into polytheism.

'You shall have no other gods but me' is the second of the Ten Commandments (Exodus 20.3). Numerous Old Testament passages warn the Israelites
not to go whoring after other gods, and it is not always clear that these other
gods are not thought to be gods at all (for example, Deuteronomy 6.14, 11.28,
28.14). The leading idea is that God is a jealous God and will not tolerate
rivals for worship among his people. This theme was still causing anxiety in
the New Testament. I Corinthians 10.20–2 begs Christians to have nothing
to do with the worship of idols and hints at the divine jealousy.

All this was not a great anxiety to the Church in the West at first. Pope
Gregory the Great tended to think that icons were a useful medium for
the education of an illiterate laity. But concern had gained a new impetus
with the rise of Islam. Islam forbade any making of images of living things
in case they became a temptation to worship any but the one God, and
in the east of Europe and the Middle East, Christian and Muslim lived
in the same territories, so that Christians were reminded visually of the
self-imposed restraints of art in Islam. John of Damascus (c.660–750) had
begun his career at Damascus as a civil servant known as Mansur, in the
fiscal department of the court of the caliph. This was in a family tradition,
and many Christians worked comfortably in the service of the regime in a
similar way, but he left when the caliph began to insist on running things in
a more thoroughgoing Muslim manner and he ceased to be able to accommodate himself to the new requirements as a Christian. It is not impossible
that his attitude to icons was influenced by a reaction, understandable in
the circumstances, against the Islamic rejection of the use of images, for he
wrote three treatises in favour of icons while he was a monk in a monastery
near Jerusalem (and probably not a subject of the Byzantine emperor at
all).[9]

John argues that Scripture must be read 'with discretion' and it has to be
recognized that it speaks in various ways. Its instructions need not be taken
as though they applied to everyone in the same way at all times. He argues
that the ban on image-making was designed for the Jews, who were 'still
infants and ill with a diseased inclination to idolatry, apt to regard idols as
Gods and venerate them as gods and reject the veneration of god and offer
his glory to the creation'.[10] It was not the making of the images but the uses
to which they were put that was forbidden, suggests John.

In putting his case for the opposite view, that images are not only
allowed but desirable, John gives extensive definitions of 'icon' and 'veneration'. His first proposition is that creation itself is a divine image-making
activity, since God made man in his own image and likeness. (There was
to be much medieval theorizing about the proper 'use' of images, taking as
a key text Genesis 1.26 with its statement that human beings were made in

the image and likeness of God, and its implication that it is their life's task to enhance that likeness as far as they can.) Even the Son can be seen as an image, suggests John: 'God himself first begat his Only-begotten Son and Word, his living and natural image, the exact imprint of his eternity.'[11]

The theory he was framing was that glimpses of God in the Old Testament were figures and images of 'one who was yet to come. For the invisible Son and Word of God was about to become truly human, that he might be united to our nature and seen upon earth.'[12] Image-making thus becomes an action of God himself, authorized and approved by him and fundamental to the Trinity itself. In his third treatise John of Damascus sets about the definition of veneration. 'Veneration ... is a sign of submission, that is of subordination and humility.'[13] The first kind of veneration is worship, which is to be offered to God alone and may take the form of service or of wonder and desire or of thanksgiving or repentance.[14]

He approves of veneration being extended to creatures, on the principle that some saints have so 'worked with God', with God indwelling in them, that veneration for the saint is veneration for God. He also approves of veneration of those 'creatures' through which God worked our salvation, such as the wood of the Cross or the holy place of Golgotha.[15]

The essence of his argument is that the veneration of icons is something quite different from the worship of idols. It does not distract from but leads back to the worship of God which is the only proper activity of Christians. John's understanding of these matters was undoubtedly influenced by his knowledge of the thinking of the Palestinian monks whose life he had embraced, and who were highly conscious of their responsibilities as curators and protectors of the holy places of Christendom.

The first serious outbreak of 'official' concern in the East occurred when in 726 Leo III, the Byzantine Emperor, ordered the destruction of icons; thus began more than 50 years of controversy over icons and outright iconoclasm in the Church in the East. The Patriarch of Constantinople, Germanus I, objected and the Emperor sought to force him to resign. The Patriarch appealed to Rome. Germanus was deposed in 730, when the Emperor set about systematic persecution of those who would not obey his decree. He issued an edict in 730 formalizing his insistence that icons be destroyed.

Rome disapproved of the Emperor's action, for in the West icons remained important to the faithful, and they still tended to be regarded as a help rather than a dangerous distraction, a pastoral aid for those who did not have enough learning to master a written theology. Two synods were held in Rome in 731 which condemned the iconoclasts. Nevertheless some effort was made in Rome to consider the positions of both sides. The fifth- and sixth-century translation of the Greek Canons by Dionysius Exiguus was put into the Roman Chancery in 774, together with papal decretals. The events which follow underline the extent to which the Church in the two ends of the old Roman Empire was now drifting into two increasingly distinct parts.

The Second Council of Nicaea of 787 invited representatives from Rome. Those who attended do not seem to have understood very clearly what was going on, for the language divide was by now a serious impediment to discourse between East and West. The Council decreed that icons should be allowed again and set out careful rules for the way they were to be venerated and how much. The 'Definition of the Faith' made by the Council emphasizes that Christ 'redeemed us from the darkness of idolatrous insanity'. It goes on to argue that some have misunderstood this and have set their faces against 'the beauty pleasing to God established in the holy monuments'. They have mistakenly held that 'the icons of the Lord and his saints were not different from the wooden images of satanic idols'. Therefore the present Council has been held and it has decreed that 'the production of representational art ... is quite in harmony with the history of the spread of the Gospel, as it provides confirmation that in becoming man the Word of God was real and not just imaginary, and as it brings us a similar benefit. For, things that mutually illustrate one another undoubtedly possess one another's message.'[16]

The Latins' incomprehension is understandable, for the exact meaning to be placed on certain key words was not easily rendered in Latin. A translation containing errors was sent to the Emperor Charlemagne by Pope Hadrian (772–95). The word *latreia* had been misunderstood and the West was led to believe that the Council had sanctioned the worship of idols. Indeed the West had got the impression that it had been decided at Nicaea that images were to be worshipped in the same way as the Trinity. In reality the text spoke merely of doing honour to icons and makes a clear distinction between such showing of a proper respect and the worship proper to the Trinity.

Indignantly the *Libri Carolini*, 'Charles's Books' or the 'Caroline Books', were issued as a manifesto against the Council by Theodulph, Bishop of Orléans, with the Emperor's sanction. Theodulph was a Visigoth by origin, who came from Spain, where Islam was already conqueror of the territory. His *Opus Caroli Regis contra Synodum* ('Work of Charles the King against the Council') condemned councils which allowed images any spiritual value or permitted any use to be made of them except for purposes of instruction of the unlettered.[17] The pictorial narratives of Bible stories had been approved for teaching purposes by Gregory the Great, so it was difficult for him to disapprove of that.

There the matter rested for much of the earlier Middle Ages, with an uneasy sensitivity on the subject in the Eastern Church and a tendency to robust acceptance of the benefits in the West. In the West the assumption that images and objects both holy and beautiful might be pastorally helpful and aids to right living persisted. But it did not go unexamined.

A positive construction was placed on the work of the artist by some. A treatise on painterly techniques (*De diversis artibus*) by 'Theophilus' is difficult to date. It has been positioned in the ninth, tenth, eleventh and even twelfth centuries. It is chiefly concerned with practical questions about the mixing of paints. Yet the author explains painstakingly that although humankind lost the privilege of immortality when Adam sinned, there was no loss of that capacity for artistic expression (*artis ingeniique capacitatem*) in which man was made in God's image. It was the divine disposition (*dispositio divina)* which created this capacity in man for the glory of his name, and a devout people use this talent as God intended. He has therefore written a book on how to mix paints and like subjects.[18]

Theophilus thus proposes a theory which constitutes a riposte to the concerns of the iconoclasts, though there is no reason to suppose that he was consciously answering them from his Western vantage point: 'Whoever you may be, whose heart is inspired by God to investigate the vast field of the various arts and apply your mind and care in order to gather from it what pleases you, ... if you will diligently examine it, you will find ... whatever kinds and blends of various colours Greece possesses: whatever Russia knows of workmanship in enamels or variety of Niello: whatever Arabia adorns with repoussé or cast work, or engravings in relief: whatever gold embellishments Italy applies to various vessels or to the carving of gems and ivories: whatever France esteems in her precious variety of windows: whatever skilled Germany praises.'

Another form of positive approval in the West derived from the pervasive enthusiasm for relics. The question Guibert of Nogent seeks to address is whether it is desirable to show these reverence and honour. This question could arise with reference not only to the relics themselves but to their containers. Richly decorated reliquaries as well as Gospel books and antiphonaries made for cathedrals and wealthy monasteries, could be regarded as holy objects in their own right and be revered like relics. A relic is not in itself an artefact, but holy objects tended to be enclosed in lovely boxes, and the faithful have their senses teased by the reliquary while their minds were supposed to be fixed on the relic within. The 'structure' was analogous with that of an outward and visible sign or an inward and spiritual truth in Augustine's doctrine of the sacraments. Guibert of Nogent, writing *De pignoribus* ('On Relics'), takes as his starting point salvation and what is required to achieve it. Some things are essential (things without which one cannot live rightly). Others are beneficial but are not requirements (for example, fasting or singing psalms).[19] Among those things which are not counted among the essentials are the veneration of the saints and relics of those bodies. So veneration of relics in beautiful boxes is not required but it is by no means forbidden, and the message Guibert has for his readers about such things is positive.

Much later in the medieval West the question of inappropriate veneration of things which were meant to stand for God and not to be treated as gods became controversial, but that story belongs to the next volume in this series.

Aesthetic principle

The Arts and Crafts Movement in late nineteenth- and early twentieth-century Britain involved a group of painters and craftsmen and designers who shared the belief that good design is beautiful because it is useful, and that, conversely, the useful need not be ugly. John Ruskin (1819–1900) ran drawing classes for working men, and there were aspirations to transform society as well as the appearance of houses and their interiors. On this understanding, beauty and the value of all members of society and the dignity of what each person did were essentially one. Medieval aesthetics began from a similarly Platonic-and-utilitarian conception of the harmony of all that is good and useful with a beautiful appearance. This harmony was symmetrical. The balance involved tended to exclude the jagged excitements of a modern aesthetic of the unexpected, the challenge of the ugly and distorted.

Utilitas in the medieval West had a different emphasis from John Stuart Mill's utilitarianism, and different again from the 'utility' of the twentieth century. Modern 'utility' implies a plain functionality in which considerations of aesthetics need not be important. Mill had a notion of 'utility' which included 'usefulness' in the sense of 'benefit'. This was closer to the medieval idea, but for the Middle Ages the benefit was spiritual.

Within the general aesthetic Christianity inherited from antiquity and made its own was a conscious sense of 'style'. This was perhaps most developed in the realm of letters, where every educated Roman was taught to adapt his style to the subject matter and purpose of what he was writing, ranging from plain language to elaborate use of decorative figures. But the notion of style was broader. There were fashions in visual design and liturgical and theatrical performance.

A more publicly visible focus of stylistic change was architectural. In architecture, influences went far beyond the local. The guilds of masons were a notable exception to the pattern in other 'trades' of setting up in business in one place, whether as the local fishmongers or the local goldsmiths, and defending the territory stoutly against invasion by other guilds practising the same craft. When it came to building cathedrals there would eventually come a time to move on. Each diocese needed only one. In the building and decoration of cathedrals and sometimes the more important churches, there was an incentive to be up-to-the-minute, and styles travelled, with the result that 'Romanesque' and 'Gothic' developed recognizable common features as the fashion changed, but at the same time the local craftsmen left their idiosyncratic marks.[20] In the later Middle Ages, the Venetians were particularly prominent in borrowing styles from other places. Artistic influence is still visible in the surviving architecture. St Mark's in Venice is a Byzantine church.

Issues of theological principle could arise in architecture and building as in other branches of the visual arts. The Cistercians chose to build simply, precisely because they did not want their order to go the way of the Benedictines until the purity of its conception was sullied by an accretion of wealth. Hélinand of Froidmont mistrusted cities. He was more comfortable in the Cistercian wilderness, for the city seemed to him to embody all that was antithetical to the simplicity of life Cistercians should aspire to. Big building projects he considered the work of the Devil. Hélinand had studied in the cathedral school at Beauvais when Ralph of Beauvais was teaching there, and he was critical of greedy students and hypocritical teachers who did not seek to maintain standards of integrity of life among their students. Cities foment heresy.[21] Peter of Celle regarded Paris as an attractive deceiver of souls.[22]

In church buildings, even within such dangerous environments, as well as in the humbler depictions in small rural churches, pictures in the form of frescoes could provide a visual narrative for the instruction of the faithful. Both Eastern and Western Churches favoured this method, but the East kept the outsides of church buildings plain, while in the West decoration is also to be found on the outside in the form of soaring pinnacles stretching to heaven. Western travellers and diplomats had brought Greek ideas of the latest in design in pictures to the West, especially in the tenth and eleventh centuries, and Eastern design makes its mark on painting in particular.[23]

Music, performance and liturgy as a form of theatre

More than the visual impact of pictures and buildings was at issue. There was sound, too, and especially 'performance' art. The annual round of worship during the liturgical year, its great feasts and fasts, commemorating important episodes in the Christian story, all involved the arts.

Augustine had mistrusted theatrical performances because he had, personally, found them so seductive. But that was because they involved the acting out of unedifying stories. Christian worship, especially hymn singing, indeed the whole 'scene' of the liturgy, struck him quite differently. Here was the natural forum for the 'performance art' of the medieval Church. The Studios monastery in Constantinople became a main centre of Byzantine hymn-writing from early in the ninth century. It already had a reputation for orthodoxy because of the stand it had taken during the iconoclast period, it had a major school of calligraphy and its monks were known as 'sleepless' because the community prayed perpetually, day and night. In the century when the West was crusading, Byzantium under the Comnenian Emperors was busy developing an iconography which celebrated the Greek liturgy as an act of worship in which earth and heaven were joined together. Angels sang overhead and bishops were portrayed in the apse celebrating the Eucharist.[24] For Eastern Christians, such pictures and their significances had immense vitality. Liturgy visibly held theology by one hand and life by the other. The iconography of the same period in Byzantium encouraged private as well as public devotion. Family churches and privately sponsored monasteries multiplied. For these a new iconography of affecting scenes and strong personal emotion was found appropriate. The Virgin Mary faints at the crucifixion of her Son.[25]

There was 'liturgical' art in the West too. Jacques de Vitry sees liturgical drama as a teaching aid, and also as echoing the courtroom drama of forensic rhetoric. St Trond was founded in about 660 by the saint who gave the house his name, who had been educated at Metz. In 1108 Rudolf became abbot and encouraged the compilation of a chronicle which was continued until his death in 1138 and then brought up to date to 1180. The same period of lively intellectual activity in the abbey saw the production of a lectionary with seven miniatures.[26] There was an enthusiasm for singing in the West, too, including the singing of the congregation.[27] Liturgical drama could include actual theatrical performances. Then there were the *Comediae*, versified dialogues surviving from the Loire valley in the mid-twelfth century, which may never have been performed, although their liveliness and dramatic tightness make it tempting to suspect that they were an early form of secular theatre, inspired by Roman comedies, of which copies were to be had even in sober monastic libraries.[28]

This visual theatre was not supposed to spill over into dress and behaviour which could secularize. Early canon law had required that clerics should dress soberly in public and wear a tonsure.[29] Red and green were especially prohibited for priestly wear, as was the wearing of stripes.[30] In the Middle Ages members of monastic orders were routinely forbidden fancy clothing, which suggests that the restriction had to be enforced, as it must have been where so many came from noble families and were used to fine clothing. For example, nuns were forbidden to work their sewing in silks except where the embroideries were for liturgical or other strictly religious use. Canon 16 of the Fourth Lateran Council sets out restrictions with regard to dress[31] which especially needed enforcement in the case of priests and canons who were not living in enclosed orders with an appropriate habit. A cleric had to look sober and not be dressed like a young man-about-town.[32] Canon 16 of the Fourth Lateran Council stated that 'Clerics should not practice callings or business of a secular nature, especially those that are dishonourable. They should not watch mimes, entertainers and actors. Let them avoid taverns altogether ... not play games of chance or of dice, not be present at such games.' Then clothes rules follow. Bishops who have been monks should wear habits.[33]

Patronage

Nor could the arts be separated from the social and economic considerations which encouraged the wealthy and influential to want to associate their names with the production and bestowal of lovely religious objects. Some patron bishops were anxious not only to get copies of books made for the cathedral libraries of the Carolingian world, but also to make them beautiful.[34] The visual difference between fine copies and scholars' working books becomes obvious at a glance in the later Middle Ages, but even much earlier, important questions about respect for the text itself were inseparable from the urge of patrons to provide books. Charlemagne ordered that the Gospel text be purged of the mistakes of copying which had got into it, and copies made and distributed which would be worthy of the importance of the text. The scholarly work seems to have been carried out under the supervision of Alcuin and when the pope sent him a copy of the Roman Sacramentary, Charlemagne gave instructions that copies be made for use in churches. Patrons connected with the court of Louis the Pious were continuing a practice which had been under way since 794 at Aachen, where a court school was producing and illuminating books.[35]

There was a transition from patronage of this Carolingian sort, focused on the provision of books where there was a lack of copies and the future of learning was at stake, to patronage directed less at needs than at desires. While he was on crusade (1248–54), St Louis, King of France, heard that a great sultan of the Saracens had given instructions that there should be a systematic search for copies of all the books his philosophers might find useful. These he had copied and kept them in his library where scholars might consult them. Louis decided that when he returned to France he would do the same, for otherwise the children of darkness would outdo the children of light. His own instructions were that copies should be made of the Bible and any writings which would throw light upon its meaning, and his idea was that the members of his own household (*familiaris sui*) should be able to study the result. In his will he distributed the library to the houses of the religious orders. Blanche of Castile, Louis's mother, had educated him herself and had a hand in the creation of the Bible *moralisée*, which illustrated both the actual passage and its moral sense. It was the view of Alfonso X of Castile, Blanche's great-nephew, that it was one of the duties of a royal wife to educate her children herself and ensure that they could read and understand the Psalter. Gospel books with full-page frontispieces and cycles of illustration[36] had a 'user-friendliness' for rich patrons, perhaps comparable in their devotional attractiveness with the coffee-table books of the later medieval West, such as books of hours.

Pictures in books were less likely to 'reach' the ordinary faithful in the earlier medieval period. The arrival in the late Middle Ages of a class of wealthy bourgeoisie who could commission works of art for their own delight led to the creation of lavishly illustrated books of hours. In one sense these were still being made beautiful for the glory of God. But they were undoubtedly also being made beautiful for the fame of the owner and to keep up with the Joneses.[37]

It would be a mistake to think of such popular interest in books with pictures as entirely confined to these later generations or pious lay patrons, however. Matilda, Countess of Tuscany (1055–1115), became her father's sole heiress in 1055 at the age of six when her brother died. She had the benefit of the support of a stepfather, Godfrey of Lorraine, but in her own right she was a cultivated woman, a tough ruler and a great supporter of the papacy in its wars with the Empire. Her piety was responsible for a number of benefactions to the monastery of San Benedetto di Polirone, which gave her body a resting-place and promised that as long as the community lasted a place should be laid for her at the monastery's table and the food of one monk should be given on her behalf to the poor. In gratitude the community gave her a Gospel book in which are some of the most important early examples of scenes from the Life of Christ.[38] The visions of Hildegard of Bingen (1098–1179) had accompanying pictures in copies held in houses of religious women, portraying Love and the Trinity or Christ in the Trinity, in striking diagrams.[39] She herself wrote of the inward meaning revealed to her, uneducated though she was, in visions which she experiences as flames striking her soul and teaching it to understand.[40] Manuscripts of saints' Lives were sometimes beautifully illuminated and provided with pictures representing episodes.

An underlying question is what purpose a picture served for someone who was able to read the words. Pictures could reinforce the message of the text, even interpret it. The portraits of the Evangelists in the earliest surviving Gospel books tend to be derived from representations of philosophers in antiquity. This continued even when such pictures would have lost their natural associations for the generation they were made for. Such a sixth-century manuscript of the Gospels[41] was owned by the community of St Augustine's, Canterbury, probably from early in its life. It has corrections of the seventh or eighth century made in England, and it was certainly at the monastery by the eleventh century. It may even have been used by Augustine of Canterbury himself, for Bede says that Gregory the Great sent him books to assist him in his mission.[42]

Pictures could even form a parallel 'text' in their own right. Beatus of Liébana in the Asturias (d.798) challenged Elipandus of Toledo to a debate on Christological questions. The text survives.[43] But he is most famous for his Apocalypse commentary, which suggests that he had access to a good library even in a remote part of Spain where people fled to the mountains as the Muslims invaded in 711 and the Visigothic kingdom collapsed. Possibly books were brought north by the fugitives. Beatus's preface declares his reliance on 'the holy Fathers' in explaining the way the Old Testament looks forward to the new in the prophecies of Revelation. The first copy seems to have been illustrated and the illustrations fully integrated into the text.[44]

The notion of 'illumination', throwing light on the meaning of the words by striking the eye with the beauty of a picture, did not necessarily require the use of representational imagery. In fine Islamic texts the script is used so decoratively that it adds a layer or dimension of visual beauty.

So the arts were not mere surface decoration upon the Christian life and the life of the Church, but were intimately involved in both its most profound and its most worldly aspects.

Conclusion

This volume of the series has covered a grand sweep of centuries and taken the reader through some of the most important transitions in the history of Christianity. This is one of the periods when Christianity 'found itself' in a time of radical change, discovered its capacity to fit into the culture of a changing world and was forced to think seriously about what it could change within itself in response, without ceasing to be the faith for which the early martyrs had died, and risking compromising its integrity. It is also the period in which the complexity of interfaith relations became apparent, in ways which sometimes foreshadow the problems of the modern world. In the earliest period only Judaism could be regarded as an alternative system of life and belief which stood apart as Christianity insisted on doing from the comprehensive syncretistic mix the Roman Empire made of all other faiths and religions and cultures in the territories it conquered. Judaism was essentially the religion of a 'people', and although Jews were to be found all over the world, it was not in the same sense as Christianity a 'world religion'. But Islam was.

Above all, early medieval Christianity got its bearings intellectually. It preserved the heritage of the ancient world as Islamic scholarship also did, but worked on it in different and complementary ways. It continued the endeavour of the first Christian thinkers to place an increasingly sophisticated, refined and abstract set of theological ideas within the highest philosophical traditions. But in these centuries we have seen that Christian thought attracted the best minds of Europe and became the driving force of civilization, colouring political thought as well as political realities, the visual arts and music as well as the arts of language. It formed Western civilization and it gave the coming generations of rebels something to challenge which was worth the challenge, and which withstood the challenge while adapting to it.

Notes

Introduction. Out of the Ancient World

1. Bernard of Clairvaux, *De consideratione*, IV.vii.23, LTR III, pp 465–6.
2. *Ibid.*, III.v.19, LTR III, pp 446–7.
3. Dorothy Sayers, 'On Translating the Divina Commedia', *Nottingham Medieval Studies* 2 (1958), pp 38–66 (p 38).
4. Cicero, *De inventione*, II.liii.159; *De officiis*, 15–17.
5. F. Cumont, *The Oriental Religions in Roman Paganism* (Chicago, 1911; reprint Dover, 1956); see also F. Cumont, *Les mystères de Mithra* (Brussels, 1913).
6. P.R.L. Brown, *The Making of Late Antiquity* (Harvard, 1978).
7. Peter Garnsey, 'Religious Toleration in Classical Antiquity', in W.J. Shiels (ed), *Persecution and Toleration*, Studies in Church History 21 (Oxford, 1984), pp 1–27.
8. Frederick Behrends (ed and trans), *The Letters and Poems of Fulbert of Chartres* (Oxford, 1976), Letter 1, p 3.
9. Ailred of Rievaulx, *De spiritali amicitia*, CCCM 1.
10. See, for example, Acts 20.28; I Corinthians 1.2, 10.32, 11.22, 15.9; Galatians 1.13; I Timothy 3.5.
11. See the first volume in this series.
12. Peter Brown, *Authority and the Sacred* (Cambridge, 1995), p 35.
13. Judith Herrin, *The Formation of Christendom* (Oxford, 1987).

Chapter 1. The Medieval History of the Church in Time and Space

1. *Magna vita Sancti Hugonis*, Prologue, ed Decima L. Douie and D.H. Farmer (Oxford, 1985), vol. i, p 1.
2. Henry Bracton, *De legibus et consuetudinibus Angliae*, fol. 33b, ed. T. Twiss, RS 70 (London, 1878–83), vol. ii, p 108, and M. Clanchy, *From Memory to Written Record: England 1066–1307* (Oxford, 1997; 2nd ed, 1993), p 146.
3. Ps-Isidore, *Decretales Pseudo-Isidorianae* (Leipzig, 1863).
4. *Gesta Abbatum Monasterii S. Albani*, ed H.T. Riley, RS 28 (1867), vol. i, pp 26–7.
5. Giraldus Cambrensis, *De invectionibus*, *Opera*, vol. iii, RS 21 (1863) pp 76ff. (p 78).

6. See Clanchy, *From Memory to Written Record*, on some of these transitions.
7. R.S. Loomis and L.H. Loomis, *Arthurian Legends in Medieval Art* (OUP, 1938).
8. See Clanchy, *From Memory to Written Record*.
9. Bede, *Ecclesiastical History*, ed B. Colgrave and R.A.B. Mynors (Oxford, 1969), preface, pp 3–5.
10. Gervase of Tilbury, *Otia imperialia*, ed and trans S.E. Banks and J.W. Binns (Oxford, 2002).
11. *Ibid.*, p xcii.
12. John of Salisbury, *Historia pontificalis*, ed M. Chibnall (Oxford, 1986), pp 1–4.
13. The majority of Rupert's *Opera* are available in the CCCM series.
14. PL 176.183–4.
15. Anselm of Havelberg, *Dialogues*, ed G. Salet (Paris, 1966).
16. Tanner, vol. i, pp 231–3. See also Marjorie Reeves, *The Influence of Prophecy in the Later Middle Ages* (Oxford, 1969).
17. Ralph Glaber, *Historiarum libri quinque*, ed John France (Oxford, 1989).
18. *Ibid.*, pp 2–3.
19. *Ibid.*, pp 50–1.
20. Orderic Vitalis, *Ecclesiastical History*, ed Marjorie Chibnall (Oxford, 1980), vol. i, pp 130–3.
21. Cf. Cato, *Distichs*, iii.13, *aliena vita est nobis magistra*; John of Salisbury, *Historia pontificalis*, p 3.
22. Thomas of Marlborough, *History of the Abbey of Evesham: Historia Ecclesie Abbedonensis*, ed and trans John Hudson (Oxford, 2002), III.1.
23. Tarif Khalidi, *Arabic Historical Thought in the Classical Period* (Cambridge, 1994), pp 178–9.
24. *Ibid.*, p 221.
25. Orderic Vitalis, *Ecclesiastical History*, vol. i, pp 130–3.
26. Bede, *Ecclesiastical History*, pp 3–7.
27. John of Salisbury, *Historia pontificalis*, p 3. Cf. Cato, *Distichs*, iii.13, *aliena vita est nobis magistra*.

Chapter 2. Spreading the Gospel: The Missionary Centuries

1. Benjamin Isaac, *The Limits of Empire* (Oxford, 1990; revised, 1992), pp 19–20.
2. *Ibid.*, p 245.
3. On the Christological controversies at issue in Arianism, see Rowan Williams, *Arius: Heresy and Tradition* (London, 2nd ed, 2001).
4. Kathleen Hughes, *Early Christian Ireland* (Ithaca, New York, 1972), p 69.
5. See the discussion in David Dumville (ed), *Saint Patrick, 493–1993* (Woodbridge, 1993), pp 179–81.
6. *Ibid.*, pp 191–2.
7. Bede, *Ecclesiastical History*, I.23–6, pp 68–79.
8. *Ibid.*, I.27, pp 78–9.

9. The authenticity of this *Libellus responsionum* has been questioned, but apart from some points which may be later interpolations, the evidence seems secure enough that these are really the questions and answers they purport to be.

10. Bede, *Ecclesiastical History*, I.27, pp 79–103.

11. *Ibid.*, III.25, pp 294–309.

12. *The Book of Kells*, Proceedings of a Conference at Trinity College, Dublin, 6–9 September 1992 (TCD Library and Scolar Press, 1994), pp 1–2.

13. Bede, *Ecclesiastical History*, V.21, pp 547ff.

14. *Vita S. Bonifatii*, 6, MGH Scriptores II (1829), p 340.

15. *Ibid.*, p 341.

16. *SS Bonifatii et Lulli epistolae selectae* I (Berlin, 1955), pp 40–1.

17. Guibert of Nogent, *Gesta Dei per Francos*, I.ii, ed R.B.C. Huygens, CCCM 127A, p 89.

18. R.W. Southern, *The Making of the Middle Ages* (Hutchinson, 1953), p 51.

19. *Ibid.*, p 36.

Chapter 3. The Church Defines the Outsider

1. Cyprian, Letter 73.21.2, CCSL 3C, p 555.

2. Augustine *De baptismo*, IV.xvii.24, CSEL 51, p 250.

3. Brian Briggs, '*Expulsio, Proscriptio, Exilium*: Exile and Friendship in the Writings of Osbert of Clare', in Laura Napran and Elisabeth van Houts (eds), *Exile in the Middle Ages*, International Medieval Research 13 (Brepols, 2002), pp 131–45 (p 135).

4. Alan of Lille, PL 210.305–430.

5. PL 210.307.

6. Bernard of Clairvaux, *Sermons*, 64–6, LTR II.

7. David Abulafia and Nora Berend (eds), *Medieval Frontiers: Concepts and Practices* (Ashgate, 2002).

8. Anna Abuafia and G.R. Evans (eds), *The Works of Gilbert Crispin*, British Academy Medieval Texts (London, 1986), pp 61–4.

9. Severus of Minorca, *Letter on the Conversion of the Jews*, ed Scott Bradbury (Oxford, 1996), pp 82–5.

10. *Ibid.*, pp 92–103.

11. The Jews are the subject of Book III, particularly their denial of the doctrines of the Trinity and Incarnation.

12. Peter Abelard, *Collationes*, ed John Marenbon and Giovanni Orlandi (Oxford, 2001), pp 18–21.

13. *Ibid.*, pp 24–5.

14. *Lettres des premiers chartreux*, ed by a Carthusian, SC 88 (1962), p 90.

15. Hermannus Judaeus, *De conversione*, ed G. Niemeyer, MGH Quellen zur Geschichte des Mittelalters, 4 (Weimar, 1963), pp 88–93, and trans K.F. Morrison, *Conversion and Text* (London: Virginia University Press, 1992), pp 88–91.

16. Alfons Hilka and Werner Söderhjelm (eds), 'Petri Alfonsi *Disciplina clericalis, I: Lateinischer Text*', in *Acta Societatis Scientiarum Fennicæ* 38/4 (1911); J. Tolan, *Petrus Alfonsi and His Medieval Readers* (Gainsville: University of Florida Press, 1993).

17. Abuafia and Evans (eds), *The Works of Gilbert Crispin*.

18. Anna Sapir Abulafia, *Christians and Jews in the Twelfth-Century Renaissance* (Routledge, 1995).

19. Peter Abelard, *Collationes*, pp 8–9.

20. *Ibid.*, pp 14–17.

21. *Ibid.*

22. *Ibid.*

23. See James Muldoon, *Popes, Lawyers and Infidels: The Church and the Non-Christian World, 1250–1550* (Philadelphia, 1979).

24. Aquinas *Summa theologiae*, Iia,Iiae, QQ.10–12.

25. Isidore, *Etymologiae*, IX.ii.57, ed W.M. Lindsay (Oxford, 1911).

26. John Victor Tolan, *Medieval Christian Perceptions of Islam: A Book of Essays* (New York, 1996), p xi.

27. *Ibid.*, pp xii–xiii.

28. Richard Fletcher, *The Cross and the Crescent* (London, 2003), pp 12–13.

29. *Ibid.*, map on pp 2–3.

30. Khalidi, *Arabic Historical Thought in the Classical Period*, pp 28ff.

31. Umayyad caliphs, 661–750.

32. Abbasid caliphs, 750–1258.

33. Hugh Kennedy, *The Prophet and the Age of the Caliphates. The Islamic Near East from the 6th to the 11th Century* (London and New York, 1986).

34. Tolan (ed), *Medieval Christian Perceptions of Islam*, pp xiv–xv.

35. Craig L. Hanson, 'Manuel I Comnenus and the "God of Muhammad": A Study in Byzantine Ecclesiastical Politics', in Tolan (ed), *Medieval Christian Perceptions of Islam*, pp 55–82 (p 55).

36. On the Nestorians, see A.R. Vine (ed), *The Nestorian Churches* (London, 1932).

37. Al Kindy, *Apology*, ed and abridged W. Muir (London, 1887), p 35.

38. *Ibid.*, pp 53–65.

39. *Ibid.*, p 84.

40. *Ibid.*, p 90.

41. *Ibid.*, pp 69–70.

42. Embricon de Mayence, *La vie de Mahomet*, ed Guy Cambier (Latomus, Brussels, 1962).

43. *Nam gens exosa Christo, gens perniciosa,*
    Gens Mahumet parens et ratione carens,
    Certat adhuc stultum defendere sedula cultum.

44. Embricon de Mayence, *La vie de Mahomet*, p 56. See also Alberto Ferreiro, *Simon Magus in Patristic, Medieval and Early Modern Traditions* (Brill, 2005), pp 221, 224, 226.

45. Khalidi, *Arabic Historical Thought in the Classical Period*, p 147.

46. *Ibid.*, p 157.

47. Liutprand, *The Embassy to Constantinople and Other Writings*, ed John Julius Norwich (London, 1993). The Latin text of *Relatio de legatione constantinopolitana* (ed P. Chiesa) is in CCCM 156.

48. *Vita Johannis Abbatis*, MGH Scriptores IV, 335–77, pp 71ff.

49. R.M. Thomson, *William of Malmesbury* (Boydell, 1987; reprint, 2003), pp 170–7.

50. In the Bodleian Library, Oxford, MS Arch. Seld. B.16.

51. Thomson, *William of Malmesbury*, p 169, gives the Latin text.

52. *Ibid.*, pp 174–5.

53. *Ibid.*, pp 184–5.

54. PL 155.825–9.

55. M.T. D'Alverny, 'Deux traductions latines du Coran au MA', AHDLMA 16 (1948), pp 69–131.

56. L. Minio-Palluelo, *Opuscula: The Latin Aristotle* (Amsterdam, 1972) and *Aristoteles Latinus* (Rome, 1951–), on the methods of the medieval translators of Greek philosophical works into Latin.

57. D'Alverny, 'Deux traductions latines du Coran au MA', p 71.

58. *Ibid.*, p 87.

59. Peter Venerable, *Letters*, Letter iii, ed Giles Constable (Cambridge, Mass., 1967), pp 294ff.

60. *Ibid.*, p 275.

61. Giraldus Cambrensis, *De principis instructione*, *Opera*, RS (1891), vol. viii, pp 68–70.

62. *Cuius Mahometic monstruosa vita, monstruosior secta, monstruosissimus finis. Mahomet maligno spiritu inspiratus, sectam abominabilem invenit, carnalibus voluptatibus consonam.*

63. PL 210.422.

64. Jacques de Vitry, *Lettres de la cinquième croisade*, ed R.B.C. Huygens and trans G. Duchet-Suchaux. (Brepols, 1998), p 46.

65. *Ibid.*, p 48.

66. *Ibid.*, p 50.

67. *Ibid.*, p 54.

68. Norman Daniel, *Islam and the West* (Edinburgh, 1960; new edition, 1993), p 275.

69. Jacques de Vitry, *Lettres de la cinquième croisade*, p 56.

70. S. Runciman, *The Medieval Manichee* (Cambridge, 1947; London, 1961).

71. Michel Roquebert, *Les Cathares: de la chute de Montségur aux dernier bûchers (1244–1329)* (Paris: Perrin, 1998), p 539.

72. Durandus de Huesca, *Une somme anti-Cathare, Le liber contra Manicheos*, ed C. Thouzellier, SSLov 32 (1964).

73. Roquebert, *Les Cathares*, p 539.

74. Caesarius of Heisterbach *Dialogue on Miracles*, V.21, trans H. von E. Scott

and C.C. Swinton Bland (Routledge: London, 1929), pp 343–4.

75. *Livre des deux principes*, ed C. Thouzellier, SC 198 (Paris, 1973).

76. *Liber de duabus principiis*, ed A. Dondaine (Rome, 1939).

77. For the Lateran IV, 3 condemnations see Tanner, vol. i, pp 233–5.

78. Gervase of Tilbury, *Otia imperialia*, p xxvii; Ralph of Coggeshall, *Chronicon Anglicanum*, pp 121–4.

79. Walter Map, *De nugis curialium*, I.30, ed M.R. James, C.N.L. Brooke and R.A.B. Mynors (Oxford, 1983), pp 124–5.

80. *Ibid.*, pp 126–7.

81. Caesarius of Heisterbach *Dialogue on Miracles*, V.20, p 342–3.

82. Hugh Eteriano, *Contra Patarenos*, ed and trans Janet Hamilton, Sarah Hamilton and Bernard Hamilton (Brill, 2004), pp 15, 19.

83. Map, *De nugis curialium*, I.29, p 121.

84. *Ibid.*, p 119.

85. *Ibid.*, p 121.

86. Lateran IV, 68, Tanner vol. i, p 266.

87. See Muldoon, *Popes, Lawyers and Infidels*.

Chapter 4. Imposing Order

1. Southern, *The Making of the Middle Ages*, p 17.

2. *The Letters and Poems of Fulbert of Chartres*, Letter 20, mid-1008 or later, ed and trans Frederick Behrends (Oxford, 1976), pp 39–45.

3. *Ibid.*, Letter 22, 1008–1012/3, p 37.

4. *Ita variis tenentur occupationibus cives et dum sic coluntur officia singulorum ut universitati prospiciatur, dum iustitia colitue, fines omnium mellea dulcedo perfundit* (VI.22). John of Salisbury's *Policraticus*, ed C.C.J. Webb (Oxford, 1909), 2 vols., and CCCM 118, Books I–IV.

5. Dante, *Monarchia*, ed and trans P. Shaw (Cambridge, 1995), I.iii.2–3.

6. Lateran II (3), Tanner, vol. i, p 197.

7. See T.M. Charles-Edwards, 'Palladius, Prosper and Leo the Great: Missions and Primatial Authority', in David Dumville (ed), *Saint Patrick: AD 493–1993*, Studies in Celtic History 13 (Woodbridge, 1993), pp 1–12. *The Book of Kells, Proceedings of a Conference at Trinity College, Dublin, 6–9 September 1992*, pp 2–3.

8. Tanner, vol. i, p 144.

9. Lanfranc, *Monastic Constitutions*, ed and trans David Knowles (London, 1951), p 1.

10. Tanner, vol. i, pp 227–71.

11. P. Fransen, *L'autorité des conciles* (Paris, 1962), pp 58–100.

12. Gregory the Great, *Registrum*, V.37, CCSL 140, pp 308–9.

13. *Ibid.*, XIII.39, CCSL 140A, pp 1043–4.

14. H. Chadwick, *East and West* (Oxford, 2003), maps the sequence.

15. W. Ullmann, *Medieval Foundations of Renaissance Humanism* (London, 1977), p 7. See also p 14 for the notion that baptism had a particular importance in

the medieval period.

16. PL 176.441.
17. Tanner, vol. i, p 212.
18. *Ibid.*, p 143.
19. Southern, *The Making of the Middle Ages*, pp 119, 121.
20. Guibert de Nogent, *De vita sua*, I.vii, ed E.R. Labande (Paris, 1981), pp 43–91; trans J.F. Benton, *Self and Society in Medieval France* (New York, 1970).
21. Tanner, vol. i, p 194.
22. *Ibid.*, p 198.
23. *Ibid.*, p 203.
24. *Ibid.*, p 215.
25. *Ibid.*, pp 199, 202.
26. *Ibid.*, p 197.
27. Gerhoch of Reichersberg, *Letter to Pope Hadrian about the Novelties of the Day*, ed N.M. Häring (Toronto, 1974), prefatory letter, p 23.
28. I Thessalonians 2.9; II Thessalonians 3.7–8; II Corinthians 11.9; Tanner, vol. i, p 213.
29. Peter the Chanter, *Summa de sacramentis et animae consiliis*, ed J.-A. Dugauquier, *Analecta Medievalia Namurcensia* 4 (Louvain, 1956), vol. i, pp 19–20.
30. *Ibid.*, pp 19, 21.
31. Bruno, *Confession of Faith, Lettres des premiers chartreux*, ed by a Carthusian, SC 88 (1962), p 92.
32. Caesarius of Heisterbach, *Dialogue on Miracles*, II.1, pp 61–3.
33. *Ibid.*, pp 66–7.
34. Michael Staunton, 'Exile in the Lives of Anselm and Thomas Becket', in Napran and van Houts (eds), *Exile in the Middle Ages*, pp 159–180. Romedio Schmitz-Esser, 'Arnold of Bescia in Exile: April 1139–December 1143: His Role as Reformer, Reviewed', *ibid.*, pp 213–232.
35. O. Lottin, 'Nouveaux fragments théologiques de l'école d'Anselme de Laon', RTAM 13 (1946), p 206.
36. *Pippinus secundum morem Francorum electus est ad regem et unctus per manum sanctae memoriae Bonefacii … et elevatus a Francis in regno in Suessionis civitate.* *Annales Regni Francorum*, ed F. Kurze MGH (Hanover, 1895), pp 10–11, 752; see also Paul A. Jackson, 'Sicut Samuel Iunxit David: Early Carolingian Royal Anointings Reconsidered', in L. Larson-Miller (ed), *Medieval Liturgy: A Book of Essays* (New York, 1997), pp 267–304.
37. R Ralph de Diceto, *De mirabilibus britanniae, abbreviationes chronicorum, Opera historica*, ed W. Stubbs, RS lxviii, 2 vols. (1876), pp 11–15.
38. Mark Duffy, *Royal Tombs of Medieval England* (Charleston, 2003), pp 22–4.
39. T.A. Dorey, 'William of Poitiers: "Gesta Guillelmi Ducis"', in T.A. Dorey (ed), *Latin Biography* (London, 1967), pp 139–55. *The Gesta Guilelmi of William of Poitiers*, ed and trans R.H.C. Davis and Marjorie Chibnall (Oxford, 1998).

40. Gervase of Tilbury, *Otia imperialia*.

41. Hincmar of Rheims, PL 125.1071, AD 881.

42. Lorenzo Valla, *De falso credita et ementita Constantini Donatione declamatio* (1520).

43. *Historia Ecclesie Abbedonensis*, II, ed and trans John Hudson (Oxford, 2002), pp 2–5.

44. *The 'Epistolae Vagantes' of Pope Gregory VII*, ed H.E. Cowdrey (Oxford, 1972), pp 2–3.

45. Uta-Renata Blumenthal, *The Investiture Controversy* (Philadelphia, 1988).

46. *The Letters of Peter of Celle*, ed Julian Haseldine (Oxford, 2001), Letter 1, vol. i, pp 5–6.

47. Bernard of Clairvaux, *De consideratione*, III.i.1, LTR III, p 431.

48. PL 217.653–60.

49. Brenda Bolton, 'The Caravan Rests: Innocent III's Use of Itineration', in Anne J. Duggan, Joan Greatres and Brenda Bolton (eds), *Omnia Disce: Medieval Studies in Memory of Leonard Boyle, O.P.* (Ashgate, 2005), pp 41–61.

50. C.R. Cheney and W.H. Semple (eds), *Selected Letters of Innocent III* (London, 1953), pp 63–5.

51. PL 216.1186–91.

Chapter 5. Church and People

1. O. Lottin, 'Nouveaux fragments théologiques de l'école d'Anselme de Laon', RTAM 13 (1946), p 206.

2. *Ibid.*

3. P. Buc, 'Vox clamantis in deserto', *Revue Mabillon* 65 (1993), pp 5–45.

4. Demetrios J. Constantelos, 'Liturgy and Liturgical Daily Life in the Medieval Greek World: The Byzantine Empire', in Thomas J. Heffernan and E. Ann Matter (eds), *The Liturgy of the Medieval Church* (Kalamazoo, 2001), pp 109–44 (p 112).

5. *Ibid.*

6. *Ibid.*

7. *Ibid.*

8. Samuel H. Cross and Olgerd P. Sherbowitz-Wetzor (eds and trans), *The Russian Primary Chronicle* (Cambridge, Mass., 1953), pp 110–11.

9. See Eamon Duffy, *The Stripping of the Altars* (Yale, 2nd ed, 2005).

10. P.S. Barnwell, Claire Cross and Ann Rycroft (eds), *Mass and Parish in Late Medieval England: The Use of York* (Reading: Spire, 2005), p 13.

11. Thomas of Celano, *Vita et miracula: Life of Francis of Assisi*, ed P.E. Alençon (Rome, 1906). II.90.

12. David Farmer, *Oxford Dictionary of Saints* (Oxford, 1978; reprint, 2004), pp xff.

13. *Ibid.*

14. Bruno, *Profession of Faith*, pp 90–3.

15. *Miracles of Sainte Aebbe of Coldingham and Saint Margaret of Scotland*, ed R. Barnett (Oxford, 2003), pp xxiii–xxiv.

16. *Ibid.*, pp xxiii–xxiv.

17. *Ibid.*, p xxx.

18. Goscelin of Saint-Bertin, *The Hagiography of the Female Saints of Ely*, ed Rosalind C. Love (Oxford, 2004), pp 96–7.

19. Bernard of Clairvaux, *Vita sancti Malachiae*, Praefatio, LTR III, p 307.

20. Anselm, Prayers 5, 6, 7, *Opera omnia*, ed F.S. Schmitt, 6 vols. (Rome, 1938–68), vol. iii, pp 13–25.

21. Ronald C. Finucane, *Miracles and Pilgrims: Popular Beliefs in Medieval England* (London, 1977 and 1995), pp 13–14.

22. Bede, *Ecclesiastical History*, III.ix–xiii, pp 241–53.

23. Michael Staunton, 'Exile in the Lives of Anselm and Thomas Becket'.

24. Finucane, *Miracles and Pilgrims*, p 157.

25. *Ibid.*, pp 152ff.

26. Farmer, *Oxford Dictionary of Saints* (Oxford, 1978, reprint, 2004), pp xff.

27. Finucane, *Miracles and Pilgrims*, p 49.

28. Farmer, *Oxford Dictionary of Saints* (Oxford 1978; 5th ed, 2003) p ix.

29. Bede, *Ecclesiastical History*, I.

30. Farmer, *Oxford Dictionary of Saints* (Oxford, 1978, reprint, 2004), pp xff.

31. *Miracles of Sainte Aebbe of Coldingham and Saint Margaret of Scotland*, p xxx.

32. Caesarius of Heisterbach *Dialogue on Miracles*, V.1–2, pp 314–7.

33. *Ibid.*, I.5, p 322.

34. Gervase of Tilbury, *Otia imperialia*.

35. *Ibid.*, p xcii.

36. *Ibid.*, iii.11, pp 576–7.

37. I am grateful to K.R. Chambers for several of the references which follow. See her forthcoming doctoral thesis, University of Cambridge.

38. Referred to in Leo Carruthers, 'The Word Made Flesh: Preaching and Community from the Apostolic to the Late Middle Ages', in Georgiana Donavin, Cary J. Nederman and Richard Utz (eds), *Speculum Sermonis: Interdisciplinary Reflections on the Late Medieval Sermon* (Turnhout, 2004), pp 3–28 (p 12); James R. Blaettler, 'Preaching the Power of Penitence in the Silos Beatus', in J. Hamesse, Beverly M. Kienzle, Debra Stoudt and Anne Thayer (eds), *Medieval Sermons and Society: Cloister, City, University* (Louvain, 1998), pp 35–61 (p 40).

39. Gísli Sigurdsonn and Vésteinn Olason (eds), *The Manuscripts of Iceland* (Reykjavik, 2004), pp 18–19.

40. *The Later Letters of Peter of Blois*, 28–30, ed E. Revell, British Academy Medieval Texts (Oxford, 1993), pp 126–59.

41. In a letter written in 441 to Theodoret, Bishop of Cyrrhus, cited in the decretal collection of Ivo of Chartres (*c.*1040–1116), and Distinction 23, Canon 19 of Gratian's *Decretum* (compiled in the 1140s).

42. Cf. John 17.18.

43. PL 210.379.

44. Walter of St Victor, *Sermones*, XVIII, 3, ed J. Châtillon, CCCM 30, p 151.

45. LTR, vol. viii, p 129.

46. *Quia vero nonnulli sub specie pietatis virtutem eius iuxta quod ait apostolus abnegantes auctoritatem sibi vendicant praedicandi cum idem apostolus dicat quomodo praedicabunt nisi mittantur.* So everyone who preaches without papal authority or the authority of the local bishop, whether publicly or privately *praedicationis officium usurpare praesumpserint* and will be excommunicated. Lateran IV, c.3, Tanner, vol. i, pp 233–5.

47. Brian Stock, *The Implications of Literacy* (Toronto, 1982).

48. *Fidem catholicam quae apostolorum symbolo continetur, et dominicam orationem, quam sancti evangelii nos scriptura edocet.* Letter to Egbert, 5, PL 94.657, and *Opera historica*, ed C. Plummer, p 408.

49. *Illiterati mittuntur ad predicandum ne fides credentium non virtute dei sed eloquentia atque doctrina fieri putaretur. … Idiotae enim dicebantur, qui propria tantum lingua naturalique scientia contenti litterarum studia nesciebant.* Bede, *Expositio super Acta*, 4.13, CCCM 121 (1983), p 26.

50. *Et quidem omnes, qui Latinam linguam lectionis usu didicerunt, etiam haec optime didicisse certissimum est; sed idiotas, hoc est, eos qui propriae tantum linguae notitiam habent, haec ipsa sua lingua discere, ac sedulo decantare facito.*

51. *Non solum de laicis, id est in populari adhuc vita constitutes, verum etiam de clericis sive monachis, qui latinae sunt linguae expertes, fieri oportet.* Bede, Letter to Bishop Egbert, *Opera historica*, ed C. Plummer (1896; 2nd ed, 1946), pp 408ff.

52. *Propter quod et ipsi multis saepe sacerdotibus idiotis haec utraque, et symbolum videlicet et dominicam orationem, in linguam Anglorum translatum optuli.* Bede, Letter to Bishop Egbert, *ibid.*

53. MGH Legum I, c.14 (Hanover, 1835), p 190.

54. Herbert Grundmann, 'Litteratus-illiteratus', *Archive für kulturgeschichte* 40 (1958), pp 1–65. *The Development of Literate Mentalities in East Central Europe*, ed Anna Adamska and Marco Mostert (Brepols, 2004). Philippe Buc, 'Vox clamantis in deserto? Pierre le Chantre et la predication laïque', *Revue Mabillon* 4 (1993), pp 5–48. Rolf Zerfass, *Der Streit um die Laienpredigt* (Frieberg, 1974). Sedulius Scottus, *Collectaneum in Apostolum*, PL 103.249: *nos qui latini sumus Latina nomina et origines de lingua nostra habentia facilius memoriae tradimus ita illi a parva aetate vernacula sui sermonis vocabula peritissimis sensibus imbiberunt et ab exordio Adam usque ad extremum Zorobabel omnium generations ita memoriter velociter que percurrunt ut eos suum putes referre nomen.*

55. *Decretals*, ed G. Friedberg, II.789, X.5, 7, 14; see also Zerfass, *Der Streit um die Laienpredigt*, pp 254–5. 1. *Sicut in uno corpore multa sunt membra, que unum et eundem actum non habent, ita sunt ordines in ecclesia, sed non omnes habent officium.* 3. *Cum igitur nonnulli laici in Lombardia predicare presumant.* 6. *Doctorum ordo est in ecclesia quasi precipuus.* 7. The *predicationis officium* must

not be usurped by those not 'sent'.

56. P.B. Roberts, 'Preaching in/and the Medieval City', in Hamesse et al (eds), *Medieval Sermons and Society: Cloister, City, University*, pp 151–64 (p 163).
57. I owe this observation to K.R. Chambers.
58. Thomas à Kempis, *Dialogi noviciorum*, II.21, *Opera omnia*, VII, ed M.J. Pohl (1922), p 167.
59. *Annales monastici*, ed H.R. Luard, RS (1864–9), vol. ii of 5 vols., p 277.
60. Letter 241, LTR VIII, p 126.
61. PL 210.377.
62. PL 210.378.
63. I am grateful to K.R. Chambers for these references.
64. PL 214.695C.
65. Walter Simon, 'Staining the Speech of Things Divine: The Uses of Literacy in Medieval Beguine Communities', in Thérèse de Hemptinne and María Eugenia Góngora (eds), *The Voice of Silence: Women's Literacy in a Men's Church* (Turnhout, 2005), pp 85–111.
66. Sarah S. Poor, *Mechthild of Magdeburg and Her Book* (University of Pennsylvania Press, 2004), p 1.
67. PL215.1510–13, trans *Heresies of the High Middle Ages: Selected Sources Translated and Annotated*, by W. L. Wakefield and A. P. Evans (New York, 1969), pp 224–26.

Chapter 6. The Church Divided: East and West

1. Henry Chadwick, *East and West: The Making of a Rift in the Church* (Oxford, 2003), p 83.
2. Rowan Williams, *Arius: Heresy and Tradition*.
3. CCSL 142 (1971), ed. M. Adraian, p 3.
4. Bede, *Ecclesiastical History*, p 299.
5. *Ibid.*, p 297.
6. PG 102.279–392, and trans J.P. Farrell (Brookline, Mass, 1987).
7. PL 100.864.
8. *Homiliae*, I.10, CCCM 116, p 82.
9. PL 129.1259.
10. Guibert of Nogent, *Gesta Dei per Francos*, I.ii, p 89.
11. Giraldus Cambrensis, *De principis instructione*, *Opera*, vol. viii, p 75.
12. Lateran IV, 4, Tanner, vol. i, p 235.
13. *De processione spiritus sancti*, S.II.
14. S.II.223–5, to Walram, Bishop of Nuremberg.

Chapter 7. Bringing the Outsiders In

1. Tanner, vol. i, p 145.
2. Robert Dodaro, *Christ and the Just Society in the Age of Augustine* (Cambridge, 2004).
3. Guibert of Nogent, *Gesta Dei per Francos*, I.1, p 87.

4. *Ibid.*

5. *The Historia vie Hierosolomitane of Gilo of Paris and a Second Anonymous Author*, ed and trans C.W. Grocock and J.E. Siberry (Oxford, 1997), pp 70–1.

6. Ronald Finucane, *Soldiers of the Faith: Crusaders and Moslems at War* (London, 1983).

7. Thomson, *William of Malmesbury*, pp 178–9.

8. *Historia vie Hierosolomitane*, p 4.

9. Guibert of Nogent, *Gesta Dei per Francos*, I.1, p 86.

10. *Gesta Francorum et aliorum*, ed Rosalind Hill (Oxford, 1962), p 11.

11. *Ibid.*, p 18.

12. *Ibid.*, pp 20, 22.

13. Finucane. *Soldiers of the Faith*, p 157.

14. *Gesta Francorum et aliorum*, p 22.

15. *Ibid.*, p xxix.

16. Letter 37, S.III.145–6.

17. Letter 117, S.III.252–5.

18. Guibert of Nogent, *Gesta Dei per Francos*, I.1, p 87.

19. On the authorship, see *Gesta Francorum et aliorum*.

20. *Ibid.*, p 1.

21. Tudebod, *Historia de Hierololymitano itinere*, PL 155.763–820, PL 155.763, and ed J. Richard (Paris, 1977).

22. Raymond of Agiles, *Historia Francorum*, PL 155.591–666.

23. *Gesta Francorum et aliorum*, p 85. See also Fulcher of Chartres, *Gesta Francorum Iherusalem peregrinantium*, PL 155.821–40.

24. Letter CCCLXI, *Opera*, vol. viii, p 318.

25. Letter 210, PL 214.765 ff.

26. Letters 208, 209, PL 214.756–8.

27. Letters 212, 213, PL 214.772ff.

28. Letter 11, PL 214.9.

29. Letter 505, PL 214.466.

30. Letter 73, PL 214.64.

31. Letter 467, PL 214.467.

32. Map, *De nugis curialium*, I.18, p 56.

33. *Ibid.*, I.23, p,69.

34. Bernard of Clairvaux, *Opera omnia*, III.205–39.

35. *Ibid.*, p 220.

36. *Ibid.*, pp 217–18, 222.

37. Letter of Guigo to Hugh of Paiens, founder of the Templars (1128), 4, *Lettres des premiers chartreux*, SC 88 (1962), p 156.

38. Joinville and Villehardouin, *Chronicles of the Crusades*, trans M.R.B. Shaw (Penguin, 1963), chapter 15.

39. Lateran IV, Canon 5, Tanner, vol. i, p.236.

40. Christoph T. Maier, *Preaching the Crusades*, Cambridge Studies in Medieval Life and Thought (Cambridge, 1994), pp 2–3; F.H. Russell, *The Just War in*

the Middle Ages, *Preaching the Crusades*, Cambridge Studies in Medieval Life and Thought (Cambridge, 1975), pp 112–26, 195–212.

41. C. Morris, *The Papal Monarchy: The Western Church from 1050–1250* (Oxford, 1989), pp 417–51.

42. Jacques de Vitry, *Lettres de la cinquième croisade*, p 94.

43. Maier, *Preaching the Crusades*, pp 96–9.

44. *Ibid.*, pp 170–4.

45. J.B. Freed, *The Friars and German Society in the Thirteenth Century* (Medieval Academy of America, Cambridge, Mass., 1977).

46. Maier, *Preaching the Crusades*, pp 82–4.

47. *Ibid.*, pp 167–8.

Chapter 8. Extreme Lives: The Religious Orders

1. Caesarius of Heisterbach *Dialogue on Miracles*, IV.1, p 194.

2. *Sermo ad abbates*, 1, LTR V, p 288.

3. *Apologia ad Guillelmum Abbatem*, 5, LTR VIII, p 84.

4. Caesarius of Heisterbach *Dialogue on Miracles*, I.16, p 24.

5. Guibert de Nogent, *Autobiographie*, I.9, ed Edmond-René Labande (Paris, 1981), p 52.

6. *Ibid.*, p 57.

7. Anselm, Letter 134, S.III, pp 276–8.

8. The best description of the way this sense is used alongside 'conversion' as an experience of personal transformation is to be found in the early chapters of Guibert of Nogent, *De vita sua*; see J.F. Benton, *Self and Society in Medieval France* (New York, 1970). See also Guibert de Nogent, *Autobiographie*, I.9.

9. Caesarius of Heisterbach, *Dialogue on Miracles*, I.39–40, pp 50–1, 55.

10. *Ibid.*

11. *Ibid.*, p 10.

12. *Ibid.*, pp 8–10.

13. *Libellus de diversis ordinibus*, ed G. Constable and Bernard S. Smith (Oxford, 2nd ed, 2003), p 3.

14. Map, *De nugis curialium*, I, pp 52–3.

15. Elizabeth Dawes and Norman H. Baynes (trans), *Three Byzantine Saints* (Oxford, 1948).

16. PL 76.149ff.

17. *Sentences of Sextus*, ed Henry Chadwick (Cambridge,1959); *Apophthegmata patrum*, ed J.G. Friere (Coimbra, 1971).

18. Their biographies have survived only in a derived version with additions by Leontius about the middle of the seventh century, in language designed to be accessible to ordinary people. See John Moschus, *Pratum spirituale*, ed and trans John Wortley (Kalamazoo, 1992).

19. Dawes and Baynes (trans), *Three Byzantine Saints*.

20. *Ibid.*

21. *Ibid.*

22. Symeon the New Theologian, *Catecheses*, ed and trans B. Krivochéine and J. Paramelle, SC, 96 (1963).

23. *The Book of Kells, Proceedings of a Conference at Trinity College, Dublin, 6–9 September, 1992*, pp 5–9.

24. Bede, *Ecclesiastical History*, iv.25, p 423.

25. B. Colgrave (ed), *Two Lives of Saint Cuthbert* (Cambridge, 1940), p 95.

26. PL 66.125ff.

27. Bede, *Ecclesiastical History*, iv.6, p 355.

28. *Ibid.*, iv.25, p 427.

29. *Ibid.*, iv.25, p 421.

30. Tim Pestell, *Landscapes of Monastic Foundation: The Establishment of Religious Houses in East Anglia, c.650–1200* (Woodbridge, 2004), p 155.

31. Emilia Jamroziak, *Rievaulx Abbey and its Social Context, 1132–1300*, Medieval Church Studies 8 (Turnhout, 2005).

32. *Ibid.*, p 111.

33. Caesarius of Heisterbach, *Dialogue on Miracles*, I.42–3, pp 58–9.

34. *Vita Anselmi*, I.v, ed R.W. Southern (Oxford 1962), p 9.

35. *Libellus de diversis ordinibus*, pp 84–5.

36. Map, *De nugis curialium*, 1.24, pp 73ff.

37. *The Letters of Peter the Venerable*, ed G. Constable (Harvard, 1967), vol. i, p 62.

38. Caesarius of Heisterbach, *Dialogue on Miracles*, I.1, pp 5–7.

39. G. Lawless (ed), *Augustine of Hippo and His Monastic Rule* (Oxford, 1987).

40. R.W. Southern, *Robert Grosseteste: The Growth of an English Mind in Medieval Europe* (Oxford, 1992).

41. One of Grosseteste's most important disciples was another intellectual pioneer and linguist, Roger Bacon, but there were others, for example Adam Marsh, Thomas Docking, Franciscans, and Dominicans too, who maintained the standards and adhered to the methods of instruction he had laid down to ensure that friars were properly educated for their preaching. Competition ensured that the Carmelites and the Augustinian friars all set up comparable structures (*studia generalia*) which could provide advanced teaching for students.

42. Map, *De nugis curialium*, 1.25, p 84.

43. Gregory the Great, *Regula pastoralis*, I.1, PL 177.14.

44. *Ibid.*

45. *Ibid.*, I.2, PL 177.15.

46. *Ibid.*, I.5, PL 177.18.

47. Bernard of Clairvaux, *De consideratione*, I.i.1, *Opera omnia*, vol. iii, p 394.

Chapter 9. The Church and the Intellectuals

1. Grosseteste, *Hexaemeron*, ed R.C. Dales and S. Gieben (London, 1982), and *The Six Days of Creation*, trans C.F.J. Martin (London, 1996), p 13.

2. *The Minor Declamationes Ascribed to Quintilian*, ed with commentary

M. Winterbottom (Berlin, 1984). See introduction for the question of authorship.

3. Macrobius, *Saturnalia*, ed. J. Willis (Leipzig, 2nd ed, 1994).

4. Cassiodorus, *Variarum*, CCSL 96.

5. Cassiodorus, *In Psalmos*, CCCSL 97 (2), preface, p 3.

6. Cassian, *Collationes*, ed J.-C. Guy, SC 109 (Paris, 1965).

7. Aristotle, *De interpretatione*, ed C. Meiser, II.79, pp 16ff.

8. Cassiodorus, *Institutiones*, ed R.A.B. Mynors (Oxford, 1937), preface, p 3.

9. N.R. Ker (ed), *The Pastoral Care: Early English Manuscripts in Facsimile* (Copenhagen, 1956).

10. Adhemar de Chabannes, *Chronicon*, ed J. Chavanon (Paris, 1897), III.54, p 176 ff.

11. Map, *De nugis curialium*, I.10, p 13.

12. Guibert de Nogent, *De vita sua*, I.iv–v, pp 25–35.

13. PL 163.759–70; H.E. Salter, *Medieval Oxford*, OHS 100 (1936), p 29.

14. J.I. Catto (ed), *The History of the University of Oxford* (Oxford, 1984), vol. i, p 8.

15. *Ibid.*, pp 47–8.

16. See Gaines Post, 'Parisian Masters as a Corporation', *Speculum* 9 (1934), pp 421–45 (pp 424, 437–8), on attempts to excommunicate the University of Paris.

17. John of Salisbury, *Historia pontificalis* is John's memoirs.

18. Cassiodorus, *Institutiones*, p 4.

19. Irena Backus (ed), *The Reception of the Church Fathers in the West* (Leiden, 1997), 2 vols.

20. *Discant ergo Celsus, Porphyrius, Julianus, rabidi adversus Christum canes, discant eorum sectatores (qui putant Ecclesiam nullos philosophos et eloquentes, nullos habuisse doctores). De viris illustribus*, ed E. Cushing (Leipzig, 1896) and PL 23.602.

21. Gennadius of Marseilles, *De viris illustribus*, PL 58.1059–1120, and ed W. Herding (Teubner, 1924).

22. PL 160.547–580.

23. Boethius, *Theological Tractates and the Consolation of Philosophy*, ed and trans H.F. Stewart, E.K. Rand and S.J. Tester (London, 1973).

24. Clarembald of Arras, *Commentary on Boethius de Trinitate*, ed N.M. Häring (Toronto, 1965), p 63.

25. Derek Krueger, *Writing and Holiness: The Practice of Authorship in the Early Christian East* (University of Pennsylvania, 2004), p 1; Frank D. Gilliard, 'More Silent Reading in Antiquity: non omne verbum sonabat', *Journal of Biblical Literature* 112 (1993), pp 689–94.

26. *Ibid.* See also Paul Sanger, *Space between Words: The Origins of Silent Reading* (Stanford UP, 1997), p 201.

27. Bede, *Expositio Actuum Apostolorum et retractatio*, ed. M.L.W. Laistner (Cambridge, Mass., 1939), p 3.

28. 'The widespread adoption of the alphabetical subject index, beginning in the 1240s to 1260s, was, again, the application of a known device – alphabetical order – to meet the need for a new kind of access to the authoritative text – the kind of alternative access required for constructing sermons and letters.' And alphabetical order was used again in the 1230s and 1240s in developing the concordances to the Bible or 'dictionaries of theological terms' which had begun to appear in the lifetime of Alan of Lille in the late twelfth century. See R.H. Rouse and M.A. Rouse, '*Ordinatio* and *compilatio* revisited', in *Ad litteram: Authoritative Texts and their Medieval Readers* (Notre Dame/London, 1992), pp 113–34 (pp 126–7); G.R. Evans, *Alan of Lille* (Cambridge, 1983); P.R. Robinson and R. Zim (eds), *Of the Making of Books: Essays Presented to M.B. Parkes* (Aldershot: Scolar, 1997); D.L. D'Avray, *The Preaching of the Friars* (Oxford, 1983), pp 64–131.

29. R.H. and M.A. Rouse, 'Biblical Distinctions in the Thirteenth Century', AHDLMA 41 (1974), pp 27–37.

30. *Dialogus de Scaccario, of Richard FitzNigel*, ed Charles Johnson (London, 1950). See also Thomas Haye, *Das Lateinische Lehrgedicht im Mittelalter* (Brill, 1997).

31. See R.B.C. Huygens, *Accessus ad auctores* (Leiden, 1970), for examples.

32. *Cum apostolus fidelibus scribat* (I Corinthians 1.10), *ut idem sapient et idem dicant omnes, et scisma nullum inter eos appareat, non parvo scismate dividuntur, qui de misterio corporis sanguinisque Christi non eadem sentientes elocuntur.* Ratramnus of Corbie, *De corpore et sanguine Domini*, II, ed J.N. Bakhuizen van den Brink (Amsterdam, 1973), p 42.

33. See G.R. Evans, *Augustine on Evil* (Cambridge, 1983).

34. *Petri Pictaveniensis allegoriae super tabernaculum Moysi*, ed P.S. Moore and J.A. Corbett (Notre Dame, 1938), p 1.

35. Hugh of St Victor, *Didascalicon*, VI.3, ed C. Buttimer (Washington: Catholic University Press, 1939), p 116.

36. Thomas of Chobham, I, *Summa de commendatione virtutum et extirpatione vitiorum*, ed F. Morenzoni, CCCM 82B (Turnhout, 1997), p 6.

37. Peter Abelard, *Historia calamitatum*, ed J. Monfrin (Paris, 1967), pp 68–9.

38. Simon of Tournai, *Disputationes, Disputatio*, XCVII, ed J. Warichez, SSLov 12 (Louvain, 1932), p 281.

39. Robert of Melun, *Quaestiones de divina pagina*, 103, *Oeuvres*, ed R. Martin, SSLov 13 (Louvain, 1932), p 52.

40. James Ginther, *Master of the Sacred Page: A Study of the Theology of Robert Grosseteste, ca. 1229/30–1235* (Ashgate, 2004).

41. Rowan Williams, *Arius: Heresy and Tradition*.

42. *Nec propter aemulorum decractationes obliquasque invidorum corrosiones nostro decrevimus proposito cedendum nec a communi doctrinae usu desistendum.* Peter Abelard, *Dialectica*, ed L.M. de Rijk (Assen, 1956), p 156.

43. Gerhoch of Reichersberg, *Letter to Pope Hadrian about the Novelties of the Day*, Prefatory letter, ed N.M. Häring (Toronto, 1974).

44. John of Salisbury, *Historia pontificalis*, pp 22–3.

45. *Ne in eorum predicatione discordia vel dissonantia inveniretur et ne alter ab altero in fide tenenda et praedicanda et docenda dissentirent.*

Chapter 10. Arts to the Glory of God

1. Translation taken from *De doctrina Christiana*, ed and trans R.P.H. Green (Oxford, 1995), II.iii.4.5.

2. *Mira quaedam deformis formositas ac formosa deformitas.* Bernard of Clairvaux, *Apologia ad Willelmum*, XXIX, *Opera omnia*, III, p 106.

3. Augustine, *De doctrina Christiana*, I.ii.2.4.

4. *Ibid.*, II.xx.30.74.

5. *Ibid.*, II.xxiii.36.89.

6. *Ibid.*, III.ix.13.31.

7. Clanchy, *From Memory to Written Record*, pp 154–5. Books could be kept in different places: liturgical ones in the church, books for reading at meals in the refectory, a monastery's books for personal reading in the cloister, a cathedral's teaching books with the chancellor, who was *ex officio* head of the school (Clanchy, p 157).

8. George Herbert, 'The Elixir', st. 5, 'The Temple' (1633), *The Works of George Herbert*, ed Helen Gardner (1961).

9. St John of Damascus, *Three Treatises on the Divine Images*, trans and intro Andrew Louth (New York, 2003).

10. *Ibid.*, pp 62–3.

11. *Ibid.*, p 101.

12. *Ibid.*, p 102.

13. *Ibid.*, p 104.

14. *Ibid.*, pp 104–5.

15. *Ibid.*, p 107–9.

16. Tanner, vol. i, pp 133–4.

17. MGH Concilia II, Supp. 1 (1998).

18. Theophilus, *De diversis artibus*, ed and trans C.R. Dodwell (Oxford, 1986), pp 1–2.

19. Guibert of Nogent, *De pignoribus*, ed R.B.C. Huygens, CCCM 127 (1993), p 85.

20. Theophilus, *De diversis artibus*, p 3; Robert Fossier, *Le France romane au temps des premiers Capétiens (987–1152)* (Louvre, Paris, 2005), p 66.

21. Beverly Mayne Kienzle, 'Cistercian Views of the City in the Sermons of Hélinand of Froidmont', in J. Hamesse, Beverly M. Kienzle, Debra Stoudt and Anne Thayer (eds), *Medieval Sermons and Society: Cloister, City, University*, pp 165–182.

22. Letter 73 to John of Salisbury: (*suo clerico suus abbas*), *ubi major et amplior voluptas corporum, ibi verum exsilium animarum*, PL 202.519–20.

23. The Ottonian Emperors sent enquiries after Byzantine princesses as brides. Liutprand the Lombard had been sent to Constantinople before,

in 949, and had been welcomed with honour by the Emperor Constantine Porphyrogenitus, a fellow intellectual. In 968 he was sent on an embassy to Constantinople to arrange a dynastic marriage between the future Emperor Otto III and a Byzantine princess. By this time the imperial throne was occupied by Nicephoras Phocas, a man of more warlike bent, with a military man's impatience with such conversation, and Liutprand, although he was now Bishop of Cremona, was not welcomed with honour at all, but left in unsatisfactory accommodation to wait. He died in 969 and it was possible to complete the mission quite quickly and arrange with the new Emperor, John Tzimisces, that there should be a marriage with the princess Theophano. and the Byzantine taste for brooding dark eyes is reflected in contemporary portraits.

24. Annemarie Weyl Carr, *Cyprus and the Devotional Arts of Byzantium*, vol. iii, p 1.

25. *Ibid.*.

26. *The Trond Lectionary*, ed E.G. Millar (Oxford: Roxburghe Club, 1949).

27. Congregational singing is discussed by Edward Foley, 'The Song of the Assembly in the Medieval Eucharist', in L. Larson-Miller (ed), *Medieval Liturgy: A Book of Essays*, pp 203–34. See also Gary Macy, *Commentaries on the Mass during the Early Scholastic Period* (Oxford, 1984).

28. Keith Bate (ed), *Three Latin Comedies* (Toronto, 1976). On gesture see C.R. Dodwell, *Anglo-Saxon Gestures and the Roman Stage* (Cambridge, 2000).

29. See Bonnie Effros, 'Appearance and Ideology: Creating Distinctions between Clerics and Laypersons in Early Medieval Gaul', in D.G. Koslin and J.E. Snyder (eds), *Encountering Medieval Textiles and Dress: Objects, Texts, Images* (New York, 2002), pp 7–24.

30. Thomas M. Izbicki, 'Forbidden Colours in the Regulation of Clerical Dress from the Fourth Lateran Council (1215), to the time of Nicholas of Cusa (d.1464)', in R. Netherton and Gale R. Owen-Crocker (eds), *Medieval Clothing and Textiles* (Boydell, 2005), vol. i, pp 105–9.

31. Tanner, vol. i, p 243.

32. Susan M. Carroll-Clark, 'Bad Habits: Clothing and Textile References in the Register of Eudes Rigaud, Archbishop of Rouen', in Netherton and Owen-Crocker (eds), *Medieval Clothing and Textiles*, vol. i, pp 81–103.

33. Tanner, vol. i, p 243.

34. Florentine Müterich, 'Carolingian Manuscript Illumination in Rheims', in *Studies in Carolingian Manuscript Illumination* (London, 2004), pp 306–7.

35. Florentine Müterich, *Studies in Carolingian Manuscript Illumination* (London, 2004), pp 98ff.

36. Annemarie Weyl Carr, *Cyprus and the Devotional Arts of Byzantium in the Era of the Crusades* (Variorum, 2005), vol. iii, p 2.

37. Robert Maniura, *Pilgrimage to Images in the Fifteenth Century* (Woodbridge, 2004); Paul Binski, *Becket's Crown: Art and Imagination in Gothic England, 1170–1300* (Yale, 2004).

38. *Gospels of Matilda, Countess of Tuscany, 1055–1115*, intro G. Warner (Roxburghe Club, 1917).

39. Barbara Newman 'Die visionären texte und visuellen welten religiöser frauen', in Ulrich Borsdorf (ed), *Krone und Schleier* (Bonn, 2005), pp 105–17. John of Salisbury, *Policraticus*, IV.6.

40. Hildegard of Bingen, Letter to Bernard, PL 197.190.

41. Now MS Corpus Christi College Cambridge, 286.

42. F. Wormald, *The Miniatures in the Gospels of St Augustine*, Sanders Lectures in Bibliography, 1948 (Cambridge 1954).

43. *Adversus Elipandum*, CCCM 69.

44. John Williams, *The Illustrated Beatus* (London, 1994), 5 vols., vol. i, pp 19–31.

Bibliography

Primary sources

Abelard, Peter, *Collationes*, ed John Marenbon and Giovanni Orlandi (Oxford, 2001)

—, *Dialectica*, ed L.M. de Rijk (Assen, 1956)

—, *Historia calamitatum*, ed J. Monfrin (Paris, 1967)

Acta et scripta quae de controversies ecclesiae Graecae et Latinae saeculo undecimo composita extant, ed J.K.C. Will (Leipzig and Marburg, 1861; reprinted Frankfurt, 1963)

Adelard of Bath, *De eodem et diverso*, ed H. Willner (Münster, 1903)

Adhemar de Chabannes, *Chronicon*, ed J. Chavanon (Paris, 1897)

Ailred of Riveaulx, *De spiritali amicitia*, CCCM 1

Al Kindy, *Apology*, ed and abridged W. Muir (London, 1887)

Alan of Lille, PL 210

Alfonsus, Petrus, 'Petri Alfonsi *Disciplina clericalis*', ed Alfons Hilka and Werner Söderhjelm, I: Lateinischer Text, in *Acta Societatis Scientiarum Fennicæ* 38/4 (1911)

Anna Comnena, *The Alexiad*, trans E.R.A. Sewter (Penguin, 1969)

Annales Judensis, MGH Scriptores I (1826)

Annales monastici, ed H.R. Luard, RS (1864–69), 5 vols.

Annales Regni Francorum, ed F. Kurze MGH Sciptores (Hanover, 1895)

Anselm of Canterbury, *Opera omnia*, ed F.S. Schmitt (Rome, 1938–68), 6 vols.

Anselm of Havelberg, *Dialogues*, I, ed G. Salet (Paris, 1966)

—, *Dialogues*, II, PL 188.1163–1210

Anselm of Laon, *Sententie*, RTAM 13 (1946)

Apophthegmata patrum, ed J.G. Friere (Coimbra, 1971)

Aristotle, *De interpretatione*, ed C. Meiser (Leipzig, 1877–78)

Augustine, *Augustine of Hippo and His Monastic Rule*, ed G. Lawless (Oxford, 1987)

—, *De baptismo*, CSEL 51

—, *De civitate Dei*, CCSL 14 (Turnhout, 1955)

Bacon, Roger, *Opus maius*, ed J.H. Bridges (Oxford, 1970)

Bate, Keith (ed), *Three Latin Comedies* (Toronto, 1976)

Bede, *Ecclesiastical History*, ed B. Colgrave and R.A.B. Mynors (Oxford, 1969; reprinted, 1991)

—, *Expositio Actuum Apostolorum et retractatio*, ed M.L.W. Laistner (Cambridge, Mass., 1939)

—, *Expositio super acta*, CCCM 121 (1983)

—, *Opera historica*, ed C. Plummer (1896; 2nd ed, 1946)

Bernard of Clairvaux, *Opera omnia*, ed J. Leclerq, C.H. Talbot and L.M. Rochais (Rome, 1967–77), 8 vols.

Boethius, *Theological Tractates and the Consolation of Philosophy*, ed and trans H.F. Stewart, E.K. Rand and S.J. Tester (London, 1973)

The Book of Kells, *Proceedings of a Conference at Trinity College, Dublin, 6–9 September 1992* (TCD Library and Scolar Press, 1994)

Bracton, Henry, *De legibus et consuetudinibus Angliae*, fol.33b, ed T. Twiss, RS 70 (London, 1878–83)

Bruno of Chartres, 'Confession of Faith', *Lettres des premiers chartreux*, ed by a Carthusian, SC 88 (1962)

Caesarius of Heisterbach *Dialogue on Miracles*, trans H. von E. Scott and C.C. Swinton Bland (London: Routledge, 1929)

Cassian, *Collationes*, ed J.-C. Guy, SC 109 (Paris, 1965)

Cassiodorus, *In Psalmos*, CCCSL 97 (2)

—, *Institutiones*, ed R.A.B. Mynors (Oxford, 1937)

—, *Variarum*, CCSL 96

Cato, *Disticha*, ed Paolo Roos (Brescia, 1984)

Cicero, *De officiis*, ed C. Atzert (Leipzig, 1923)

Clarembald of Arras, *Commentary on Boethius de Trinitate*, ed N.M. Häring (Toronto, 1965)

Conciliorum oecumenicorum decreta, ed Norman Tanner (Georgetown, 1990), 2 vols.

Crispin, Gilbert, *The Works of Gilbert Crispin*, ed Anna Abulafia and G.R. Evans, British Academy Medieval Texts (London, 1986)

Cross, Samuel H., and Olgerd P. Sherbowitz-Wetzor (eds and trans), *The Russian Primary Chronicle* (Cambridge, Mass., 1953)

Cyprian, *Letters*, CCSL 3C

D'Alverny, M.T., 'Deux traductions latines du Coran au MA', AHDLMA 16 (1948), pp 69–131

Dante, *Monarchia*, ed and trans P. Shaw (Cambridge, 1995)

Dawes, Elizabeth and Norman H. Baynes (trans), *Three Byzantine Saints* (Oxford, 1948)

Durandus de Huesca, *Une somme anti-Cathare, Le Liber contra Manicheos*, ed C. Thouzellier, *Spicilegium Sacrum Lovaniense* 32 (1964)

Embricon de Mayence, *La vie de Mahomet*, ed Guy Cambier (Latomus, Brussels, 1962)

Eusebius, *Historia ecclesiastica*, ed and trans K. Lake and J.E.L. Oulton (Loeb, 1926–32)

Fulbert of Chartres, *The Letters and Poems of Fulbert of Chartres*, ed and trans Frederick Behrends (Oxford, 1976)

Fulcher of Chartres, *Gesta Francorum Iherusalem peregrinantium*, PL 155.821–40

Garlandus Comptista, *Dialectica*, Prologue, ed L.M. de Rijk (Assen, 1959)

Gennadius of Marseilles, PL 58.1059–1120 and ed W. Herding (Teubner, 1924)

Gerbert of Aurillac, *Opera omnia*, ed N. Bubnov (Hildesheim, 1963)

Gerhoch of Reichersberg, *Letter to Pope Hadrian about the Novelties of the Day*, Prefatory letter, ed N.M. Häring (Toronto, 1974)

Gesta Francorum et aliorum, ed Rosalind Hill (Oxford, 1962)

Gervase of Tilbury, *Otia imperialia*, ed and trans S.E. Banks and J.W. Binns (Oxford, 2002)

Gesta abbatum Monasterii S. Albani, ed H.T. Riley, RS 28 (1867)

Gilo of Paris, *The Historia vie Hierosolomitane of Gilo of Paris and a Second Anonymous Author*, ed and trans C.W. Grocock and J.E. Siberry (Oxford, 1997)

Giraldus Cambrensis, *De invectionibus*, *Opera*, vol. iii, RS 21 (1863)

—, *De principis instructione*, *Opera*, vol. viii, ed G.F. Warner, RS 8 (1891)

Glaber, Ralph, *Historiarum libri quinque*, ed John France (Oxford, 1989)

Goscelin of Saint-Bertin, *The Hagiography of the Female Saints of Ely*, ed Rosalind C. Love (Oxford, 2004)

Gospels of Matilda, Countess of Tuscany, 1055-1115, intro G. Warner (Roxburghe Club, 1917)

Gregory the Great, *Registrum*, CCSL 140 and140A

—, *Regula pastoralis*, PL 177.14 and London, 1872

Gregory VII, *The 'Epistolae Vagantes' of Pope Gregory VII*, ed H.E. Cowdrey (Oxford, 1972)

Grosseteste, Robert, *Hexaemeron*, ed R.C. Dales and S. Gieben (London, 1982)

—, *The Minor Declamationes Ascribed to Quintilian*, ed with commentary M. Winterbottom (Berlin, 1984)

—, *The Six Days of Creation*, trans C.F.J. Martin (London, 1996)

Guibert de Nogent, *Autobiographie*, I.9, ed Edmond-René Labande (Paris, 1981)

—, *De pignoribus*, ed R.B.C. Huygens, CCCM 127 (1993)

—, *De vita sua*, ed E.R. Labande (Paris, 1981)

—, *Gesta Dei per Francos*, ed R.B.C. Huygens, CCCM 127A

—, *Self and Society in Medieval France*, J.F. Benton (New York, 1970)

Hermannus Judaeus, *De conversione*, ed G. Niemeyer, MGH *Quellen zur Geschichte des Mittelalters*, 4 (Weimar, 1963), and trans K.F. Morrison, *Conversion and Text* (London: Virginia University Press, 1992)

Hildegard of Binghen, *Letter to Bernard*, PL 197.190

Hincmar of Rheims, *Opera*, PL 125

Hugh Eteriano, *Contra Patarenos*, ed and trans Janet Hamilton, Sarah Hamilton and Bernard Hamilton (Brill, 2004)

Hugh of St Victor, *Didascalicon*, ed C.H. Buttimer (Washington, 1939)

Huygens, R.B.C., *Accessus ad auctores* (Leiden, 1970)

Innocent III, *Selected Letters of Innocent III*, ed C.R. Cheney and W.H. Semple (London, 1953)

Isidore, *Etymologiae*, IX.ii.57, ed W.M. Lindsay (Oxford, 1911)

Ivo of Chartres, *Decretum*, PL. 161.498

Jacques de Vitry, *Lettres de la cinquième croisade*, ed R.B.C. Huygens and trans G. Duchet-Suchaux. (Brepols, 1998)

Jerome, *De viris illustribus*, ed E. Cushing (Leipzig, 1896)

John of Damascus, St, *Three Treatises on the Divine Images*, trans and intro Andrew Louth (New York, 2003)

John of Ephesus, *The Third Part of the Ecclesiastical History*, trans R. Payne Smith (Oxford, 1860), from the Greek text of W. Cureton (Oxford, 1853)

John of Salisbury, *Historia pontificalis*, ed M. Chibnall, Oxford Medieval Texts (Oxford, 1986)

—, *Metalogicon*, ed J.B. Hall, CCCM 98 (1991)

—, *Policraticus*, ed C.C.J. Webb (Oxford, 1909), 2 vols., and CCCM 118, Books I–IV

Joinville and Villehardouin, *Chronicles of the Crusades*, trans M.R.B. Shaw (Penguin, 1963)

Kempis, Thomas à, *Dialogi noviciorum*, II.21, *Opera omnia*, VII, ed M.J. Pohl, (1922)

Ker, N.R. (ed), *The Pastoral Care: Early English Manuscripts in Facsimile* (Copenhagen, 1956)

Lanfranc, *The Monastic Constitutions of Lanfranc*, ed David Knowles (London 1951)

Lettres des premiers chartreux, ed by a Carthusian, SC 88 (1962)

Libellus de diversis ordinibus, ed G. Constable and Bernard S. Smith (Oxford, revised edition, 2003)

Liber de duabus principiis, ed A. Dondaine (Rome, 1939)

Liutprand, *Die Werke Liudprands von Cremona*, ed J. Becker, MGH Scriptores (Hanover, 1883)

—, *The Embassy to Constantinople and Other Writings*, ed John Julius Norwich (London, 1993)

—, *Relatio de legatione Constantinopolitana*, ed P. Chiesa, CCCM 156

Livre des deux principes, ed C. Thouzellier, SC 198 (Paris, 1973)

Macrobius, *Saturnalia*, ed J. Willis (Leipzig, 1994, 2nd ed)

Magna vita Sancti Hugonis, ed Decima L. Douie and D.H. Farmer (Oxford, 1985), 2 vols.

Map, Walter, *De nugis curialium*, ed M.R. James, C.N.L. Brooke and R.A.B. Mynors (Oxford, 1983)

Mill, John Stuart, *The Protagoras*, ed J.M. Robson (Toronto, 1978)

Millar, E.G. (ed), *The Trond Lectionary* (Oxford: Roxburghe Club, 1949)

Minio-Palluelo, L. (ed), *Aristoteles Latinus* (Rome, 1951–)

—, (ed), *Opuscula: The Latin Aristotle* (Amsterdam, 1972)

Miracles of Sainte Aebbe of Coldingham and Saint Margaret of Scotland, ed R.

Barnett (Oxford, 2003)

Moschus, John, *Pratum spirituale*, ed and trans John Wortley (Kalamazoo, 1992)

Mostert, Marco, *The Library of Fleury, A Provisional List of Manuscripts* (Hilversum, 1989)

Nicetas Stethatos, *Opuscula and Letters*, ed J. Darrouzès, SC (Paris, 1961)

Orderic Vitalis, *Historia Ecclesiastica*, ed Marjorie Chibnall (Oxford, 1969–80), 6 vols.

Peter of Blois, *The Later Letters of Peter of Blois*, ed E. Revell, British Academy Medieval Texts (Oxford, 1993)

Peter of Celle, The *Letters of Peter of Celle*, ed Julian Haseldine (Oxford, 2001)

Peter of Poitiers, *Petri Pictaveniensis allegoriae super Tabernaculum Moysi*, ed P.S. Moore and J.A. Corbett (Notre Dame, 1938)

Peter the Chanter, *Summa de sacramentis et animae consiliis*, ed J.-A. Dugauquier, *Analecta Medievalia Namurcensia* 4 (Louvain, 1956)

Peter the Venerable, *The Letters of Peter the Venerable*, ed G. Constable (Harvard, 1967), 2 vols.

Ps-Isidore, *Decretales pseudo-Isidorianae* (Leipzig, 1863)

Ralph de Diceto, *De mirabilibus Britanniae, abbreviationes chronicorum, Opera historica*, ed W. Stubbs, RS lxviii (1876), 2 vols.

Raymond of Agiles, *Historia Francorum*, PL 155.591–666

Robert of Melun, *Quaestiones de Divina Pagina, Oeuvres*, ed R. Martin, SSLov 13 (Louvain, 1932)

Rupert of Deutz's *Opera* are available in the CCCM series

Sedulius Scottus, *Collectaneum in Apostolum*, PL 103.249

Severus of Minorca, *Letter on the Conversion of the Jews*, ed Scott Bradbury (Oxford, 1996)

Simon of Tournai, *Disputationes, Disputatio*, ed J. Warichez, SSLov 12 (Louvain, 1932)

SS Bonifatii et Lulli epistolae selectae I (Berlin, 1955)

Sextus, *Sentences of Sextus*, ed Henry Chadwick (Cambridge,1959)

Symeon the New Theologian, *Catecheses*, ed and trans B. Krivochéine and J. Paramelle, SC 96 (1963)

Theophilus, *De diversis artibus*, ed and trans C.R. Dodwell (Oxford, 1986)

Thomas of Celano, *Vita et miracula, Life of Francis of Assisi*, ed P.E. Alençon (Rome, 1906)

Thomas of Chobham, I, *Summa de commendatione virtutum et extirpatione vitiorum*, ed F. Morenzoni, CCCM 82B (Turnhout, 1997)

Thomas of Marlborough, *History of the Abbey of Evesham: Historia Ecclesie Abbedonensis*, ed and trans John Hudson (Oxford, 2002)

Tudebod, *Historia de Hierololymitano itinere*, PL 155.763–820, PL 155.763, and ed J. Richard (Paris, 1977)

Valla, Lorenzo, *De falso credita et ementita Constantini Donatione declamatio* (1520)

Vita Johannis Abbatis, MGH Scriptores IV, 335–77

Vita S. Bonifatii, 6, MGH, Scriptores II (1829)

Walter of St Victor, *Sermones*, XVIII, 3, ed J. Châtillon, CCCM 30

William of Malmesbury, *Gesta regum*, ed R.A.B. Mynors et al (Oxford, 1998–89)

—, *Polyhistor deflorationum*, ed H. Testroet Ouellette (Binghampton, New York, 1982)

William of Poitiers, *The Gesta Guilelmi of William of Poitiers*, ed and trans R.H.C. Davis and Marjorie Chibnall (Oxford, 1998)

Selected secondary sources

Abulafia, Anna Sapir, *Christians and Jews in the Twelfth-Century Renaissance* (Routledge, 1995)

Abulafia, David and Nora Berend (eds), *Medieval Frontiers: Concepts and Practices* (Ashgate, 2002)

Backus, Irena (ed), *The Reception of the Church Fathers in the West* (Leiden, 1997), 2 vols.

Barbero, Alessandro, *Charlemagne: Father of a Continent*, trans Allan Cameron (Berkeley: University of California Press, 2004)

Barnwell, P.S., Claire Cross and Ann Rycroft (eds), *Mass and Parish in Late Medieval England: The Use of York* (Reading: Spire, 2005)

Bartlett, Robert, *The Making of Europe: Conquest, Colonisation and Cultural Change 950–1350* (London, 1993)

Berman, Constance Hoffman (ed), *Medieval Religion: New Approaches* (Routledge, 2005)

Binski, Paul, *Becket's Crown: Art and Imagination in Gothic England, 1170–1300* (Yale, 2004)

Blaettler, James R., 'Preaching the Power of Penitence in the Silos Beatus', in J. Hamesse, Beverly M. Kienzle, Debra Stoudt and Anne Thayer (eds), *Medieval Sermons and Society: Cloister, City, University* (Louvain, 1998)

Blumenthal, Uta-Renata, *The Investiture Controversy* (Philadelphia, 1988)

Bolton, Brenda, '"The Caravan Rests": Innocent III's Use of Itineration', in Anne J. Duggan, Joan Greatres and Brenda Bolton (eds), *Omnia Disce: Medieval Studies in Memory of Leonard Boyle, O.P.* (Ashgate, 2005)

Briggs, Brian, 'Expulsio, Proscriptio, Exilium: Exile and Friendship in the Writings of Osbert of Clare', in Laura Napran and Elisabeth van Houts (eds), *Exile in the Middle Ages*, International Medieval Research 13 (Brepols, 2002)

Brightman, F.E., *Liturgies Eastern and Western* (Oxford, 1896)

Brown, P.R.L., *The Body and Society: Men, Women and Sexual Renunciation in Early Christianity* (London, 1989)

—, *The Cult of the Saints: Its Rise and Function in Latin Christianity* (Chicago, 1981)

—, *The Making of Late Antiquity* (Harvard, 1978)

Brown, Peter, *Authority and the Sacred* (Cambridge, 1995)

Buc, Philippe, 'Vox clamantis in deserto? Pierre le Chantre et la predication laïque', *Revue Mabillon* 4 (1993)

Cameron, Averil, *Agathias* (Oxford, 1970)

Carr, Annemarie Weyl, *Cyprus and the Devotional Arts of Byzantium in the Era of the Crusades* (Variorum, 2005)

Carroll-Clark, Susan M., 'Bad Habits: Clothing and Textile References in the Register of Eudes Rigaud, Archbishop of Rouen', in R. Netherton and Gale R. Owen-Crocker (eds), *Medieval Clothing and Textiles* (Boydell, 2005), vol. i

Carruthers, Leo, 'The Word Made Flesh: Preaching and Community from the Apostolic to the Late Middle Ages', in Georgiana Donavin, Cary J. Nederman and Richard Utz (eds), *Speculum Sermonis: Interdisciplinary Reflections on the Late Medieval Sermon* (Turnhout, 2004)

Catto, J.I. (ed), *The History of the University of Oxford* (Oxford, 1984), vol. i

Chadwick, Henry, *East and West: The Making of a Rift in the Church* (Oxford, 2003)

Charles-Edwards, T.M. 'Palladius, Prosper and Leo the Great: Missions and Primatial Authority', in David Dumville (ed), *Saint Patrick: AD 493–1993*, Studies in Celtic History 13 (Woodbridge, 1993)

Ciggaar, K.N., *Western Travellers to Constantinople. The West and Byzantium, 962–1204* (Leiden, 1996)

Clanchy, M., *From Memory to Written Record: England 1066–1307* (Oxford, 1997; 2nd ed, 1993)

Constantelos, Demetrios J., 'Liturgy and Liturgical Daily Life in the Medieval Greek World: The Byzantine Empire', in Thomas J. Heffernan and E. Ann Matter (eds), *The Liturgy of the Medieval Church* (Kalamazoo, 2001)

Cumont, F., *Les mystères de Mithra* (Brussels, 1913)

—, *The Oriental Religions in Roman Paganism* (Chicago, 1911; reprint, Dover, 1956)

Daniel, Norman, *Islam and the West* (Edinburgh, 1960; new ed, 1993)

D'Avray, D.L., *The Preaching of the Friars* (Oxford, 1983)

Dodaro, Robert, *Christ and the Just Society in the Age of Augustine* (Cambridge, 2004)

Dodwell, C.R, *Anglo-Saxon Gestures and the Roman Stage* (Cambridge, 2000)

Dorey, T.A, 'William of Poitiers: "Gesta Guillelmi Ducis"', in T.A. Dorey (ed), *Latin Biography* (London, 1967)

Duffy, Eamon, *The Stripping of the Altars* (Yale, 2nd ed, 2005)

Duffy, Mark, *Royal Tombs of Medieval England* (Charleston, 2003)

Dumville, David (ed), *Saint Patrick, 493–1993* (Woodbridge, 1993)

Dunn, Marilyn, *The Emergence of Monasticism* (Blackwell, 2000; reprint, 2003)

Effros, Bonnie, 'Appearance and Ideology: Creating Distinctions between Clerics and Laypersons in Early Medieval Gaul', in D.G. Koslin and J.E. Snyder (eds), *Encountering Medieval Textiles and Dress: Objects, Texts, Images*

(New York 2002)

Evans, G.R, *Augustine on Evil* (Cambridge, 1983)

—, *Alan of Lille* (Cambridge, 1983)

Farmer, David, *The Oxford Dictionary of Saints* (Oxford, 1978; reprint, 2004)

Ferreiro, Alberto, *Simon Magus in Patristic, Medieval and Early Modern Traditions* (Brill, 2005)

Finucane, Ronald C., *Miracles and Pilgrims, Popular Beliefs in Medieval England* (London, 1977 and 1995)

—, *Soldiers of the Faith: Crusaders and Moslems at War* (London, 1983)

Fletcher, Richard, *The Cross and the Crescent* (London, 2003)

Foley, Edward, 'The Song of the Assembly in the Medieval Eucharist', in L. Larson-Miller (ed), *Medieval Liturgy: A Book of Essays* (New York, 1997)

Fossier, Robert, *Le France romane au temps des premiers Capétiens (987–1152)* (Louvre, Paris, 2005)

Fransen, P., *L'autorité des conciles* (Paris, 1962)

Freed, J.B., *The Friars and German Society in the Thirteenth Century* (Cambridge, Mass.: Medieval Academy of America, 1977)

Garnsey, Peter, 'Religious Toleration in Classical Antiquity', in W.J. Shiels (ed), *Persecution and Toleration*, Studies in Church History 21 (Oxford, 1984)

Gilliard, Frank D., 'More Silent Reading in Antiquity: non omne verbum sonabat', *Journal of Biblical Literature* 112 (1993)

Ginther, James, *Master of the Sacred Page: A Study of the Theology of Robert Grosseteste, ca. 1229/30–1235* (Ashgate, 2004)

Gretsch, M., *Aelfric and the Cult of Saints in Late Anglo-Saxon England* (Cambridge, 2005)

Grundmann, H., *Religiöse Bewegungen im Mittelalter* (1935); English translation, S. Rowan, *Religious Movements in the Middle Ages* (Notre Dame and London, 1995)

—, 'Litteratus-illiteratus', *Archive für kulturgeschichte* 40 (1958), in Anna Adamska and Marco Mostert (eds), *The Development of Literate Mentalities in East Central Europe* (Brepols, 2004)

Hanson, Craig L., 'Manuel I Comnenus and the "God of Muhammad": A Study in Byzantine Ecclesiastical Politics', in John Victor Tolan (ed), *Medieval Christian Perceptions of Islam: A Book of Essays* (New York, 1996)

Haye, Thomas, *Das Lateinische Lehrgedicht im Mittelalter* (Brill, 1997)

Herrin, Judith, *The Formation of Christendom* (Oxford, 1987)

Hughes, Kathleen, *Early Christian Ireland* (Ithaca, New York, 1972)

Isaac, Benjamin, *The Limits of Empire* (Oxford, 1990; revised, 1992)

Izbicki, Thomas M., 'Forbidden Colours in the Regulation of Clerical Dress from the Fourth Lateran Council (1215), to the Time of Nicholas of Cusa (d.1464)', in R. Netherton and Gale R. Owen-Crocker (eds), *Medieval Clothing and Textiles* (Boydell, 2005), vol. i

Jackson, Paul A., 'Sicut Samuel Iunxit David: Early Carolingian Royal Anointings Reconsidered', in L. Larson-Miller (ed), *Medieval Liturgy: A*

Book of Essays (New York, 1997)

Jamroziak, Emilia, *Rievaulx Abbey and Its Social Context, 1132–1300*, Medieval Church Studies 8 (Tournhout, 2005)

Johnson, Charles, *Dialogus de Scaccario of Richard FitzNigel* (London, 1950)

Kaelber, Lutz, *Schools of Asceticism: Ideology and Organization in Medieval Religious Communities* (Pennsylvania, 1998)

Kennedy, Hugh, *The Prophet and the Age of the Caliphates. The Islamic Near East from the 6th to the 11th Century* (London/New York, 1986)

Khalidi, Tarif, *Arabic Historical Thought in the Classical Period* (Cambridge, 1994)

Kienzle, Beverly Mayne, 'Cistercian Views of the City in the Sermons of Hélinand of Froidmont', in J. Hamesse, Beverly M. Kienzle, Debra Stoudt and Anne Thayer (eds), *Medieval Sermons and Society: Cloister, City, University* (Louvain 1998)

Krueger, Derek, *Writing and Holiness: The Practice of Authorship in the Early Christian East* (University of Pennsylvania, 2004)

Lapidge, Michael, *The Anglo-Saxon Library* (Oxford, 2006)

Lauwers, M., 'Praedicatio-Exhortatio. L'Église, la réforme et les laics (XIe-XIIIe siècles),' in R.M. Dessi and M. Lauwers (eds), *La parole du prédicateur: Ve–XVe siècle* (Paris, 1997)

Linder, Amnon, *Raising Arms: Liturgy in the Struggle to Liberate Jerusalem in the Late Middle Ages* (Turnhout, 2003)

Loomis, R.S. and L.H., *Arthurian Legends in Medieval Art* (OUP, 1938)

Lottin, O., 'Nouveaux fragments théologiques de l'école d'Anselme de Laon', RTAM 13 (1946)

Macy, Gary, *Commentaries on the Mass during the Early Scholastic Period* (Oxford, 1984)

Maier, Christoph T., *Preaching the Crusades*, Cambridge Studies in Medieval Life and Thought (Cambridge, 1994)

Maniura, Robert, *Pilgrimage to Images in the Fifteenth Century* (Woodbridge, 2004)

Markus, Robert, *Gregory the Great and His World* (Cambridge, 1997)

Morris, C., *The Western Church from 1050–1250* (Oxford, 1989)

Muldoon, James, *Popes, Lawyers and Infidels: The Church and the Non-Christian World, 1250–1550* (Philadelphia, 1979)

Murphy, J.J., 'The Teaching of Latin as a Second Language in the Twelfth Century,' *Historiographia Linguistica* 7 (Amsterdam, 1980)

Müterich, Florentine, 'Carolingian Manuscript Illumination in Rheims', in *Studies in Carolingian Manuscript Illumination* (London, 2004)

Newman, Barbara, 'Die visionären texte und visuellen welten religiöser frauen', in Ulrich Borsdorf (ed), *Krone und Schleier* (Bonn, 2005)

Patchovsky, A., 'The Literacy of the Waldensians', in P. Biller and A. Hudson (eds), *Heresy and Literacy, 1000–1530* (Cambridge, 1994)

Pestell, Tim, *Landscapes of Monastic Foundation: The Establishment of Religious Houses in East Anglia, c.650–1200* (Woodbridge, 2004)

Peuchmaurd, M., 'Le prêtre ministre de la parole dans la théologie du XIIe siècle (canonistes, moines et chanoines)', RTAM 29 (1962)

Poor, Sarah S., *Mechthild of Magdeburg and Her Book* (University of Pennsylvania Press, 2004)

Post, Gaines, 'Parisian Masters as a Corporation', *Speculum* 9 (1934)

Reeves, Marjorie, *The Influence of Prophecy in the Later Middle Ages* (Oxford, 1969)

Renard, J.-P., *La formation et la désignation des prédicateurs au début de l'Ordre des Prêcheurs* (Fribourg, 1977)

Roberts, P.B., 'Preaching in/and the Medieval City', in J. Hamesse, Beverly M. Kienzle, Debra Stoudt and Anne Thayer (eds), *Medieval Sermons and Society: Cloister, City, University* (Louvain 1998)

Robinson, P.R, and R. Zim, *Of the Making of Books: Essays Presented to M.B. Parkes* (Aldershot: Scolar, 1997)

Robson, Michael, *St Francis of Assisi* (London, 1997)

Roquebert, Michel, *Les Cathares: de la chute de Montségur aux dernier bûchers (1244–1329)* (Paris: Perrin, 1998)

Rouse, R.H. and M.H., 'Ordinatio and compilatio revisited', in *Ad litteram: Authoritative Texts and Their Medieval Readers* (Notre Dame and London, 1992)

Runciman, S., *The Medieval Manichee* (Cambridge,1947; London, 1961)

Russell, F.H., *The Just War in the Middle Ages: Preaching the Crusades*, Cambridge Studies in Medieval Life and Thought (Cambridge, 1975)

Salter, H.E., *Medieval Oxford*, OHS 100 (1936)

Sanger, Paul, *Space between Words: The Origins of Silent Reading* (Stanford UP, 1997)

Sayers, Dorothy, 'On Translating the Divina Commedia', *Nottingham Medieval Studies* 2 (1958)

Schmitz-Esser, Romedio, 'Arnold of Bescia in Exile: April 1139–December 1143: His Role as Reformer, Reviewed', in Laura Napran and Elisabeth van Houts (eds), *Exile in the Middle Ages*, International Medieval Research 13 (Brepols, 2002)

Sheenan, M.W., 'The Religious Orders, 1220–1370', in J.I. Catto (ed), *History of the University of Oxford* (Oxford, 1984), vol. i

Sigurdsonn, Gísli and Vésteinn Olason (eds), *The Manuscripts of Iceland* (Reykjavik, 2004)

Simon, Walter, 'Staining the Speech of Things Divine: The Uses of Literacy in Medieval Beguine Communities', in Thérèse de Hemptinne and María Eugenia Góngora (eds), *The Voice of Silence: Women's Literacy in a Men's Church* (Turnhout, 2005)

Southern, R.W., *The Making of the Middle Ages* (Hutchinson, 1953)

—, *Robert Grosseteste: The Growth of an English Mind in Medieval Europe* (Oxford, 1992)

Staunton, Michael, 'Exile in the Lives of Anselm and Thomas Becket', in Laura

Napran and Elisabeth van Houts (eds), *Exile in the Middle Ages*, International Medieval Research 13 (Brepols, 2002)

Stock, Brian, *The Implications of Literacy* (Toronto, 1982)

Thomson, R.M., *William of Malmesbury* (Boydell, 1987, reprint 2003)

Thouzellier, C., *Catharisme et Valdéisme en Languedoc à la fin du XIIe et au début du XIIIe siècle*, (Louvain-Paris, 1969)

Tolan, John Victor, *Petrus Alfonsi and His Medieval Readers* (Gainsville: University of Florida Press, 1993)

—, (ed), *Medieval Christian Perceptions of Islam: A Book of Essays* (New York, 1996)

Trout, J.M., 'Preaching by the Laity in the Twelfth Century', *Studies in Medieval Culture* 4 (1973)

Ullmann, W., *Medieval Foundations of Renaissance Humanism* (London, 1977)

Wakefield, W.L. and A.P. Evans (eds), *Heresies of the High Middle Ages: Selected Sources Translated and Annotated* (New York, 1969)

Ward-Perkins, Bryan, *The Fall of Rome and the End of Civilization* (Oxford, 2005)

Wellesz, Egon, *A History of Byzantine Music and Hymnography* (Oxford, 2nd ed, 1961)

Williams, John, *The Illustrated Beatus* (London, 1994), 5 vols.

Williams, Rowan, *Arius: Heresy and Tradition* (London, 2nd ed, 2001)

Wormald, F., *The Miniatures in the Gospels of St Augustine*, Sanders Lectures in Bibliography, 1948 (Cambridge 1954)

Zerfass, Rolf, *Der Streit um die Laienpredigt* (Frieberg, 1974)

Index